SO-AAB-221

Entrepreneur
MAGAZINE'S

# LEGAL GUIDE

# Buying and Selling a Business

# Additional Titles in Entrepreneur's Legal Guides
## Helen Cicino, Esq.
## Managing Editor

*Bankruptcy for Businesses: The Benefits, Pitfalls, and Alternatives*

*Business Contracts: Turn Any Business Contract to Your Advantage*

*Business Structures: How to Form a Corporation, LLC, Partnership, or Sole Proprietorship*

*Estate Planning, Wills, and Trusts*

*Forming an LLC: In Any State*

*Forming a Partnership: And Making It Work*

*Harassment and Discrimination*

*Hiring and Firing*

*Incorporate Your Business in Any State*

*Intellectual Property: Patents, Trademarks, Copyrights, Trade Secrets*

*Principles of Negotiation: Strategies, Tactics, Techniques to Reach Agreements*

*The Operations Manual for Corporations*

*The Small Business Legal Tool Kit*

*Small Claims Court Guidebook*

*Tax Planning for Business: Maximize Profit, Minimize Taxes*

Entrepreneur
MAGAZINE'S

LEGAL
GUIDE

Ira Nottonson
Attorney at Law

658.1
Nottonson

# Buying and Selling a Business

- Choose the Right Transactions
- Maximize the Value of Your Sale or Purchase
- Strategically Negotiate and Win

Publisher: Jere Calmes
Cover Design: Desktop Miracles, Inc.
Production: CWL Publishing Enterprises, Inc., Madison, Wisconsin,
www.cwlpub.com

Advisory Editor for the Entrepreneur Press Legal Guide Series: Helen Cicino, Esq.

This publication is designed to provide accurate and authoritative information in
regard to the subject matter covered. It is sold with the understanding that the publisher is not engaged in rendering legal, accounting, or other professional services. If
legal advice or other expert assistance is required, the services of a competent professional person should be sought.

—From a Declaration of Principles jointly adopted by
a Committee of the American Bar Association
and a Committee of Publishers and Associations

ISBN  13: 978-1-59918-172-1
        10: 1-59918-172-X

**Library of Congress Cataloging-in-Publication Data**
Nottonson, Ira N., 1933-
  Buying and selling a business / by Ira Nottonson.
    p. cm. — (Legal guide series)
  Includes index.
  ISBN-13: 978-1-59918-172-1
  ISBN-10: 1-59918-172-X
  1. Sale of small businesses. 2. Small business--Purchasing. 3. Sale of small
businesses—Law and legislation--United States. 4. Small business—Purchasing—
Law and legislation—United States. I. Title.
  HD1393.25.N675 1999
  658.1'64—dc22

                                                        2008004596

12  11  10  09  08                          10  9  8  7  6  5  4  3  2  1

# Contents

| | Preface | xi |
|---|---|---|
| | About the Author | xix |
| Part One | Introduction to Buying and Selling a Business | 1 |
| Chapter 1 | The Buyer-Seller Relationship | 3 |
| | The Buyer Wants an Income | 4 |
| | It Is the Seller's Problem | 6 |
| | Methods of Valuation | 6 |
| | Family Business Transitions | 9 |
| | Key Points to Remember | 17 |
| Chapter 2 | The Financial Picture | 19 |
| | Financial Considerations for the Buyer | 21 |
| | Financial Considerations for the Seller | 24 |
| | Key Points to Remember | 29 |
| Chapter 3 | Negotiating Price and Pricing Variables | 33 |
| | Financing Methods | 34 |
| | Negotiating the Down Payment | 36 |
| | Negotiating the Length of the Note | 38 |
| | Negotiating the Interest Rate | 39 |

| | | |
|---|---|---:|
| | Price Structuring Begins with the Buyer's Perspective | 41 |
| | The Personal Side to Negotiations | 45 |
| | Creative Financing Options | 45 |
| | Key Points to Remember | 49 |
| **Chapter 4** | **Your Team of Professionals** | **51** |
| | Accountants and Attorneys | 52 |
| | Business Brokers | 54 |
| | Key Points to Remember | 58 |
| **Chapter 5** | **The Information Game** | **61** |
| | What the Buyer Needs to Know | 63 |
| | What the Seller Needs to Know | 68 |
| | Legal Aspects of the Transaction | 70 |
| | Body Language | 70 |
| | Key Points to Remember | 71 |
| **Part Two** | **The Buyer's Perspective** | **73** |
| **Chapter 6** | **Committing to a Market Niche** | **75** |
| | Consider a Homebased Business | 76 |
| | How to Make a Smart Business Investment | 82 |
| | Key Points to Remember | 87 |
| **Chapter 7** | **The Asset Variables** | **89** |
| | Just What Is for Sale? | 90 |
| | What to Request from Your Seller | 101 |
| | Key Points to Remember | 104 |
| **Chapter 8** | **Investors and Partners** | **105** |
| | The Investor Profile | 106 |
| | The Partner Mystique | 110 |
| | Forms of Participation | 114 |
| | Key Points to Remember | 115 |
| **Chapter 9** | **The Franchise Decision** | **117** |
| | Franchising—Past and Present | 119 |
| | The Variables Involved in Your Decision | 121 |
| | A Franchisor's Marketing and Advertising Capabilities | 123 |
| | Making the Decision | 126 |
| | Key Points to Remember | 132 |

| | | |
|---|---|---:|
| **Chapter 10** | **Finding the Help You Need** | **133** |
| | The Franchise Option | 135 |
| | The Dilemma | 137 |
| | Insider Experience | 138 |
| | Key Points to Remember | 141 |
| **Chapter 11** | **Don't Let Your First Mistake Be Your Last** | **143** |
| | Feeling the Pressure | 144 |
| | A Potential Partner or Consultant | 146 |
| | Check on Your Available Tools | 148 |
| | When Your Money Won't Buy the Dream You Want | 149 |
| | Full Disclosure for Both Husband and Wife | 150 |
| | Making the Hard Comparisons and the Harder Judgments | 152 |
| | Key Points to Remember | 152 |
| **Part Three** | **The Seller's Perspective** | **153** |
| **Chapter 12** | **Your Retail Business and How to Package It** | **155** |
| | The Franchise Comparison | 157 |
| | A Good Customer Mix | 158 |
| | What Is Your Competition? | 159 |
| | Parking | 162 |
| | Key Points to Remember | 163 |
| **Chapter 13** | **Selling the Bottom Line** | **165** |
| | Your Operating Profit | 167 |
| | Operating Profit Leads to an Asking Price | 168 |
| | Key Points to Remember | 178 |
| **Chapter 14** | **Finding the Right Buyer and Protecting the Sale** | **179** |
| | Finding the Buyer | 182 |
| | Protecting the Sale | 185 |
| | Key Points to Remember | 193 |
| **Chapter 15** | **The Motivations Behind the Sale** | **201** |
| | Starting or Buying a Business | 201 |
| | Why Are You Selling? | 204 |
| | The Buyer's Motivations | 205 |
| | Key Points to Remember | 213 |

| | | |
|---|---|---:|
| **Chapter 16** | **Before the Sale** | **215** |
| | Bankruptcy: Not Yet | 215 |
| | Preparation for a Sale | 217 |
| | A Successful Business | 217 |
| | A Good Business with Insufficient Operating Profit | 219 |
| | A Good Business with Some Standing Debt | 221 |
| | A Business with Serious Solvency Problems | 221 |
| | Business Disaster Pending | 222 |
| | The Bankruptcy Alternative | 224 |
| | Key Points to Remember | 232 |
| **Chapter 17** | **Negotiating the Sale of a Troubled Business** | **235** |
| | Preparing a Business for Sale | 236 |
| | What a New Owner Offers a Troubled Business | 237 |
| | Your Legal Obligation to Disclose | 240 |
| | At the Negotiating Table | 242 |
| | Bankruptcy as a Selling Posture | 245 |
| | Key Points to Remember | 246 |
| **Chapter 18** | **How to Value and Sell a Professional Practice** | **247** |
| | Professional Practice Is Unique | 247 |
| | Special Concerns for Transfer of Ownership | 249 |
| | Valuation of a Specialty Practice | 259 |
| | Key Points to Remember | 266 |
| **Part Four** | **Legal and Financial Considerations** | **267** |
| **Chapter 19** | **The Accountant's Job** | **269** |
| | Representing the Seller | 270 |
| | Representing the Buyer | 274 |
| | Key Points to Remember | 281 |
| **Chapter 20** | **The Lawyer's Job** | **283** |
| | Limited Liability | 284 |
| | Attorneys in General | 285 |
| | Creating the Client Relationship | 285 |
| | Representing the Seller | 286 |
| | Representing the Buyer | 289 |
| | Key Points to Remember | 296 |

| | | |
|---|---|---|
| Chapter 21 | **The Broker's Job** | **297** |
| | Representing the Seller | 299 |
| | Representing the Buyer | 305 |
| | Key Points to Remember | 310 |
| Chapter 22 | **The Lender's Job** | **311** |
| | Writing a Business Plan | 311 |
| | Approaching the Lender | 313 |
| | Know the Bank and the Banker | 314 |
| | The Business Plan | 315 |
| | Make Your Case | 316 |
| | The Essentials of Your Application | 321 |
| | The Big Decision | 322 |
| | The Bankruptcy Loan | 323 |
| | Key Points to Remember | 324 |
| **Part Five** | **Contract Elements** | **325** |
| Chapter 23 | **The Noncompete, Nondisclosure Issue** | **327** |
| | When a Business Is Transferred | 328 |
| | When an Employee Leaves | 329 |
| | What Will the Courts Say? | 331 |
| | Key Points to Remember | 335 |
| Chapter 24 | **The End of the Franchise Contract** | **337** |
| | All Franchise Contracts Are Not the Same | 338 |
| | Key Points to Remember | 347 |
| **Part Six** | **Revisiting the Essentials and Valuing an Internet Business** | **349** |
| Chapter 25 | **Revisiting the Financial Issues** | **351** |
| | The Balance Sheet | 352 |
| | The Profit and Loss Statement | 357 |
| | The Comparative Analysis | 366 |
| | Key Points to Remember | 369 |
| Chapter 26 | **Revisiting the Core Elements of This Book** | **371** |
| | For a Seller: Why Does Someone Buy a Business? | 373 |
| | For a Buyer: Why Does Someone Sell a Business? | 375 |

| | | |
|---|---|---:|
| | Why Value a Business? | 377 |
| | Key Points to Remember | 379 |
| **Chapter 27** | **Valuing an Internet Business** | **381** |
| | The Bottom Line in Terms of Valuation | 383 |
| | How to Value an Internet Business | 384 |
| | The Internet | 385 |
| | The Phenomenal Growth Potential | 386 |
| | Key Points to Remember | 390 |
| | **Glossary** | **391** |
| | **Index** | **403** |

# Preface

The only magic contained in this book is in understanding the reality that exists between a buyer and a seller. You cannot plug in a magic formula that will make your purchase or sale of a business successful. You need to establish a working relationship with the person opposite you at the negotiating table. Your ability to work together toward a mutually acceptable result, coupled with your ability to adjust your expectations about what that result will be, will determine your success or failure. Adjusting expectations is the key to successful negotiation.

If a sale requires the seller to receive a substantial portion of the purchase price over an extended period—in the form of a purchase money promissory note—the relationship between buyer and seller will likely last five to ten years. In this case, the seller depends on the buyer to succeed in the business and make regular payments on the note. In turn, the buyer depends on the seller to have been truthful about the business elements. Signing a note rather than paying cash for a business creates a greater sense of codependency. It requires buyer and seller to perform careful research before the sale and establish a common psychological and emotional understanding as sale negotiations proceed. How to establish this mutual understanding, along being aware of the legal ramifications of your agreement, is the secret to buying or selling a business.

This book, therefore, presents both the buyer's and the seller's perspectives. I urge you to take advantage of this fact and read the entire book, regardless of the category to which you belong.

Making a judgment about the value of the business is just the beginning. The presentation, negotiation, and documentation of the sale are the critical elements. You will find the basic strategies to valuing a business in Chapters 1 to 4. The remainder of the book takes you through the preparation, decision-making, and negotiating process. You will find worksheets on the accompanying CD and sample profit and loss statements throughout the book to help you pinpoint key issues involved in your particular situation and figure out how to deal with them.

I have woven into the context wherever appropriate the methods by which a seller can reduce costs and maximize equity potential. Most of these methods focus on how to prepare the business for sale. Consequently, if you are considering selling, you will benefit from working through the exercises on the CD that accompanies this book whether you ultimately sell the business or not. More importantly, the book will help you decide when a potential sale does not look good, saving you more time and money in the long run.

The book will teach you enough of the buzzwords and basic concepts to understand what your professionals are talking about. It will position you to frame a decent presentation as a seller and give you the tools necessary to understand the fundamentals as a buyer.

Finally, if complicated legal issues arise in your particular situation, this book should not take the place of using competent legal counsel. On the contrary, it is one of my strongest recommendations that you employ the services of professionals, such as an attorney and an accountant, early in the process. You will save money by avoiding costly mistakes!

Remember: your success as a buyer or a seller will depend on the frame of mind you take to the process. By the time you finish this book and the worksheet exercises on the accompanying CD, you will know how much work you have yet to do to make your purchase or sale successful and where to find the help you need if you cannot do it all yourself.

## How to Use This Book

This book was developed by tying together the things that are appropriate to buyers, sellers, entrepreneurs, and professionals and putting them into one package. Certain chapters have more information specific to one type of individual than to others. However, if you are a seller and only read Part Three, The Seller's Perspective, you will completely lose the perspective of the buyer, an absolutely essential and necessary part of your thinking. The reverse is also true: if you are a buyer and only read Part Two, The Buyer's Perspective, you will never have the necessary understanding of the seller's motivations that is so essential to the negotiating process. The only way to fully benefit from what this book has to offer is to read both the buyer's and the seller's perspectives.

## Organization

For the sake of clarity, the book is divided into six parts. The first is an introduction that focuses on financial issues and the preliminary issues any buyer or seller should consider before entering negotiations. Parts Two and Three focus on the concerns of buyers and sellers. Later in Part Five you'll read about the contract that brings them together. Part Four is for both you and the professionals—to become more familiar with the different roles they play in the buy-sell process. Part Six is a revisiting of the financial basics, together with an understanding of the principal elements involved in the core factors of the book. It also contains Chapter 27, answering the all-important question of how to properly understand the valuation aspects of an internet business.

## Part One. Introduction to Buying and Selling a Business

Part One sets out some very specific language and concepts you need to know to properly negotiate a purchase price. If you are not close enough to that stage of the process, you may want to read Parts Two and Three first and then return to Part One after you understand all the elements involved in preparing for and negotiating the purchase and sale of a business.

## Part Two. The Buyer's Perspective

The buyer's section discusses strategies for initial market research, the emotions that sometimes interfere with a buyer's good business sense, and different ways to get into a business, such as buying a franchise start-up, buying an existing franchise, or buying an existing independent business.

The buyer's section also offers sellers important information. It enables a seller to prepare a selling portfolio that appeals to the right buyers and to recognize when a buyer is not right for the sale. Distinguishing between the right buyer and wrong buyer is a subtle but vital part of a business sale. If a buyer fails after taking over the business and defaults on promissory note payments, the business is not sold, and the seller may return to a business so poorly managed in the interim that it is not salvageable. With this in mind, it is important for sellers as well as buyers to read Part Two.

## Part Three. The Seller's Perspective

The seller's section walks you through the finer points of preparing a business for sale. You will run cost analyses, compare profit and loss statements, reconstitute your own financial data, and calculate an asking price. Chapters 16 and 17 also take you through the possibility of selling a business that is losing money or even operating under bankruptcy protection.

Because a buyer's success depends on taking over a sustainable business, buyers must recognize when a seller's financial information does not coincide with industry standards. Buyers will find in Part Three all of the processes sellers must perform to prepare their business for sale. Buyers can then look for discrepancies in the disclosure documents they receive during sale negotiations and perform their own research into competition, customer base, location, lease, advertising methods, and product and labor costs. All of this research will not only help buyers secure the best deal during the sale, but also get them started in the right direction when they take over business operations.

If a buyer finances the purchase with a promissory note to the seller, the buyer-seller relationship will likely last several years. When a buyer knows how a seller prepares a business for sale, reconstitutes the profit and loss statement, and presents all the information, the relationship will be based on mutual understanding and trust rather than suspicion or misunderstanding.

## Part Four. Legal and Financial Considerations

Part Four takes a unique twist in its point of view. Throughout the first three parts, the text is addressed directly to you, the reader, whether you are a buyer or seller. In Part Four, however, the "you" is addressed directly to accountants, lawyers, and brokers. Buyers and sellers should read these very important chapters—the chapters are intentionally written this way so buyers and sellers can read them and then have their accountants, lawyers, and brokers read the chapter that applies specifically to them.

Professionals will find three significant elements in this book:

- The technical methodology for valuing a business
- The individual perspective of the buyer and seller
- The client's emotional involvement that professionals need to recognize throughout the negotiating process

Part Four will help professional advisers prepare for their role in negotiating a business transfer, learn to work as a united team on behalf of the buyer or seller they represent, and make sure buyer and seller are protected from potential post-sale problems.

Buyers and sellers can benefit from Part Four by learning what professional advisers and consultants can and should do in a business sale.

This section is also designed to better prepare you for engagements with your lender. Business growth today, in great part, is based on the ability of a business to generate the dollars necessary to reach the next level of success. This often brings many business people to the banker or other lender without a real understanding of what is expected of them. Knowing the lender's job and perspective gives the borrower a clear understanding of how to succeed in getting the necessary dollars. Buyers preparing a loan will especially benefit from its content and Worksheet 22 on the accompanying CD titled "Know the Lender's Job." Also, note the section in Chapter 25, "What Is a Borrowing Base?"

## Part Five. Contract Elements

The problem in today's small business marketplace seems to be centered, in the general business community, around competition. Fair competition is one thing; losing customers because of competition is quite another. In the franchise community, problems seem to be appearing due to the expiration of franchise contracts. The language of the contracts does not leave much room for survival of the owner/operator after the contract expires. Look to these chapters for some solid advice.

## Part Six. Revisiting the Essentials and Valuing an Internet Business

It is clear in today's competitive business environment that the businessperson must have a complete understanding of his or her business barometers. Part Six includes material that will, for many readers, clear the air of the misunderstandings relative to basic financial paperwork. It includes an explanation of the following:

- What each item on a profit and loss statement (an income statement) is designed to show and how to handle "assumptions"
- What the balance sheet is designed to show, including an understanding of the need for and the use of various ratios
- The purpose of the cash flow forecast and how it relates to the difference between accounting on a cash basis versus accounting on an accrual basis

- The cumulative aspects of a breakeven analysis
- How you can read the financial information and understand what the indicators suggest in terms of trends in the business' history and how they can be recognized, analyzed, and prepared for
- The difference between an asset sale and a stock sale

Part Six also has some additional information that should revitalize the reader in terms of what the real goals should be relative to buyer and seller and the use of the valuation concept.

## Other Helpful Resources

**Ilustrations, Tables, and Samples.** Buying or selling a business requires you to consider many different variables. Not all variables will apply to your particular situation. You will find throughout the book stories, illustrations, tables, and samples that will help clarify the various concepts and apply them to real-life examples—particularly the purchase or sale you are considering. The illustrations, tables, and samples will expose you to many negotiating points, problem issues, and potential pitfalls. Read them carefully and apply the experiences of these former buyers and sellers to your experience. The accompanying CD also contains a supplement with numerous articles, stories, and other information that provides additional insight into the content of the book.

**Worksheets.** The accompanying CD includes worksheets for each chapter. For example, if you are selling a business with a small operating profit, the worksheet for Chapter 16 will help you target problem areas and improve your cost factors. If you are buying a business that includes many different assets as part of the package, The worksheet for Chapter 7 will help you isolate and analyze those assets and their value to the business.

You may find that not all the worksheet questions require answers. Some are designed simply to make you think about the many elements involved in buying and selling a business. Sometimes, just looking over the questions and identifying the answers you don't know will prepare you to meet with your professional advisers.

**Key Points to Remember.** Finally, each chapter features a summary of the most important topics covered in the chapter. If you don't understand one or more of the points listed here after reading the chapter, go back and reread the area where the subject was covered. Understanding and feeling comfortable with the main points of each chapter may make the difference between your ultimate success and failure.

# About the Author

**Ira N. Nottonson** is a Law Review Graduate of Boston College Law School and licensed to practice in the Commonwealth of Massachusetts and the State of California. He has practiced general litigation and business/franchise law with partnerships in Boston, Massachusetts and Westwood, California. At present, he confines his consulting practice to the business of buying, selling, evaluation, and reconstruction of small businesses.

Mr. Nottonson has acted in different capacities for many companies, both private and public: chief executive officer, chief operating officer, and chief legal counsel. He has also, at various times, been head of marketing, franchise sales and has acted as consultant for hundreds of companies throughout the United States and the United Kingdom. These companies include International House of Pancakes, Orange Julius of America, House of Pies, PIP Printing, PIP/UK (the British subsidiary of PIP Printing), Quickprint of America (the Big Red Q Quickprint Centers), Copper Penny Family Restaurants, The Bryman-Sawyer Schools, United Rent-All, and Icelandic Design.

In his legal capacity, Mr. Nottonson has been responsible as a member of the management committee for all of the above companies. He has been an integral part of the planning and implementation of basic business concepts.

Mr. Nottonson's qualifications are particularly unique, as he has also been an entrepreneur in his own right. He has been the owner of an advertising agency, a television production company, a publishing company, a law practice, and a nightclub. This diverse background has given him a better understanding of the day-to-day problems of business from a very personal perspective.

Mr. Nottonson currently works with both startups and problematic situations needing negotiation and reconstruction. He has been appointed as arbiter by the court and has testified on the subjects of small business and business valuations. He has written extensively on the subject of business generally for various newspapers and periodicals and writes a business column for the *Boulder Daily Camera* in his hometown of Boulder, Colorado. In addition, he has been guest lecturer at various colleges and universities as well as a teacher at the Boulder Chamber of Commerce under the auspices of the Small Business Development Center. As an articulate exponent of business concepts, he has appeared on radio and television over the years.

He is also the author of the books, *Before You Go Into Business, Read This!* (1998), *Forming A Partnership and Making It Work* (2007), and *The Small Business Legal Tool Kit* (2007).

# PART ONE

# Introduction to Buying and Selling a Business

# CHAPTER 1

# The Buyer-Seller Relationship

### Illustration 1-1. The Art Gallery

Jonathan Calmes decided to buy an art gallery with his wife. Although they had no experience in the business end of the art world, they liked the idea of dealing with artists and collectors. They would also be moving to the city where the gallery was located. They sought the advice of a business consultant who was recommended by their attorney. Although they were looking for a valuation of the business they were considering, they got a lot more than they expected.

They began to realize that the value of the business was only one of the things they needed to know about. The consultant suggested that they examine various other aspects of the business. Who was the person who traveled around the country buying the art that the gallery was selling? What kind of experience did this person have? What relationship did this person have to the seller? Could this knowledgeable person leave whenever he wanted to? Could this person go to work for someone else or even on his own? What was the customer base? Were there many customers or only a few? What was the relationship of the customers to the seller? How strong was this loyalty and was it transferable to the buyers? Did the seller own the building that housed the business? If not, how long was the lease and did it have an option to renew on terms that would be appropriate to the revenue of the business? Did the business have any potential to grow in the future? What was the competition? Would the competitors be harmful to the business?

Based on these questions and others, Jonathan and his wife realized that buying a business involved a lot more work than they had thought.

Buying and selling a business can be very complex, but it doesn't have to be. As you prepare for and negotiate a purchase or sale, you will encounter some specialized terminology that you will need to know in order to understand the buyer's and seller's financial realities. Both buyer and seller will need to consider a number of new ideas—and consider them from each other's point of view. A third situation is the transfer of a family-owned business to the next generation. While many issues remain the same, some special issues must also be considered.

You will find in this chapter some of the ideas upon which this book's valuation method is based. This chapter is only an introduction. Each concept is explained in more detail in succeeding chapters. You will develop a fuller understanding as each concept becomes integrated with other aspects of the buy-sell process.

## The Buyer Wants an Income

Buyers consider investing in an existing business because they want a new lifestyle and a respectable income—immediately. Some are willing to delay gratification of those desires; most are not. If a buyer says at the negotiating table, "It doesn't work for me," it usually means that the business would not produce enough profit to provide the buyer with a sufficient income.

Many sellers, believe it or not, don't consider this a valid criticism of the deal they're proposing. That is why many sellers are still waiting to find buyers for their businesses.

Most buyers intend to buy a business and take an income from it the very next day. They don't want to be told that they will receive an income after they increase sales, decrease costs, or put into effect some other great plan that, for some reason or other, the seller did not or could not implement while he or she owned the business.

## The Relationship between Operating Profit and Asking Price

Unless a buyer purchases a business with cash—and that is certainly the exception rather than the rule—the buyer will make a down payment and begin a long-term monthly payment schedule with "someone."

The buyer might make payments to a lending institution, but in most cases, the buyer will be paying off a purchase money promissory note to the seller. Once the buyer takes over the business, the business itself should be able to service the purchase money debt.

To understand where these payments come from, picture a simple four-piece pie chart. Allocate a piece of the pie to fixed expenses, another piece to cost of product, and a third piece to labor. The remaining piece of pie is called *operating profit*. Although each business has its own particular percentages, this concept will help you form an idea of the percentage parameters within which any business should properly function.

For example, look at the numbers for a fictional quick-print shop. The Spry Print Shop has an annual gross revenue of $363,797. After paying for all the costs of producing the product (known as *cost of product* or cost of sales), the fixed expenses (including rent and utilities), and all salaries (including insurance, payroll taxes, and the like), there is an annual operating profit of 7.5 percent, or $27,285.

That doesn't look too bad right after the buyer takes over, does it? Well, that depends. If the buyer paid $200,000 for the business, put down 20 percent

($40,000), and financed the balance of $160,000 with the seller over a ten-year period at ten percent interest, the annual total of the monthly payments would be $25,000.

If the buyer uses the $27,285 to pay $25,000 on the promissory note to the seller, the operating profit of $27,285 is reduced to a buyer's income of $1,912. This is clearly not the respectable income the buyer is looking for, which suggests that the purchase price is probably too high.

## It Is the Seller's Problem

Some sellers respond to the above situation with "That's not my problem!" But an income that is too low for the buyer certainly is the seller's problem if it keeps the buyer from taking over the business. It is an even bigger problem if the buyer takes over the business without knowing that the resulting income will be too low.

If the buyer takes over the business and is then unable to receive a decent income and make payments on the note to the seller, both the buyer and the seller have a big problem. Some sellers will say, "Well, that's OK. I'll just take back the business." There are two things the seller needs to consider before accepting that alternative.

- The purpose of the exercise is to make a sale—a permanent sale—so the seller can collect the money and move on.
- The seller might take back the business only to find that it has seriously deteriorated during the buyer's period of operation.

If a seller has to return to a seriously mismanaged business now worth much less than the purchase price, the transaction was a costly misadventure.

## Methods of Valuation

How many methods are there to value a business? Some brokers and sellers develop selling price analyses one page long and others are dozens of pages long. Specifically, every method should involve costs of product, labor, rent, operating profit, and equipment capability and age. Generally, every method should also involve competition, geography, parking, new business, market value fluctuations for buildings, lease, location, and a variety of other considerations depending on the particular business and its relative position in the marketplace.

Some people actually use formulas like 100 percent of gross volume for 12 months. Others speak of a multiple of net profit, which depends on who created the profit and loss statement. Still others include economic values, such as the depreciated value of the equipment.

Most formulas are developed by taking the average selling price in a given trade or industry and working out a formula that fits the majority of the sales. The problem is that this method will normally give a business a bigger value if it is below average and a smaller value if it is above average. It does not necessarily represent a true value of any kind, and it certainly doesn't allow for the buyer's income as an important element.

Realistically, no formula will stand alone without some consideration of the buyer's income.

## The Business Must Pay for Itself

When you buy a house, your loan officer will ask you many detailed questions about your personal income and whether it can support the monthly mortgage payments. If you buy a business, the business will be your personal income. If the business income cannot support the monthly payments on a purchase money promissory note, you will default on the note and the sale will fail. The seller has a responsibility to set an asking price and establish a note payment structure that the business's operating profit can support.

As you will learn in the succeeding chapters, no single formula for valuing a business works without considering all the variables involved:

- Operating profit
- Buyer's income
- Asset variables—such as lease, location, equipment, competition, and customer base—and their value to the business
- Return of investment
- The three primary price adjustors—size of down payment, interest rate, and the length of the note if the sale involves a purchase money promissory note

However, as a seller, if your business shows no operating profit or shows a loss, you will not be able to use this book's method for developing an asking price. You will have to show what your business could and should do if properly operated—when the buyer brings cost of product and cost of labor within industry standards. Some buyers and sellers will face the problem of a business with no profit. Many reasons why a business has not performed well are entirely fixable under a new owner. Chapters 16 and 17 discuss this situation at some length.

## Seller's Equity vs. Buyer's Bonus

Some business brokers contend that a seller has the right to base the asking price on future profits. The more defensible position is that future profits belong to the buyer as a kind of bonus. The seller is entitled only to a purchase price based on the equity he or she has earned from building the business as the owner. The buyer's bonus is the additional profit the buyer will earn from what he or she puts into the business after taking it over.

Look at another example. Spry Print Shop's chief competitor, Bob's Printing, has a more effective management team and is paying less rent for its premises. Bob's Printing has a somewhat larger annual gross revenue than Spry, at $379,289. However, after Bob pays for all the costs of product, fixed expenses, and salaries, he has an operating profit of 25 percent, or $94,822, more than three times the 7.5 percent earned by Spry Print Shop. The price Bob can ask for his shop, based on the larger operating profit, is his earned equity.

The financial picture for Bob's Printing, therefore, looks much different. Bob has built so much equity into his business that he can justify a much higher asking price than Spry's owner, possibly as much as $500,000. Bob's Print Shop will pay for itself—enable the new owner to meet promissory note payments from operating profit—and provide the new owner with an annual income. If the buyer puts 20 percent down, or $100,000, and finances the balance of $400,000 by the seller over a ten-year period at ten percent interest, the annual total of the monthly payments would be $63,432. Deduct this from the $94,822 operating profit and the buyer gets an annual income of $31,390.

Furthermore, if you follow the manager's salary concept discussed in Chapter 2, the new owner of Bob's will eventually be able to take over management of the shop and enjoy the manager's salary in addition to this income from profit.

The format for selling is not as simple as in the two examples just shown. You will need to factor in other variables, such as lease, equipment, marketplace, customer fluctuation, competition, and industry outlook. However, if you develop a selling price without considering the buyer's perspective, you will not negotiate a successful sale.

## Family Business Transitions

One other scenario that must be considered is when children take over the family business. While all of the information in this book will be valuable to parents and children making this transition, other factors also enter into the decision-making process.

It shouldn't surprise anyone who is contemplating such a takeover that preparation is key to the success of the transition and the survival of the business.

In some cases, members of two or more generations have been working together in the business before a takeover is considered. This is not always the case, however. A business owned by a parent offers a unique job opportunity to a son or daughter as well as a potential for the future. With the limitations of job availability and the competitive element being as strong a market force as it is, many young people are looking at the family business from a new perspective. However, the responsibilities of preparation to ensure a smooth transition rest on the shoulders of the parents. This section discusses the issues that parents must consider.

### The Relationship Before the Takeover

There can be many variables in terms of relationships just before a family takeover. In some cases, the son or daughter may have been working in the business for such a long time that he or she has actually become an integral part of the operation. In other cases, although this is sometimes difficult to admit, the son or daughter may never have become an integral or necessary part of the operation, regardless of how long he or she may have been associated with the business.

With respect to a working relationship that already exists, some parents never think their children are capable, no matter how hard their children may try and how effective they might appear to their peers. Other parents give their children credit for total competence without ever having done a really objective analysis of the value of their children to the company if management were left exclusively in their hands. Other variations include having a good general manager who is not a member of the family and who is perfectly competent to maintain the continuity of the business. That person may seem to get along with the son or daughter when the parents are around, but is he or she capable of working well with the son or daughter in the absence of the parents? On the other hand, if there is a general manager and the parents give the operating responsibility to their son or daughter, will they lose the general manager and, in turn, jeopardize the continuity of the business, particularly when the parents will no longer be available for day-to-day consultation?

---

### Illustration 1-1. Identify Suitable Successors

In one situation, the owner of a business had both his son and daughter working in the business with him when he succumbed to a heart attack. Neither of his children had any intention of making the business a permanent part of his or her future. The business, however, represented so large a portion of their father's estate that both children agreed to maintain the continuity of the business for the sake of their mother. The problem of holding the pieces together during the takeover period, for which no preparation had been made, caused tremendous pressures between the children.

The daughter finally left. The son was not capable of handling much of the paperwork by himself. He was not trained for this responsibility and he did not have the inclination to handle the myriad details that had normally fallen on the shoulders of his sister. The business eventually got into trouble. It survives today, but its tempo will never be as dynamic

---

as it was under their father. Adequate preparation could have avoided many, if not most of the problems that the business and the children faced after their father's death.

## Day-to-Day Consultation After Takeover

The extent to which you will want to maintain a relationship with the business after takeover depends on your answers to a variety of questions.

- To what extent is the continuity of the business essential to your retirement?
- To what extent are you still responsible for certain contractual obligations, like the lease, even though you will no longer be connected with operations?
- Are you ready to give up the business and its equity by telling your son and daughter that it is a sink-or-swim situation?
- To what extent are you obliged to make working capital available in the event the business enters a slow period or the industry takes a downturn?
- In other words, just how quickly are you prepared to cut the cord?

You will want to keep a number of factors in mind. Primarily, there is the question of the business concept. You have run the business with a certain philosophy and with the idea that it holds a certain position or niche in its particular trade or industry. It is very easy for someone to quickly and dynamically superimpose a whole new set of principles on the business in your absence. Some of these may be only subtle changes with little long-term effect; others may well impact the very nature of the business.

But here is a place to take care. On the one hand, staying the course and maintaining continuity are important. On the other hand, you must never lose sight of the creative juices of new blood and new energy and you must recognize that the business marketplace is constantly changing. It feeds on creativity and change. The competitive element can be quickly lost by not taking advantage of change when change is necessary or appropriate. It is for this reason that you should stay in touch—not "in *charge*," but "in *touch*."

Make sure that you can monitor the changes and recognize the impact that each change will likely have on your position in the marketplace, before it is too late to cure. After all, larger companies do this by having a board of directors. Consider the next example.

### Illustration 1-2. Stay in Touch

In one situation, the son took over the business after spending many years as an apprentice under his father's supervision. Immediately after taking over, in an attempt to ensure a good competitive position, he leased some new state-of-the-art equipment. The increase in his productivity was minimal. The increase in his client base was also small. But the increase in monthly obligations was substantial. He had not generated the advertising necessary to "fill the time of the new equipment" and make the lease and the monthly payment workable.

The father would have taken a much more conservative position by saying, "Let's examine the market potential before we make the investment." The father was devastated, but the paperwork was already signed. The business, instead of generating a modest retirement income as the father had hoped, turned into a Chapter 7 bankruptcy. The father, instead of retirement, got a new job. Staying "in touch" after the takeover would, undoubtedly, have netted a different result.

## Vulnerability of Assets After Takeover

Unfortunately, when you start a business, you may sign a long-term lease for the premises, a franchise agreement for ten or 20 years, or leases and contracts for the use or purchase of equipment. If you purchase a business, you might sign a promissory note for money you borrow from a lending institution or the seller. These people might be very encouraging, from a personal standpoint, when you tell them that you are turning the business over to your son or daughter. However, they will normally not be inclined to release you from your obligation, since you are probably more stable in the community and likely have more assets than your son or daughter. In other words, your assets and your dollars will remain at risk even though you may no longer be personally involved in the business.

Remember: even though you may have a corporation that is responsible for most of those obligations, you have probably signed all the paperwork as an individual as well. Most banks, landlords, and purveyors of expensive equipment will not allow the corporate signature without either a co-signer or a guarantor. In either case, you will remain responsible until the entire debt is paid, as illustrated below.

---

### Illustration 1-3. Getting Off the Hook

A son who took over a franchise from his mother and father was extremely knowledgeable about that business. He operated it very well for a number of years. In fact, he grew it quite dramatically. Then, he hit a downturn and the business verged on the edge of disaster. The franchise company, the landlord, and the equipment companies all came after the mother and father, neither of whom was capable any longer of operating the business. They were not even aware of its day-to-day activity, but their assets were still vulnerable.

This business has made all kinds of arrangements for readjusting its debts and will probably survive. In this case of a permanent takeover, arrangements should have been made to close out certain obligations after a given time period and let the parents off the hook, providing the business showed proper stability in the early stages, which it did.

---

Moving their business into the hands of the next generation is a dream held by many parents. The children recognize the great opportunity that such a transition provides. It is unfortunate that there are pitfalls to which little or no serious consideration is given—until it is too late. If you are involved in such a situation, make sure that all the parties involved completely understand the nature of the business, its position in the marketplace, and its future in the competitive field. Make sure that you have a plan for the future and a pattern for potential growth that all parties understand thoroughly. Make sure that all of you discuss, analyze, and agree upon certain investments, particularly in the early days, rather than allowing individual, inexperienced judgments to prevail. It is in the nature of youth to reach out creatively toward the future. It is in the nature of parents to reflect on the past to ensure a conservative approach for the future. Neither is wrong. It is, in fact, in the combination of these things that you will find the most successful transitions. It is worthwhile to take the time for this exercise.

## Uncle Sam: Your New Partner After the Sale

Because of the tax implications of every sale transaction, you would be careless not to consider the methods by which you can eliminate or at least minimize the taxes that might be payable if family members inherit your business. The nature of the tax structure in this country allows for various ways to approach this problem. Here are some alternatives:

- Form a legal entity that will allow an incremental increase of ownership over a period of time.
- Give the family member participation on a gift basis, being sure not to incur a gift tax in the process.
- Set up a trust to hold the stock.
- Establish a family limited partnership.

Along with most alternatives, it will be critical to create an insurance program that will handle the tax problem by making dollars available for acquiring stock without diluting its value or the participation of ownership. Failure to do so will often defeat the intention of the original owner.

A brief analysis of some of these alternatives suggests that gifts, like irrevocable trusts, can be inappropriate, because they may cause the owner to lose active control of the enterprise during his or her lifetime. This is not usually the goal that the owner seeks to achieve. Establishing a limited partnership, on the contrary, allows the owner, as the general partner, to maintain control while having portions of the ownership in the hands of limited partners.

This brief examination should make it clear that any approach to the tax question and the owner's ability to maintain control during his or her lifetime will require the advice of an expert. Consult the team of your attorney, your accountant, and your insurance planner before any definitive move is contemplated. (See Part IV.) These are the key points for a smooth transition of a family business:

- Be sure that your children are properly trained to take charge of the daily responsibilities of the business.
- Be aware of potential conflicts with any of your current key employees.

- Take the time to set the stage with the appropriate personnel, vendors, and customers.
- Make sure that your transition period is long enough to ensure success of the turnover.
- Understand the difference between "staying in charge" and "staying in touch."
- Structure the transition to minimize tax implications.

## Adjusting Expectations

The remainder of this book will closely examine several concepts vital to buying and selling a business, including the following:

- Operating profit
- Return of investment
- Return on investment
- Reconstitution of the profit and loss statement
- Owner's compensation vs. manager's salary
- The need to adjust expectations to successfully negotiate a sale

Many of these concepts require at the very least a calculator and at the most a skilled accountant. The last issue—adjusting your expectations—may be the most important and most difficult of all. If either buyer or seller remains inflexible about the terms of the deal, negotiations will fall apart. If you are a seller, you must adjust your expectations about the value of your business to meet your buyer's income needs. If you are a buyer, you must adjust your expectations about the immediate income you may receive to meet the reality of the business's operating profit and working capital requirements.

A buyer normally enters negotiations with only a casual understanding of the business and with several misconceptions. The seller's job is to put the buyer at ease and develop a comfort zone within which the buyer can contemplate his or her future. The seller should anticipate buyer questions and give answers that make sense.

Apart from all the calculations regarding operating profit and note payments, the buyer is going to have a number of projects in mind. He or she may want to replace equipment, upgrade the cosmetics of the business, or add new personnel. The buyer will also be interested in how to increase his or her income. Again, when it comes to buyer's income, the objective valuation of a business must remain flexible.

Some buyers enter the world of business ownership after being behind a salaried desk at $40,000 per year. Others come from executive suites with compensation packages of $400,000 per year. The buyer's current or former income will play a very significant part in the conversation at the negotiating table. And the buyer will also do a lot of thinking at his or her kitchen table. The seller must therefore give the buyer and the buyer's family as many positive elements to think about as possible.

If a buyer wants an income of $100,000 per year and your business, even at its maximum potential, can offer only half that, it is not the right investment. If, on the other hand, the buyer is looking for an annual income of $80,000 and your asking price, based on current operating profit, will afford the buyer $60,000 per year, you may have the beginning of a negotiation. You must be willing to adjust your levels of expectation to make the potential sale a reality.

Examine the practical considerations apart from the technical or mathematical. The buyer needs sufficient funds to pay the purchase money promissory note and all other expenses, both in boom and in bust economic times. Although the seller's goal is to maximize his or her earned equity, the sale is never complete until the note is paid off. The margin between note payments and operating profit cannot be too narrow. If the margin is too narrow, it's not a sale: it's a gamble. If there is a bad month, or if the buyer doesn't maintain the business in the best tradition, or if an employee leaves who is difficult to replace, or if a particularly large client moves away, it could cause a glitch in the payment schedule. A seller should not let greed get in the way of his or her logic as a person.

In the succeeding pages, you will find many of these concepts repeated and explained in greater detail. However, the reigning mottos of this book will remain the same:

- If it doesn't work for the buyer, it doesn't work for the seller.
- The sale is not final until the last note payment is made.

## Key Points to Remember

- The buyer is interested in an immediate and dependable income based on the business and its profit as it exists the day it is purchased.
- Every business is based on four fundamental financial figures—cost of product, cost of labor, general administrative expenses, and profit.
- No pricing formula can be valid without considering the buyer's income.
- The seller is entitled to convert the earned equity of the business to a selling price. Any growth of the business and its profit after the sale is the buyer's bonus.
- Negotiation is the art of adjusting expectations.

# The Financial Picture

**Illustration 2-1. Converting
the IRS P&L to a Seller's P&L**

Peter Stahl wanted to sell his business and he understood that bottom-line profit was the figure he needed to decide the value and the price he should ask. He took out his tax return and found that the profit, after all expenses, on which he paid taxes was $50,000. When he applied the formula that he was using to determine the price, he found that the business was worth only about $250,000. This was much less than he expected. He went to Nathan Ross, a valuation consultant, to see if he was right. Fortunately, Peter was wrong.

Your tax return, prepared properly, is intended to minimize the tax payable within the appropriate legal parameters. But some of the allowable deductions are not going to be obligations to which a buyer would be subjected after a sale. Depreciation is a deduction that doesn't require a cash expenditure; as such, this should become a part of seller's profit. Any one-time expenses during the year (such as the accountant's fees for preparation of the financial paperwork ) would not become obligations for the buyer. And there are often expenses that are not required to operate the business properly (such as for a business trip that the seller chose to take every year but that the buyer might decide not to take). These expenses were discretionary for the seller; the buyer is not obligated to continue incurring them. When these deducted expenses were added up and removed from the profit and loss (P&L) statement, the bottom-line profit turned out to be $100,000, which raised the price of the business from $250,000 to $500,000. Peter was glad he sought the advice of Nathan Ross.

As mentioned in Chapter 1, this book discusses several concepts that may be difficult to understand at first. This chapter leads you through the financial ideas, almost as a glossary introduces and defines new terms you need to have in your vocabulary. This chapter includes the following points:

- Where buyers get their money and how much it costs
- How the risk of failure relates to the investment for success
- What the purchase money promissory note represents
- How to replace owner's compensation with an appropriate manager's salary
- How to reconstitute the profit and loss statement
- What the receivables turnover period and working capital reservoir mean to buyer and seller

One of this book's most important goals is to teach you the language of professionals and experts who work in small business investments every day. While you cannot commit to memory all the ideas and terms used by lawyers and accountants, you can become more familiar with them so you can better understand and interpret what your professionals tell you. Once you finish reading this chapter, complete Worksheet 2 on the accompanying CD to help reinforce some of the financial concepts and terminology you will need when working with your professionals.

# Financial Considerations for the Buyer

The first decision you face as you consider buying a business is how to finance it. Below are the three essential factors involved in that decision: your cash return, your level of risk, and your financing method.

## Buyer's Cash Return

Whenever you use your own cash in an investment, you lose the money you would have earned if you had left it where it was. Therefore, you need to compare the return your cash investment would yield in the business you buy and the return it would get in the stocks, mutual funds, or savings account where you have it now.

First, compare your percentage return from your current investment and the interest rate you would pay if you left your money in that investment and borrowed the money to buy the business. In this example, use a percentage return of 8 percent, which is not an unreasonable expectation for a relatively secure investment at this time. If you pay $200,000 in cash to buy a business, you lose $16,000 per year ($200,000 x .08) by not investing that money elsewhere. On the other hand, if you do not use your own cash, you have to borrow money from the seller or elsewhere at 10 percent or higher. Taking the cash out of your invested capital is actually less expensive for you. (You can benefit from other advantages when you use cash for the purchase, as discussed in Chapter 3.)

Next, compare the return you expect from the business and the return you're currently getting from your investment, again using 8 percent as your current rate of return. If you invest $200,000 in a business with $200,000 gross revenues and 10 percent operating revenues, the $20,000 operating profit is the cash return on your investment. If you invest your own money, essentially borrowing money from yourself, you lose $16,000 per year ($200,000 x .08), but you gain $20,000 per year in operating profit. You get a better return on investment by paying cash for the business than you would get if you had the same $200,000 in another investment at 8 percent. If, on the other hand, the operating profit is only $15,000, you will make more money by leaving your money invested and earning 8 percent, $16,000 per year on $200,000, or negotiating a lower purchase price for the business.

No matter where the money comes from, it will cost you something. The trick is to compare all the percentages and come to the negotiating table knowing exactly what you can risk and how much it will cost.

## High Risk

The interest, or return, you receive from an investment is often based on the level of risk involved in the investment. You can get a heck of a return by investing in the third race at Churchill Downs, but there is also a high risk of losing. High potential return represents high risk.

When you buy a business, there are other risks involved besides the financial percentages. For some businesses, a change in ownership can mean a dramatic change in stability—for example, if the business depends on the ability of the owner to go out and sell. On the other hand, if the business is a retail shop that depends primarily on location and longevity for its growth, a change in ownership could make little difference. If the business's success depends more on location, you face less uncertainty in your investment as long as the location stays the same. If the business relies on the previous owner's contacts or personality, your risk is higher if you cannot use similar resources or otherwise compensate. If the business you are considering buying has these types of risk, you want to negotiate a lower asking price to enjoy higher returns after you overcome the initial risks. The seller will counter your arguments by assuring you that your investment is secure. The seller will explain the history of the industry, the growth of the marketplace, and the need for the product or service. Learn what each of these things represents in terms of risk or the stability of the business.

## Financing Methods

Businesses rarely sell for cash. The buyer is more likely to make a cash down payment and have the seller carry a note for the remainder of the purchase price, a purchase money promissory note. When this happens, it is certainly in the seller's best interest that the buyer succeed with the business. Otherwise, the seller may be left with much litigation and aggravation. Ultimately, the sale has to work for the buyer in order to work for the seller as well. Remember: the sale is not final until the last check clears in final payment on the purchase money promissory note.

If you obtain the necessary money from a lending institution, that third-party lender will have an investment in your success because it will hold the purchase money promissory note instead of the seller. Because payment of the promissory note depends so much on the buyer's success, banks and other lenders are normally not so inclined to put their money at risk in the purchase of a business. The third-party lender can normally find a more secure investment in the real estate community involving hard assets that do not depend on the energies and abilities of an individual. The seller, on the other hand, has fewer alternatives if he or she wants to sell the business.

There are many methods for adjusting the purchase price or the payment schedule on a note. The list is endless. If you consider any of the following methods, you may want to have an accountant by your side.

- Increase or decrease in the down payment
- Special arrangements for the buyer to pay the down payment in increments
- Services or products made available at a discount to the seller after the sale, so long as the seller does not remain in a competitive position
- Responsibility retained by the seller to pay certain payables, some of which may not be accrued
- An agreement that the buyer will pay the seller for a percentage of receivables in cash (rather than, as is usually the case, the seller being responsible for all accrued payables and entitled to all accrued receivables)

- Change in the length of time to pay the purchase money promissory note
- Lowering the interest rate on the purchase money promissory note
- Particular assets to be retained by the seller or purchased separately by the buyer—often including personal computers, software, and office furniture
- Security given by the buyer in addition to the business itself, such as a second trust deed on personal real estate holdings
- Secondary elements, such as professional fees, to be absorbed by one party or the other
- An agreement by the buyer to pay the seller's broker's fees in part or in full
- A transition period in which the seller remains with the business after the sale as a paid consultant

Chapter 3 discusses some of these price adjustments in more detail, particularly the length of the note and the size of the down payment.

Both buyer and seller will have to be engaged in mathematical calculations and percentages. As a result, both need to know the many factors that can become a part of financing the purchase.

## Financial Considerations for the Seller

Because your asking price is based on operating profit, you want to do everything in your power to make that operating profit look good. For most of your career, however, you have reported to the Internal Revenue Service (IRS) an operating profit that you wanted to look as small as possible because you paid taxes on it. Changing your profit and loss statement (P&L) from one used for tax purposes to one used for selling purposes is called *reconstituting* your P&L. It is your first step to selling your business.

### Reconstituting the Profit and Loss Statement

As a seller, you must reconstitute your P&L to present all the financial pieces in the right light and with the right continuity. Some things in your P&L are irrelevant to the buyer. As you know, a good P&L for the IRS is one that contains all the possible deductions the tax code allows, so your business shows a minimum of profit and the taxes you pay are lower. On the other hand, by taking out expense items allowed by the tax code that were appropriate but not essential to the operation of the business, your business will show a bigger profit. As a result, your business will be valued higher.

Keep in mind that both P&Ls are legal and legitimate. You are not committing any deception here. In fact, you will probably show the buyer and/or the buyer's accountant both sets of numbers at some point, so that they understand how you prepared them and how the buyer can prepare a P&L for the IRS in the future.

Under no circumstances, however, do you have any flexibility relative to gross revenues or the cost of sales. These cannot be changed! While better marketing may increase revenues and greater attention to detail may decrease cost of sales, these are not items personal to the owner. The profit and loss statement at the end of this chapter—presented before and after reconstitution—illustrates this point.

The time to present your financial information in the form most effective and most positive for a potential sale is during the initial negotiations. You want to look at the financials from your potential buyer's perspective. How will the bottom line work for him or her? Will there be enough left to feed the family after the payments on the purchase money promissory note? Is there enough potential in the business to satisfy the buyer's expectations now and in the future?

Some buyers are more sophisticated than others. If your buyer wants to discuss profit and loss only, you should be prepared with concrete figures. Be careful not to confuse the buyer with information you think is pertinent, but that the buyer has not requested or shown an inclination to examine.

## Depreciating Equipment

Can you ask your buyer to pay for equipment that has depreciated to zero? Again, the Internal Revenue Code may allow a piece of equipment to be completely depreciated in five to seven years, but that does not mean the equipment is really worth zero at the end of that time. The notion that equipment the IRS allows you to depreciate is really worth nothing is one of the biggest fictions in negotiating a business sale. The depreciation period is an arbitrary life span given to equipment and periodically changed by the legislature for tax purposes. You may depreciate your car over a relatively short period as allowed by the IRS, but it doesn't mean that your Ford, Cadillac, or Mercedes is then worth zero.

Some equipment simply does not change much over the years. You must examine and evaluate the life of equipment, including replacement parts, depending on the particular industry involved. The real question is the relevance of the technology applied in the equipment.

If buyers understand the business, a discussion about the equipment's value will be easy and productive. If they don't, the negotiations will be more difficult because buyers will be looking at depreciation as essential to the calculations. After all, they always see it in the P&L prepared for tax purposes. Remember: depreciation is designed to anticipate the cost of replacing equipment as it becomes necessary. Since nobody knows when replacement will be necessary, the legislature has given it an arbitrary time period. In any case, you should be prepared to explain the role your equipment plays in the total picture of your business, its adequacy to perform the job for which it was designed, and the requirements for repair and replacement over a given period.

## Owner's Compensation Package

In addition to equipment depreciation, another figure that affects your operating profit is the figure you use to represent the owner's salary. Each owner is likely to take a different compensation package; you are not responsible for what your buyer decides to include as owner's compensation after buying the business. An owner can enhance his or her personal income in many ways, such as having the business pay for cars, insurance, travel, or other benefits. If you have included similar items in your compensation package, you will have a badly distorted set of costs and your operating profit will reflect these costs, unless you remove them from the P&L.

When you remove the P&L enhancements and equipment depreciation from your P&L, your business will show a higher operating profit. You will be able to show the buyer more easily that the business can stand on its own and pay its new obligations, like the note to the seller, out of current revenues.

## The Absentee Owner Concept and Manager's Salary

One of the most important steps toward that goal is to establish an appropriate manager's salary in place of any inflated owner's salary you may currently enjoy. Although absentee ownership is not appropriate for most businesses, it is the basic concept used to develop an appropriate manager's salary. You need a manager's salary for one simple reason—because you deduct cost of labor to calculate your operating profit, you must create a standard for measuring the cost of labor that is consistent with the other financial elements of the business.

Just about every industry has developed a comparison of manager's salary and gross sales at some point in its history, and you can obtain industry information on which to base your ratio of manager's salary to gross sales. For example, in one industry, a manager might make $20,000 per year on sales of $2 million, or one percent of sales. In another industry, a manager might make $20,000 per year on sales of only $200,000, ten percent of sales. You need to establish a standard appropriate for your industry and marketplace that is separate from the items you, as owner, have included in your compensation package. Make this a priority item—it is that important!

Once you develop a formula, you won't have to allocate a manager's salary arbitrarily to show your true operating profit. If, for example, you are paying your son three times what you would pay another manager, there is no reason to include that salary in your selling formula. You should use a manager's salary in all the P&Ls and refrain from talking about owner's compensation at all.

During the initial transition period, the buyer may retain the manager and act as an absentee owner. The new owner can spend time learning about the business and the industry and stabilizing and building the business. After completing this initiation or training period, the new owner may then choose to take on the manager's role and the manager's money. By adding this salary to the net profit and the P&L enhancements, the new owner will have an idea what the business can mean to his or her family in terms of total income.

The concept of manager's salary is vital to the valuation process. Many variables go into determining manager's salary, including industry standards, levels of responsibility, dollar volume, and cost of living in a specific geographical area. For example, the salary for a manager in San Francisco who handles a gross volume of $300,000 may not be the same as for a manager in Kansas City handling the same gross volume of $300,000. In San Francisco, $27,000 represents much less purchasing power than $27,000 in Kansas City. Also, the manager's salary you choose must be appropriate to the talent necessary to handle the responsibilities of the business.

## Receivable Turnover Period and Working Capital Reservoir

Finally, one last set of terms you need to be familiar with relates to the cash requirement you want your buyer to bring to the negotiating table.

Years ago, people used to talk about certain businesses as *cash businesses*. The customers paid for the product or service at the counter in cash when they picked it up. Times have changed! Very few service businesses and only some product businesses can claim to be cash businesses today. Now, if IBM wants you to do its printing, but it pays its bills 90 days after receiving the invoices, you will probably still take the job because you feel secure that IBM will pay. You are carrying its receivable for 90 days. IBM will not immediately reimburse you for the paper you used for that job, or the ink, or the labor, or, in some cases, outside work such as typesetting that you had to pay for right away. Some businesspeople call this the *receivable turnover period*.

Credit cards can decrease the gamble of collection and eliminate the turnover period. However, credit cards represent another percentage loss on the bottom line, because of the amount credit card companies charge for their service.

The buyer must always have a *working capital reservoir*. The amount you designate for this purpose can vary depending on the particular client mix for your business. Just as an example, a reasonable request in the printing industry is an amount equal to a month and a half of gross revenues. In the case of a shop doing approximately $25,000 per month, this amounts to $37,500. Before your buyer can begin to think about making a down payment, he or she must have a minimum of $37,500 in an operating account. So, to put a $50,000 down payment on the purchase of the business, the buyer needs $87,500 in cash.

A cash requirement that size may be too big for many potential buyers. Chapter 3 will discuss some of the variables involved in getting past the cash requirement and making the sale. It shows you some of the more creative and complex methods for financing or price structuring the sale of a business.

Before you move on, however, look at the reconstituted P&L on the following pages and the effect it has on operating profit and asking price.

## Key Points to Remember

- The buyer must consider risk as one of the elements involved in business investment and recognize the effect it may have on his or her return of investment.
- Many elements can be adjusted in the buy-sell negotiation, apart from the price.
- Reconstituting the P&L will maximize the profit picture in the seller's favor.
- The owner's compensation package must be converted to a manager's salary in order for the profit equation to make any sense in valuing the business.
- Both buyer and seller must be sure that the buyer has a strong working capital reservoir to ensure continuity and success of the business takeover.

---

### Sample of a Reconstituted P&L—Alice's Print 'n' Copy

The two columns on the profit and loss statement for Alice's Print 'n' Copy represent the figures before and after reconstituting the P&L to sell the business.

The following items are personal to the owner and not to the business and are therefore removed from the reconstituted P&L:

- The owner's draw in excess of an appropriate manager's salary

---

- The owner's auto insurance payments and bank payments on car unless delivery is part of the service
- Health insurance for the owner's spouse
- Airline tickets for a working holiday in London

Here are some other items a seller might consider eliminating:

- Legal and accounting costs attributable exclusively to preparing for the sale
- One-time equipment purchases that were expensed rather than depreciated

Be careful not to exclude things like dues and subscriptions or donations, repair and maintenance, or outside labor, all of which are integral parts of running the business no matter who owns it. If the new owner can find a way to eliminate the use of outside labor or decides to drop a membership in a trade organization, that savings is part of the buyer's bonus, not the seller's equity.

If you reconstitute your P&L carefully and reasonably, it is a very effective selling tool. Of course, the best way to raise the operating profit and thus the asking price is to actually increase sales or decrease costs—in reality and not just on paper.

The maximum asking price payable from an annual operating profit of $16,690 is $105,000 payable over ten years at 10 percent interest. (You will learn how to calculate a maximum asking price in Chapter 3.) However, an asking price as high as $105,000 will mean payments that will take all of the operating profit and leave nothing for the buyer's income. Alice's Print 'n' Copy will more likely sell for much less, possibly as little as $80,000, depending on other negotiated items, such as a transition period, the value of equipment, location, and lease, or the size of the down payment, the interest rate, or the length of the promissory note.

With a selling price of $80,000, financed with a ten-year note at 10 percent interest and a 10 percent down payment, the buyer will have to meet annual note payments of $11,418 from the operating profit of $16,690 per year. This will give the buyer an annual income of $5,272.

The manager at Alice's is receiving $16,640 per year in salary. When the new owner feels comfortable enough running the business without a manager, he or she can release the manager and add that $16,640 salary to his or her income, raising that income to $21,912 per year.

|  | BEFORE | | AFTER | |
|---|---|---|---|---|
|  | Year to Date | % | Year to Date | % |
| **Sales** | | | | |
| Printing | $101,499 | 74.5% | $101,499 | 74.5% |
| Outside Services | 31,451 | 23.11% | 31,451 | 23.11% |
| Copier | 3,431 | 2.52% | 3,431 | 2.52% |
| Returns and | | | | |
| Allowances | (275) | −0.20% | (275) | −0.20% |
| **Total Sales** | **$136,106** | **100%** | **$136,106** | **100%** |
| **Cost of Sales** | | | | |
| Beginning Inventory | $2,182 | 1.60% | $2,182 | 1.60% |
| Purchases | 18,637 | 13.69% | 18,637 | 13.69% |
| Outside Vendors | 15,208 | 11.17% | 15,208 | 11.17% |
| Ending Inventory | (1,514) | −1.11% | (1,514) | −1.11% |
| Equipment Supplies | 4,361 | 3.20% | 4,361 | 3.20% |
| **Total Cost of Sales** | **$38,874** | **28.55%** | **$38,874** | **28.55%** |
| **GROSS PROFIT** | **$97,232** | **71.45%** | **$97,232** | **71.45%** |
| **Operating Expenses** | | | | |
| Salaries & Wages[1] | $14,645 | 10.76% | $14,560 | 10.70% |
| Partners' Salaries[1] | 20,800 | 15.28% | 16,640 | 12.23% |
| Taxes on Payroll[1] | 2,718 | 2.00% | 2,392 | 1.76% |
| Advertising | 6,197 | 4.55% | 6,197 | 4.55% |
| Auto Expenses[2] | 2,152 | 1.58% | 900 | 0.66% |
| Bad Debt Expense | 320 | 0.24% | 320 | 0.24% |
| Copier Service | 906 | 0.67% | 906 | 0.67% |
| Depreciation[3] | 9,297 | 6.83% | 0 | 0.00% |
| Dues/Subscriptions | 417 | 0.31% | 417 | 0.31% |
| Franchise Royalty | 11,284 | 8.29% | 11,284 | 8.29% |
| Insurance | 2,434 | 1.79% | 2,434 | 1.79% |
| Health Insurance[4] | 1,474 | 1.08% | 874 | 0.64% |
| Legal & Accounting | 2,828 | 2.08% | 2,828 | 2.08% |
| Office Expenses | 1,813 | 1.33% | 1,813 | 1.33% |
| Over and Short | (6) | 0.00% | (6) | 0.00% |
| Promotion | 229 | 0.17% | 229 | 0.17% |
| Rent | 11,760 | 8.64% | 11,760 | 1.47% |

|  | BEFORE | | AFTER | |
|---|---|---|---|---|
|  | Year to Date | % | Year to Date | % |
| **Operating Expenses** | | | | |
| Repairs and | | | | |
| Maintenance | $2,007 | 1.47% | $2,007 | 1.47% |
| Supplies | 356 | 0.26% | 356 | 0.26% |
| Taxes and License | 920 | 0.68% | 920 | 0.68% |
| Telephone | 1,612 | 1.18% | 1,612 | 1.18% |
| Travel and | | | | |
| Entertainment[5] | 1,738 | 1.28% | 238 | 0.17% |
| Utilities | 1,861 | 1.37% | 1,861 | 1.37% |
| **Total Operating Expenses** | **$97,762** | **71.84%** | **$80,542** | **59.19%** |
| **TOTAL OPERATING PROFIT** | **($530)** | **-0.39%** | **$16,690** | **12.26%** |

1. Save $4,571 from the differential in salaries and payroll taxes.
2. Save $1,252 after deducting payments on owner's car.
3. Save $9,297 on equipment depreciation.
4. Save $600 after deducting spouse's insurance.
5. Save $1,500 on owner's business/personal trip to Europe.

# CHAPTER 3

# Negotiating Price and Pricing Variables

### Illustration 3-1. It Must Buy Itself

Alice Wallace was told by her consultant that when you value a business to buy, which Alice was in the process of doing, you must follow the philosophy that "a business must be able to buy itself." Alice didn't understand what this meant. Her consultant explained that a buyer needs to be able to take a large enough salary to take care of his or her family and have enough left over to pay back the money borrowed to buy the business. It's really simple. And, if the business can't pay back the money within a reasonable time (a maximum of ten years, even with a "no risk" business), don't buy it!

The previous two chapters covered some of the fundamental financial relationships created between a buyer and a seller in negotiating a business sale. Your accountant and attorney will likely handle the fine print and mathematical calculations involved in getting those relationships defined on paper. Nonetheless, you need to understand on what theories those calculations and provisions are based and how you, whether buying or selling, can make them work to your best advantage.

Toward that end, this chapter provides charts, graphs, and an amortization method and discusses pricing variables, such as size of down payment, interest rate, and length of note. While you should always consult your accountant and attorney before agreeing to any pricing option, this chapter gives you a good foundation for negotiating a price structure and understanding the recommendations of your accountant and your attorney.

Keep in mind that a seller is dealing with two sets of figures in the negotiations. The first figure comes from using a method of valuing the business based on the total purchase price derived from the operating profit, regardless of the amount of the down payment. The second figure is based very much on the amount of the down payment, because the size of the down payment will determine how much money the buyer would have left each month after making the payment on the purchase money promissory note (PMPN). As you read this chapter, look for how these two sets of figures work and how they will affect the asking price of a business.

## Financing Methods

A buyer usually pays for a business in cash or finances it through a PMPN. Financing is often carried by the seller, but in some cases it may be carried by a third party. Whether the buyer pays cash or finances all or part of the purchase price, some price adjustments may be necessary, depending on the figures and the percentages with which the buyer and seller are working. While pluses and minuses exist in all forms of financing, the seller will minimize later complications by getting as much cash upfront as possible.

## An All-Cash Deal

Apart from the tax consequences, it's best for a seller to receive cash for the full purchase price. Then the seller is relieved of any future responsibility to the business. An all-cash deal is very unlikely, but if it's a possibility, the seller should adjust the price to accommodate the present value of money—that is, money collected in cash now has a greater value than money paid over a ten-year period, interest notwithstanding. An all-cash deal should, therefore, offer some price advantage to the buyer in current dollars. For the seller, the obvious benefits of a cash sale also warrant that he or she consider a price break that allows a cash deal. The more buyers are willing to put down in cash—whether a large down payment or the entire purchase price—the larger the concession they will expect in the purchase price.

The negative side of a cash sale for the seller is that if the entire purchase price of the business is received in a single tax year, the capital gains tax can be devastating. The seller will also find that the rate of interest paid by a buyer on a PMPN is normally higher than the interest rate the seller can get in the investment marketplace. An accountant can be very helpful in working out the differentials for the present value of the dollar, the effects of the capital gains tax, and the interest rate potential. For the buyer, the negative side of a cash sale is that the buyer who owes nothing to the seller has no leverage for dealing with any misrepresentations the seller made during negotiations.

## A Seller-Carry Deal

The more common form of financing is for the buyer to make a cash down payment and for the seller to carry the balance of the purchase price at a specified interest rate and over a specified period of time. In this situation, these are the three primary variables:

- Size of the down payment
- Length of the note
- Interest rate

Before examining these variables in detail, remember one last important item. Whatever money the buyer uses to purchase the business, particularly what he or she puts down in cash upfront, is money taken from investment elsewhere. The seller must be prepared to factor in the buyer's lost investment income in negotiating the sale.

## Negotiating the Down Payment

If a buyer does not make a down payment or makes a small down payment, the seller will commonly adjust the payment plan to make up for the lack of cash upfront, either by increasing the interest rate on the PMPN or by decreasing the length of the note. The adjustment is to increase the return to the seller without making the payments too onerous for the buyer. Any major adjustments can jeopardize the sale by making the business simply unaffordable for the buyer. A seller cannot raise the price to a potential buyer who is otherwise qualified if the business's operating profit cannot support the larger figure.

On the other hand, a buyer who makes a large down payment should not be getting less for paying more. If the buyer makes a large down payment and thereby lowers the amount of the PMPN, the annual note payments are lower, which means the new owner is earning a larger net profit each year. The buyer is actually purchasing a higher annual income. This is the buyer's bonus.

The best negotiating position for the seller is to pursue not a higher asking price, but rather a larger down payment. By putting more cash down, the buyer reduces the loan amount that must be paid from the operating profit. The seller can show the buyer how to generate a higher annual income and the seller walks away with more cash in hand.

To demonstrate how this works, here's an example. Assume that a business with gross revenues of $300,000 per year sells for $250,000. The full purchase price is represented by a ten-year note at a 10 percent interest rate fully amortized—that is, the principal and interest will be paid completely by the end of the ten years. Assume further that the business yields a 20 percent operating profit, or $60,000. The full loan amount of the PMPN is $250,000; if the seller carries it for ten years at 10 percent, the payments are $3,303 per month, or $39,636 per year. After making the PMPN payments from the operating profit, the buyer receives a net profit of $20,364 per year.

In this scenario, the seller may reasonably ask for a 20 percent down payment, $50,000. If the seller carries the balance of the purchase price, the loan amount is only $200,000 and the annual payments drop to $31,716. With the larger down payment, it is easier for the buyer to make payments on the PMPN out of the operating profit. The buyer would then, after the payments on a ten-year note at 10 percent, enjoy a profit of $28,284. The larger down payment, in addition to any possible concession in the purchase price, gives the buyer a larger annual income from the business.

In negotiating the size of the down payment, the seller should recognize that the buyer is using his or her own money, $50,000 in this example, for the down payment and is losing money every year in passive income that the $50,000 could have generated. If the buyer's investment income was earning 8 percent, the buyer loses $4,000 on the cash down payment, $50,000 times 8 percent. The seller could reasonably lower the purchase price by $4,000 as a concession in recognition of the loss in passive income.

As you can see in Table 3-1, a $60,000 operating profit could also support an asking price of $300,000, 100 percent of gross revenues. The payments, with the same 10 percent interest rate, are $47,568 per year, which still leaves $12,432 in the buyer's pocket after payments on the PMPN.

However, $12,432 may not leave the buyer enough room to handle a bad season, an unexpected employee problem, or the loss of a big customer. The seller can counter the buyer's concern that the operating profit after note payments would be too small by illustrating the larger annual net profit the buyer would have in the future if he or she made a larger down payment now. The seller does not have to lower the price—the size of the down payment leaves plenty of room for negotiation.

The buyer's annual net profit can rise substantially with a larger down payment. Table 3-1 shows how a 20 percent down payment on a $300,000 asking price will nearly double the buyer's net profit from what it would be with no down payment—from $12,432 to $21,948.

| Asking Price | Down Payment | Size of PMPN | PMPN Payments per year | Buyer's Net Profit per Year* |
|---|---|---|---|---|
| $300,000 | No Down Payment | $300,000 | $47,568 | $12,432 |
| $300,000 | 10% ($30,000) | $270,000 | $42,816 | $17,184 |
| $300,000 | 20% ($60,000) | $240,000 | $38,052 | $21,948 |
| $250,000 | No Down Payment | $250,000 | $39,635 | $20,364 |
| $250,000 | 10% ($25,000) | $225,000 | $35,667 | $24,333 |
| $250,000 | 20% ($50,000) | $200,000 | $31,716 | $28,284 |

*After deducting PMPN from operating profit.

**Table 3-1.** Adjustments in the down payment
This table assumes gross sales of $300,000 and an operating profit of 20 percent, or $60,000 per year, and a ten-year note at 10 percent interest.

# Negotiating the Length of the Note

A buyer is concerned about the length of the PMPN period because it affects the amount of his or her monthly payment on the note. A shorter payment schedule means a bigger monthly payment and thereby a smaller monthly income available from the operating profit.

The seller is concerned about the note's length because it affects the price he or she can justify asking for the business. A longer payment period lowers the size of the monthly payments and enables the seller to ask a higher price because the buyer can handle the payments more easily. The negative side of a longer payment schedule is the added risk of collecting the entire balance. Any number of elements might cause a downturn in the business; the longer the note, the greater the chances of this happening. The seller may be more interested in getting a higher price for the business than in getting paid more quickly on a shorter payment schedule. On the other hand, if the seller wants to collect the balance of the purchase price more quickly, he or she must be prepared to lower the price so that the operating profit can handle the higher monthly payments on the shorter note.

To demonstrate how different repayment periods affect the asking price and the buyer's net profit, look at Table 3-2, which takes the same business with annual gross revenues of $300,000 and a 20 percent operating profit, but with a seven-year note at 10 percent. With a loan amount of $250,000, the payments are $49,800 per year. With a loan amount of $300,000, the payments are $59,760, just barely payable out of the $60,000 operating profit.

| Length of Note | Asking Price | Annual Note Payment | Net Profit to Buyer |
|---|---|---|---|
| 10 years @ 10% | $300,000 | $47,568 | $12,432 |
| 10 years @ 10% | $250,000 | $39,636 | $20,364 |
| 7 years @ 10% | $300,000 | $59,760 | $240 |
| 7 years @ 10% | $250,000 | $49,800 | $10,200 |
| 5 years @ 10% | $300,000 | $76,488 | ($16,488) |
| 5 years @ 10% | $250,000 | $63,740 | ($3,740) |

**Table 3-2.** Adjustments in the length of the note
This table assumes an operating profit of $60,000.

It is simple enough to look at the five-year amortization to see that trying to collect the money within this shorter time makes the obligation much more difficult for the buyer. With the figures used in this example, the business cannot pay for itself, so the seller should reduce the asking price. If the seller is willing to reduce the price to accelerate the payments and recover his or her equity value more quickly, then the sale will work for both parties.

# Negotiating the Interest Rate

A promissory note commonly has an interest rate 2 percent to 3 percent above the prime rate. Again, if you are selling, you do not want to jeopardize the sale by demanding an unreasonable rate. This book uses a standard interest rate of 10 percent for all examples. Based on prevailing rates over an extended period of time, it has proven to be a comfortable rate for both buyer and seller, based on the premise that the buyer couldn't borrow at an interest rate that low and the seller couldn't invest at an interest rate that high. Rates other than 10 percent may be appropriate as the interest rate fluctuates.

Keep in mind that, regardless of the economy or the bank rates, the buyer and the seller are always in a position to discuss and negotiate the interest rate, which may ultimately be based on personal bargaining factors. Whatever interest rate a buyer and a seller might negotiate, the concepts in this book remain valid.

Usury statutes can limit the rate of interest a seller can charge, however. These statutes and limitations vary from state to state. Check for your particular jurisdiction to ensure that the rate you want to use would be legal.

## Amortization Tables

Although amortization tables are available and you should have one, there is an easy way to have the figures handy when you need them, even without the schedule. You can use a simple method to determine the monthly and annual payments for a PMPN at any interest rate and for any period.

The payout figures shown in Table 3-3 will give you a quick idea about how the numbers will work for your business. Amortization schedules are obtainable from any savings and loan association and most banks and credit agencies as well as online. You should prepare some of these factor schedules and become familiar with their use relative to the interest and payment-period ratio before you start discussing buying or selling.

As you can see in Table 3-3, the figures of $2,124.71 for five years, $1,660.12 for seven years, and $1,321.51 for ten years are based on a $100,000 note at a 10 percent interest rate. To determine the monthly or yearly obligation on a different loan amount, divide the amount by 100,000 and multiply the result by the appropriate factor, as shown in Table 3-3. That gives a monthly payment figure. Multiply it by 12 and you get the yearly PMPN payment.

| Loan Amount | Term | Monthly Factor | Multiple (Loan/100,000) | Monthly Payments | Yearly Payments |
|---|---|---|---|---|---|
| $100,000 | 5 years | 2,124.71 | 1.00 | $2,124.71 | $25,497 |
| $100,000 | 7 years | 1,660.12 | 1.00 | $1,660.12 | $19,921 |
| $100,000 | 10 years | 1,321.51 | 1.00 | $1,321.51 | $15,858 |
| $135,000 | 5 years | 2,124.71 | 1.35 | $2,686.36 | $34,420 |
| $135,000 | 7 years | 1,660.12 | 1.35 | $2,241.16 | $26,894 |
| $135,000 | 10 years | 1,321.51 | 1.35 | $1,784.04 | $21,408 |
| $83,000 | 5 years | 2,124.71 | .83 | $1,763.51 | $21,162 |
| $83,000 | 7 years | 1,660.12 | .83 | $1,377.90 | $16,535 |
| $83,000 | 10 years | 1,321.51 | .83 | $1,096.85 | $13,162 |

**Table 3-3.** A simple amortization method
The monthly factor shown in this chart is based on a $100,000 note at 10 percent interest. You can use this monthly factor to determine the payments on any loan amount at 10 percent interest by dividing the loan amount by 100,000 and multiplying the result (shown in the fourth column) by the monthly factor.

# Price Structuring Begins with the Buyer's Perspective

By understanding the variables and their interrelationships, a seller can work backwards from operating profit to find out what yearly PMPN obligation it can support and still allow a potential buyer the yearly income he or she wants. The basic variables that will cause the figures to change are the size of the down payment, the length of the note, and the interest rate. Once a seller knows what down payment a potential buyer can offer, how long the note will be, and what interest rate to set, a workable asking price should begin to emerge. The seller will know exactly what price will work with the operating profit and the buyer's needs. If the business doesn't pay for itself and the buyer goes under, the seller hasn't made a sale.

You can determine the maximum asking price for the particular length of note you will use by applying the following formula:

Operating profit ÷ annualized payment from amortization table
x 100,000 = maximum asking price

On a note with a 10 percent interest rate, the annualized payment amount from the amortization method shown in Table 3-3 is $15,858 for a ten-year note, $19,921 for a seven-year note, and $25,497 for a five-year note. If a business is doing $200,000 gross volume and maintaining an operating profit of 20 percent, $40,000 per year, you can determine the maximum asking price as follows:

- On a ten-year note: the operating profit of $40,000 divided by the yearly figure of $15,858 (from Table 3-3) equals 2.5, which is multiplied by $100,000 to get a maximum asking price of $250,000, payable from the operating profit, leaving no income for the buyer.
- On a seven-year note: the operating profit of $40,000 divided by the yearly figure of $19,921 (from Table 3-3) equals 2, which is multiplied by $100,000 to get a maximum asking price of $200,000, payable from the operating profit, leaving no income for the buyer.
- On a five-year note: the operating profit of $40,000 divided by the yearly figure of $25,497 (from Table 3-3) equals 1.56, which is multiplied by $100,000 to get a maximum asking price of $156,000, payable from the operating profit, leaving no income for the buyer.

If you examine sales over recent years, you will find that the seven-year amortization gives you the most reasonable seller's asking price. The payments on a five-year amortization tend to be too difficult for the buyer. A ten-year amortization allows the breathing room needed by both buyer and seller. But, again, a larger down payment changes the working figures for both buyer and seller.

Table 3-4 illustrates all these variables—operating profit, down payment, asking price, and length of note. If you're selling, pay particular attention to the last column, because that is where your potential buyer is focused.

| Asking Price | Down Payment | PMPN Payment per year | Operating Profit | Buyer's Net Profit per Year |
|---|---|---|---|---|
| **10-Year Note** | | | | |
| $250,000 | No Down Payment | $39,635 | from $60,000 = | $20,364 |
| $250,000 | 10% ($25,000) | $35,667 | from $60,000 = | $24,433 |
| $250,000 | 20% ($50,000) | $31,716 | from $60,000 = | $28,284 |
| $200,000 | No Down Payment | $31,716 | from $60,000 = | $28,284 |
| $200,000 | 10% ($20,000) | $28,545 | from $60,000 = | $31,455 |
| $200,000 | 20% ($40,000) | $25,373 | from $60,000 = | $34,627 |
| $250,000 | No Down Payment | $39,635 | from $30,000* = | ($9,635) |
| $250,000 | 10% ($25,000) | $35,681 | from $30,000 = | ($5,681) |
| $250,000 | 20% ($50,000) | $31,716 | from $30,000 = | ($1,716) |
| $200,000 | No Down Payment | $31,716 | from $30,000 = | ($1,716) |
| $200,000 | 10% ($20,000) | $28,545 | from $30,000 = | $1,455 |
| $200,000 | 20% ($40,000) | $25,373 | from $30,000 = | $4,627 |
| **7-Year Note** | | | | |
| $250,000 | No Down Payment | $49,800 | from $60,000 = | $10,200 |
| $250,000 | 10% ($25,000) | $44,823 | from $60,000 = | $15,177 |
| $250,000 | 20% ($50,000) | $39,843 | from $60,000 = | $20,157 |
| $200,000 | 20% ($40,000) | $31,874 | from $30,000 = | ($1,874) |
| $150,000 | 20% ($30,000) | $23,906 | from $30,000 = | $6,094 |

**Table 3-4.** Pricing variables at work (continued on next page)
Note the change in operating profit.

| Asking Price | Down Payment | PMPN Payment per year | Operating Profit | Buyer's Net Profit per Year |
|---|---|---|---|---|
| **5-Year Note** | | | | |
| $300,000 | 20% ($60,000) | $61,192 | from $60,000 = | ($1,192) |
| $250,000 | 20% ($50,000) | $50,993 | from $60,000 = | $9,007 |
| $200,000 | 20% ($40,000) | $40,794 | from $60,000 = | $19,206 |

**Table 3-4.** Pricing variables at work (continued)

## Operating Profit Is the Key

Operating profit is the key to creating a selling price. As the examples above demonstrate, a higher operating profit enables a seller to ask a higher price. One of the ways a seller should prepare his or her business, therefore, is to reduce the operating cost percentages to maximize operating profit.

As discussed in Chapter 2, you can quickly affect the operating profit on paper by reconstituting the profit and loss statement. Figure in an appropriate manager's salary and eliminate any operating costs that are discretionary: each owner will invariably have his or her own priorities in that respect.

If all your costs and payments are properly figured into your P&L, then you will likely approach a realistic asking price through some of the methods outlined above. If, for example, a seller still has two years left on an equipment contract, he or she will have to show how the buyer can meet those equipment payments and still have money left. Then the seller can point out that, at the end of the contract period, the buyer can count on adding the payment amounts to the profit. The seller may have to lower the monthly payment schedule on the PMPN for the first two years, to allow the buyer a larger operating profit from which to pay for the equipment during the balance of the contract. At the end of that period, the seller can raise the monthly payments on the PMPN, because the buyer will no longer be paying off the equipment. It can work either way.

If the seller makes the lower payment on the PMPN a permanent concession on the purchase price, he or she can then point out that the buyer's income will increase after paying off the equipment, as the amount that had been going to the equipment payments will begin going to the operating profit and thus to his or her personal income. A seller can show a buyer wanting an annual income of $80,000 that he or she may have to settle for less annually for two years—$65,000, for example, if the equipment payments are $15,000 per year. Then, after paying off the equipment, the income will rise to $80,000. Whether you are buying or selling, work these differentials out with your accountant before you put them on the negotiating table.

## The Personal Side to Negotiations

A seller needs to assess a buyer's goals and preferences to decide which payment plan and financing scheme the buyer will be most receptive to. A seller needs to spend time with the buyer to learn about his or her perspective for the business. Trial lawyers often joke that if four people witness an accident from four street corners, you will get four different descriptions of the accident—perhaps to the point that it's hard to believe that there was only one accident. A seller should try to stand on the buyer's street corner to better understand what he or she is seeing.

People interested in buying businesses are always looking for the largest income they can generate, which they usually equate with the largest investment they can handle. This equation, by the way, is not necessarily valid, but it seems to be the foundation for most buyers' thinking.

### Don't Forget a Working Capital Reservoir

A buyer who is considering a substantial cash investment is probably looking for a business growth opportunity—not merely buying a job. The seller might, during negotiations, consider a lower down payment to ensure that the buyer has a large enough working capital reservoir to sustain the business, survive, and succeed.

## Creative Financing Options

Much of the premise of this book and its valuation concept is that the selling price depends, in great part, not on the real or perceived value of the business, but rather on the financial position of the potential buyer. If the purchase price and PMPN obligations do not work for the buyer, the sale will not work at all, regardless of what the seller thinks the business is worth. The business is really worth only what a buyer will or can pay.

For example, assume you are selling your business and the potential buyer is exactly the right kind of person to operate it, experienced in sales and ready to work hard for new customers and higher sales. In fact, this is exactly the kind of person you wish you had working for you before you decided to sell the business. But the buyer doesn't have enough cash for both the necessary working capital and a down payment. There are a number of ways to make this sale work.

## Temporary Partnerships

One creative financing option is a temporary partnership. Many buyers and sellers form temporary partnerships with each other as a short-term alternative to a sale.

If you are selling, always ensure that your buyer/partner cannot purchase or build an equity position and then back out of the deal to purchase the business. Also, ensure that your temporary partner cannot become your competitor after learning all about the business. Set a specific time and dollar amount for your buyer/partner to purchase your remaining interest in the business and make sure that, if your partner decides not to purchase the business, you can buy back his or her share of the business at a reasonable price in a reasonable time.

No partnership situation exists in which both (or all) partners are satisfied all the time with their partners. Every partnership agreement should contain a buyout clause at the beginning of the relationship. It can be based on either a specific amount of money or a formula that is easy to calculate at any time during the life of the partnership.

## Using the Buyer's Assets

Another creative finance option is for the buyer to put at risk personal assets to protect the seller. A buyer can put assets at risk in many ways, but the simplest is to execute a second trust deed or second mortgage on real property that has sufficient equity value. The trust deed could be for a period that expires with the last payment on the PMPN or for a period long enough for a specific amount to be paid on the note, such as equivalent to a 20 percent down payment, for example. Instead of a second deed of trust, a buyer could use stocks or bonds as collateral.

A buyer could even get an acceptable cosigner, but this is not so easy to do on a note that runs six figures. Finding a cosigner for a business loan is not exactly the same as having a father cosign for a Visa card for his teenager, but it could be done.

You might ask, "If the buyer has access to these assets, why not convert them to cash to meet the seller's down payment requirement?" The answer is that these assets are often difficult to convert to cash without a substantial penalty.

If the buyer cannot get to the assets because the timing is not right, the seller needs to consider what kind of protections can be put into the contract of sale or the PMPN. Seller protections are discussed in Chapter 14.

## Allocation of Purchase Price

Much of the creativity in financing comes from the need to have a particular kind of sale fit the tax position of the buyer or the seller. Depending on the state in which a business is located, you, whether you're buying or selling, may have to pay sales tax on the sale of a business that transfers some or all of its assets. (Note the difference between a *stock* sale and an *asset* sale.) Be sure to see your accountant for the difference in tax liability as well as your attorney for liability protection.

The effects of allocation of purchase price monies to equipment and goodwill are different for the buyer and the seller. For example, in some states the payment of the sales tax is the seller's responsibility while in other states the responsibility falls to the buyer.

If the seller is responsible for paying the sales tax, he or she will want a lower allocation for equipment, because the majority of the sales tax is imposed on hard assets. On the other hand, the buyer will want a higher allocation for equipment, so that he or she has more assets on which to take depreciation, which will reduce the taxable income from the operating profit. Even with the new tax law allowing depreciation of goodwill, the time allowed to depreciate hard assets is still shorter, which will be much more advantageous to the buyer for tax purposes.

If the buyer is responsible for the sales tax, he or she will have to decide whether paying a substantial tax at the time of purchase is worth taking a larger depreciation later. If the seller is responsible for the sales tax, he or she may need to negotiate the allocation, because the seller wants the hard assets lower, for sales tax purposes, and the buyer wants the hard assets higher, for depreciation purposes. *Sharing the sales tax burden may satisfy the needs of both buyer and seller.*

Other states may not have any sales tax on a bulk sale transfer. Be sure to consult your attorney as to whether there is a Bulk Sales Act in your jurisdiction.

## A Balloon Payment

The term "creative financing" has been overused in the last ten years, particularly in the real estate market when interest rates, at one point, got too high for average homebuyers to handle the payment schedule on a 30-year fully amortized mortgage. One creative method that came into existence is a balloon mortgage. This is a fixed-rate mortgage with monthly payments that are not large enough to pay off the loan during the term. Balloon mortgages terminate after a specified time, usually five to seven years, at which time the remaining balance must be paid in one balloon payment or restructured for an additional period of time.

You could equate this to taking a ten-year fully amortized note and converting it to a five-year note, amortizing the full amount over ten years but making the balance of the principal due at the end of the five years. Although a balloon payment scheme allows for reasonable payments for the five years, paying off or refinancing the entire balance of the principal at the end of that term can be a hardship for the borrower.

Balloon mortgages were quite reasonable in real estate, because many people didn't live in the same house for more than five years. They normally sold their houses, which allowed them to pay off the mortgage balance before the balloon payment came due. In addition, the housing market is relatively stable and easily financed compared with the small business market.

The balloon payment plan is much more difficult to arrange for purchasing a business because banks are not as interested in lending money on business equity. If the buyer can't make the balloon payment by the due date or refinance the balance, he or she is left to the mercy of the seller to agree to refinance the balance or take back the business on default.

Both buyer and seller must beware of any creative scheme that they do not fully discuss with professional counsel: it can prove to be equally dangerous to both parties. In addition, the balloon payment concept flies in the face of the basic valuation model: a business must be able to buy itself within a reasonable period of time based on risk.

As you continue to explore more aspects of buying and selling and, if you're looking to buy, to examine actual businesses for sale, you may want to return to this chapter. As you examine and reexamine the specifics of each potential purchase, you will become more familiar with the figures and calculations. After a while, you will feel more comfortable with the process of negotiating price and pricing variables.

Worksheet 3 on the accompanying CD will also help you build a comfort zone for working with price and payment figures.

## Key Points to Remember

- An all-cash deal carries a heavy tax burden for the seller and affords no ongoing protection to the buyer.
- The larger the down payment, the greater the discount the buyer is entitled to on the purchase price.
- A longer PMPN allows a higher asking price because the monthly payments are lower.
- If the seller helps the buyer purchase the business at the right price, the seller is more likely to be collecting the balance of the PMPN.
- Price is based on operating profit. Anything the seller can do to decrease expenses will increase the bottom line and raise the asking price.

# Your Team of Professionals

**Illustration 4-1.**
**Beware of Tricky Language**

In the recent sale of a business, the attorney representing the buyer wanted to insert the following sentence in the purchase and sale agreement and in the promissory note: "The seller has the right to take back the business in the event that the buyer defaults in his obligations under the purchase and sale agreement or the promissory note; however, the business shall be the only collateral that the seller has a right to pursue after such a default. It is understood that no other personal assets of the buyer shall, under any circumstances, be subject to such pursuit in the event of default, a deficiency judgment, or the like."

The seller's attorney explained that including this language in the agreement could leave the seller vulnerable should the buyer damage the business in some way. The seller, realizing that her lawyer's advice was correct, told the buyer that the sale was off unless the language was taken out of the agreement and the promissory note. The buyer agreed to take it out, the sale went through, and the seller was protected.

Without the advice of counsel, the seller would not have known what jeopardy was waiting around the corner. The buyer, with only the business itself at risk, would not have had a strong incentive to maintain the business at its highest efficiency. The interesting aspect to this story is that the buyer failed to maintain the business. The buyer failed to make payments on the purchase money promissory note. The seller didn't want to take back the business and brought a lawsuit for the balance of the note. The seller prevailed in the lawsuit and collected the balance.

Many buyers and sellers think it is much easier to frame and finish the purchase and sale of a business by leaving the professionals out of the loop at the beginning. Nothing could be further from the truth. Would you frame the basic structure of a house before consulting an architect and a general contractor? The most important time to consult professionals is before you structure the deal. When you develop your negotiating posture, having an accountant and attorney present can make a dramatic difference in how you arrive at the price and include the appropriate legal provisions to protect your final agreement.

## Accountants and Attorneys

With the complexity of tax laws and other legal concerns, the use of an accountant and an attorney is mandatory!

You must use an accountant to structure the sale to your best tax advantage. You may already know about certain basic tax considerations, many of which are included in this book. However, ensuring that each financial element works well with all the others is clearly the job of an accountant. If you fail to use an accountant early in the process, you may suffer from costly mistakes that are difficult if not impossible to correct later on.

If you're selling, you also need competent legal counsel to prepare all the legal protections that ensure that your sale is binding. A buyer with remorse or a good litigator can dream up many kinds of problems after a sale that you want to avoid. Even if you sell your business for cash, you certainly don't want a lawsuit down the road because of misleading or deceptive statements made in the selling documents. If your sale leads you to carry a purchase money promissory note for several years, then you certainly want the protection of knowing that your attorney has attended to all the details. The fees paid to legal counsel are the best guarantee of a good night's sleep after sale.

Sellers will sometimes argue against using an attorney, saying, "But the buyer is an old friend." It is amazing how friendships get tested when the dollar becomes part of the relationship. Be careful, not foolish. Use an attorney right from the beginning. The scenario described in Illustration 4-1 at the beginning of this chapter reinforces the importance of having an attorney on your professional team.

As this illustration points out, the business is normally used as collateral security for the purchase money promissory note so that, if the buyer defaults on the note, the seller can take the business back. The business should, however, be used only as partial collateral, not as complete collateral. A buyer can take a large amount of money out of a business before the seller becomes aware that the business is in trouble. The seller may take back the business, but it will be a far cry from the success it was when it changed hands. If this is all the seller can get as compensation, he or she is facing a horrible situation. Meanwhile, the buyer might have taken out of the business as much money as he or she put into the down payment—or even more! The buyer will walk away with a lot of money, leaving the seller with a business that can no longer survive.

Another word of admonition: listen to your lawyer's and accountant's recommendations, but make the decision using your own good judgment. Each part of the selling equation is based on your relationship to the business and your relationship to your own future. All of your professionals, even though they believe they are working strictly in your best interests, will often have views quite different from yours. Be aware that their opinions are related primarily to their particular areas of expertise and not to something that is better evaluated by your own personal instinct or through conferring with a family member or a personal advisor.

## Business Brokers

Although the ultimate decision will rest squarely on your shoulders, an attorney and an accountant are essential members of the selling or buying team. The value of a business broker, however, depends on the circumstances of the sale.

Both buyers and sellers can use the services of a business broker. However, a seller is more likely to need a broker early on, to help prepare and position the business for sale. The advice here pertains primarily to sellers. (Buyers can find more information on using a business broker in Chapter 21.)

Brokers handle many different kinds of businesses. Their experience can help you, as a seller, evaluate different types of potential buyers. Perhaps most importantly, they examine many kinds of purchase and sale arrangements and financial packages. This kind of experience might help make a weak sale strong and can be a valuable asset.

Your broker may not have extensive experience in your particular industry or business, but it is easy enough to provide your broker with the appropriate information. A good broker will know enough to use the seller's experience and knowledge. A broker may not know the intricacies of your particular business, but he or she will have more experience than you in the process of selling a business.

If you choose to handle the selling without a broker, you need to know how brokers operate in order to achieve the advantages of working with a broker.

One problem with hiring a broker is the 10 to 12 percent commission normally payable at the time the business is sold. Considering that the sale may bring only a 10 percent down payment, you could be paying more when you sell than you're receiving, especially when you consider legal and accounting fees as well. The size of the commission is certainly worth some serious consideration. You should also consider the possibility that a buyer may make no down payment, a situation that would leave you with an even larger cash deficit. (Although a no-down-payment deal may not be desirable, the situation does arise.)

You may face an even bigger concern, however. Ask yourself two basic questions:

- Is it possible that people may be interested in purchasing your business who are extremely qualified, but who do not have enough cash for a solid working capital reservoir and a substantial down payment?
- Is the broker motivated by the commission he or she will earn when the business is sold?

The answer to both these questions is clearly "Yes."

The broker's position is simple enough—if a potential buyer does not have sufficient capital for both working capital and a down payment, from which the broker will deduct his or her commission, then that person simply doesn't belong on your list of candidates. So, using a broker may eliminate potential buyers. If you feel comfortable considering only those potential buyers who appear to have sufficient dollars for both working capital and a substantial down payment, then you can easily decide that you want to use a broker. However, not only is it possible to eliminate an otherwise qualified candidate by using such a simple dollar qualifier, it is surprising what assets and cash availability are disclosed only after the first meeting of the parties. Discarding candidates too early can be a big mistake.

By reading this book and preparing for the sale of your business, you may be able to convince a broker that you are interested in working with his or her office if you can arrange for a lower commission. If you have done much of the preparatory work yourself, such as creating a business plan presentation with the appropriate valuation formulas and the proper financial documentation, a broker might very well see the logic of your suggestion. That preparation by the seller can spare a broker many hours of tedious work. If the first broker you contact does not see the logic of a lower commission, you may find another who is more inclined to think favorably about the arrangement. The broker who represents a business already prepared for sale with a seller more familiar with the process may receive a commission sooner, which might compensate for the discount.

Make no mistake, however: preparing your business for presentation requires you to do a good deal of work. You must do the following:

- Prepare your financial documentation, requiring a conference with your accountant.
- Adjust the cosmetics of the business, particularly elements that need change in anticipation of putting the business up for sale, such as repairing a shabby sign, painting the building, or replacing old and tattered point-of-purchase advertising materials. This may involve discussions with your business advisor.
- Consider legal matters affecting the business's posture for sale, such as consent to transfer the lease, which would certainly bring you to your attorney's office.
- Prepare a preliminary advertising approach, such as a letter to other franchisees if you are a franchised business. (See Chapter 14.)
- Properly evaluate the business to substantiate a fair asking price.

After you speak with your accountant and your attorney about the issues discussed in this book, you will be well on your way to preparing your business for sale. You may then be able to justify negotiating a lower commission rate from a broker.

The negative side to trying to hire a broker at a lower commission rate is that the broker normally splits the selling commission with the broker representing the buyer. If the buyer's broker has a choice between introducing a buyer/client to you through your broker, who will split a commission of 6 percent or 8 percent, and introducing the buyer/client to another business proposition through a broker who will split a commission of 12 percent, what will the buyer's broker choose? You may lose the opportunity to present your business to that potential buyer because you are trying to save some dollars on the commission.

Although the commission to the buyer's broker is normally not a substantial problem, you need to consider it. Be careful that this does not work against you. If you work without a broker, but a broker represents your buyer, you will have to negotiate your price to accommodate the buyer's broker's fee. You will be looking at a fee of 6 percent or less, however, as opposed to a fee of 11 percent or 12 percent. The key is that if you decide to work with a broker, insist on having the opportunity to meet with as many potential buyers as you want. You might want to examine all the applications to make your own decision about meeting the applicants—regardless of what their financial picture might initially look like.

It cannot be stated too often that deals are made in many ways and good buyers are not easy to find. If money is your sole requirement, you may lose some very interesting candidates. If a candidate is a little short on capital, you may be able to work out a payment plan by manipulating variables like down payment or length of note. A broker may also be helpful with adjustments of this kind if he or she has previously handled any similar negotiation.

Finally, there is no magic to what a broker does. You can advertise your business and obtain mailing lists just as easily as a broker. Sometimes, of course, the daily activity of the business itself is just too demanding for you to allocate any time at all to selling it. The choice is yours! And it may not be easy. You must also keep in mind that if you find a buyer after your broker's agreement expires, the broker may still be entitled to his or her commission. Be sure that you understand the language in your broker agreement. (See Chapter 21.)

## A Language All Their Own

Both the buyer and the seller need to understand professionals' language. Many times, people explain things that don't make sense. If they ask whether you understand, more often than you'd like to admit, you say yes when you really should say no! If the information is relatively unimportant, you avoid embarrassment and looking stupid to other people. However, selling a business is not the time to be casual about information you don't understand.

If a beloved member of your family were very ill and the doctor were explaining the alternative means of treatment, would you listen? Would you insist on understanding? Would you keep asking until you were blue in the face? If necessary, would you find someone who could interpret the doctor's language? You bet!

Your accountant, your attorney, and your broker represent you, you sought their professional advice, and you want the protection their services provide. You need to understand what they are saying.

Professionals may be very knowledgeable about their particular areas of expertise, but some of them are lousy teachers. They use the jargon of their profession every day and assume that you understand them. Sometimes, they will even ask if you do. If you don't understand, tell them—and keep telling them until you do. Nothing is so complicated that it can't be explained in simple terms if it is broken down into its basic parts. The information involved in buying or selling a business is too important for you to misunderstand or misinterpret. It may make a big difference in your financial future.

If your professional can't explain it to you so that you understand it, get someone who can. It is absolutely essential to the relationship you need for a successful transaction.

Finally, remember that professionals, just like anyone else, may be tempted to reach beyond their area of expertise and advise you on matters that are not included in their training. This can be helpful, but it can also be harmful. When dealing with attorneys, accountants, and brokers, be careful to select only the advice that is relevant to their area of expertise and beware of their advice when it is outside their field. Some professionals have some very strange things to say about businesses they know nothing about.

Nevertheless, the experience, education, and skill that professional accountants, attorneys, and brokers offer to a buyer or seller in the early stages of a business sale are invaluable. You will always save time and money by bringing professionals into the process early and avoiding the costly mistakes you might make without their help. For more specific information regarding the role of an attorney, an accountant, or a broker in a business transfer, see Part Four.

## Key Points to Remember

- An attorney and accountant are necessary members of your buying or selling team. Get the team together early in the process.
- Develop a vocabulary that both you and your professionals understand.
- If you are selling, make sure that you meet all viable buying candidates. Don't be too quick to dismiss candidates with limited financial resources after only a cursory look.

- A seller may learn the financial qualifications of a buyer only after an initial conference. Most people do not make a full financial disclosure at a first meeting.
- Document your relationship with your broker with unambiguous language.

# CHAPTER 5

# The Information Game

### Illustration 5-1. Alex Buys from Kelly

Alex was interested in buying Kelly's retail business. When he saw the advertisement in the paper, he responded in what he considered the most sophisticated fashion. He asked to see Kelly's income statements for the past five years, her income tax returns for that same five-year period, the balance sheets for each of the year-ends, the lease for the premises including any options to renew, a list of all vendors and their current balances, and a full customer list in order of annual gross purchases.

Kelly had been in business for six years and was not about to satisfy this shopping list of every aspect of her business until she established the quality and seriousness of this potential buyer. The answers to these questions could make Kelly vulnerable to someone who might want to open a competing business. Kelly, instead of complying with this question overkill, decided to give Alex only the information that she felt was appropriate at this early stage of inquiry. She told Alex that the price of the business was $635,000 and that she required a minimum down payment of 20 percent with the balance payable over no more than seven years at 10 percent interest. She also suggested that Alex have a working capital reserve of about $30,000 to handle the receivable turnover period and accommodate the first 90 days of activity after the takeover.

Kelly closed by stating that, if the same sales picture and the same expenses against revenues were maintained after the sale, without any increase in sales or decreases in expenses, the buyer should be able to take about $50,000 from the business during the year as owner's compensation.

This is really all to which the potential buyer is entitled … at the outset. Even the price is, in a sense, a secondary issue when you consider that the buyer knows how much down payment is expected, how much working capital is suggested, and how much income he or she can anticipate without even increasing business or decreasing expenses. The tax returns are also redundant at this point, because they are primarily used to confirm the representations made by the seller before the buyer would normally make any firm commitment. It is too early for the paperwork to be significant.

If the potential buyer is interested and continues the inquiry, he or she is prepared to submit some financial information before the seller is obliged to consider him or her a viable candidate. Then, the normal next step is a meeting to ensure that all parties understand what each party expects. The detail of the financial paperwork is a secondary issue and the customer list is just about the last disclosure that a seller should make.

To establish a negotiating relationship, both the buyer and the seller need some initial information. However, both parties are often reluctant to reveal information, particularly sensitive financial data, without proper proof that it will lead to serious and legitimate negotiations.

This early stage often sets the tone for the rest of the negotiating process. When mutual trust is established early, the process proceeds more smoothly. Many factors can prevent that trust from forming, however. This chapter discusses some of those factors, the type of information the buyer and the seller can expect early in the process, and the danger signals to look for during initial disclosures.

If you're buying, keep in mind that a good makeup job by a seller can hide many important elements you need to know about a business. The business that you are considering might not be all that it appears to be. The seller will probably not tell you all the negatives about the business. He or she may inadvertently obscure or even intentionally hide them.

Although intentional nondisclosure can be the grounds for good legal action, you are trying to find and procure a stable business with immediate income and growth potential, not to find a good cause for a lawsuit. Your job as a businessperson is to use your best efforts and exercise your best judgment to find and purchase a stable and income-generating business.

If you're selling, keep in mind that financial stability, business experience, and ethical stature are the three key elements you want in any buyer. If you are taking cash for the business and leaving the country, you may not care about the treatment of your old customers, vendors, and neighbors. If, on the other hand, you are going to be collecting the purchase price or a portion of it over an extended time, you need to examine your buyer's financial and employment background with great care. The secret agenda of a buyer can ruin a seller who negotiates in good faith.

## What the Buyer Needs to Know
### The Competition

As a buyer interested in a particular trade or industry, you must look at what the competition is offering. Who else is in the marketplace? How do the competitors present their businesses and what embellishments have they made to attract customers? In some cases, an owner is happy to discuss his or her success. In other cases, you will find it difficult to get beyond the front counter.

Some market research is easy. Look at the furniture and the fixtures. Look at the marketing materials presented to the public. Certain other items, however, may be difficult to access without the owner's permission. You may want to examine a competitor's equipment to ensure that the equipment included with the business you are buying is state-of-the-art and sufficient to put you on a level playing field with competitors. You want to look at the quality of the personnel.

If you want to make a line-by-line comparison of the business you are considering purchasing and its competitors, you will need specific information from the seller. It would not be unusual, however, for a seller to be somewhat reluctant to share all of this information with you, particularly financial information, solely because you indicate an interest in the business. It is not uncommon for businesspeople to shop their competitors, to pose as buyers and examine financial information to compare just how their own businesses are doing—such as to determine whether rent, cost of product, and/or labor factors are too high relative to what their competitors are spending.

You will need to convince the seller that you are a serious candidate before he or she is willing to share information about the business. If you present yourself as a serious and qualified buyer and the seller is still reluctant to share information, you may need to proceed with the purchase more cautiously.

## The Customer Base

Most businesses depend on their current customer base for stability and growth. A potential buyer is going to be interested in the customer base for a variety of reasons.

Perhaps the most important reason is to see if the business basically depends on a small cadre of important customers who may easily shift their allegiance to a competitor after the sale. The defection of a few big customers would make a business vulnerable.

Another concern is whether you want to deal with the kind of customers on which the business depends. Fast-food operations, for example, have relatively insignificant contact with their customers and generate very little allegiance. On the other hand, many retail operations have a very close rapport with their customers, who come in for advice and counsel as well as products or services. In considering buying a business, you need to recognize the difference and have the personality and inclination to involve yourself in the customer relationships necessary to maintain the business.

The danger that a competitor also wants to obtain this kind of information from a seller makes it more difficult for you as a legitimate buyer. If the competitor is close enough geographically, he or she may want a peek at some of the customers or at a particular group of customers with the intention of stealing the business. Again, the seller should be very cautious before releasing any customer information. If you disclose your financial statement, that may help close the credibility gap and convince the seller that you are a legitimate potential buyer and not someone who could put the business in jeopardy.

## Curiosity Seekers

In addition to the problem of competitors, there are many "buyers" who, frankly, are just curious to know what profits businesses show based on their dollar investment. Some of these "buyers" have actually developed portfolios of business opportunities. Some of them, believe it or not, will never buy a business of any kind. They are merely amateur analysts who don't have the gumption or, in some cases, the dollars to make the investment.

Sellers don't want to expose their financials to curiosity seekers. The time devoted to each conversation with a fake buyer is a waste most sellers can't afford. You must understand the frustration of the seller in this context and be careful to create an environment of trust before you can expect to enjoy a seller's time, energy, expertise, and disclosure.

One of the other problems with amateur analysts who spend time in a seller's business is that, in many cases, the employees are unaware that the business is for sale. The more questions about the business, the more difficult it is for the seller to keep this situation under control.

On the other hand, if a seller is serious about putting the business in front of real buyers, he or she is obliged to have certain information available under certain conditions. You should understand these conditions and know what you can expect to see and when.

## Inspect the Business in Person

Sometimes the buyer will ask the seller over the phone to send a package of information concerning the business. A big business may have this information prepared, but small entrepreneurs rarely have time to put together packets of information while they're running the business. It is more appropriate, particularly if you are calling from out of town, to visit the business. After all, if buying the business involves moving to a new area, you won't make that decision unless that area satisfies a number of personal needs and desires—yours and your family's.

If you are a serious buyer, you will also want to see the building, the traffic pattern, the surrounding area, and the general population mix. Some people don't mind working in a depressed environment; others do. Bars on the windows can often be a danger signal to a buyer about the nature of the neighborhood, particularly if personnel may be working different shifts or leaving after dark. You can't see those bars over the telephone.

So which comes first, the chicken or the egg? The seller does not want to disclose a lot of information unless he or she feels the buyer is a serious prospect. The buyer does not want to make the trip unless he or she can expect the business to fulfill certain basic requirements. Many circumstances may alter the sequence, and these will vary from industry to industry. However, certain guidelines normally prevail.

The buyer is entitled, on the first round, to know the gross volume, the profit (even though "profit" is defined in various ways), the amount of cash required for the down payment and the working capital reservoir, and the amount of the balance of the purchase price the seller is willing to carry, if any.

Profit and loss statements, balance sheets, and cash-flow analyses should not be necessary at this point. If you have a face-to-face conversation with the seller, you will resolve many questions. The seller should discuss whatever additional information he or she needs from you in order to permit you to continue examining the business.

Both parties can learn a lot without a single piece of paper changing hands, just by meeting and getting familiar with each other's general demeanor. When all is said and done, the dynamics of the negotiations will depend largely on the relationship and the trust that develops or fails to develop between the parties.

## The Franchise and Mandatory Disclosure

If the business is a franchise, the same basics apply. The buyer should certainly visit the location and meet the owner. However, it is a good deal easier to obtain general industry information that a potential buyer would normally want.

When a franchise is offered for sale anywhere in the United States, the franchisor is required to release a disclosure document to the buyer. In some states, it is called a *Uniform Franchise Offering Circular (UFOC)*; in others, a *Federal Trade Commission disclosure document.* This document contains information about the basic business concept, the people involved, the number and location of units, any pending litigation, and the history, financial stability, management structure, and operation of the franchise (parent) company.

If you are buying a franchise, new or existing, directly from the franchisor, the required language at the top of the disclosure document indicates when you should receive it. "At the earlier of (1) the first personal meeting; or (2) ten business days before the signing of any franchise or related agreement; or (3) ten business days before any payment." Although this language is currently undergoing some changes, the import remains the same. (See Chapter 14 for the complete language.)

If you are buying an existing franchise from an individual franchisee, two schools of thought exist regarding the disclosure document. On the one hand, the more conservative franchisors will insist that you get the document in timely fashion. One of the document's purposes is, after all, to protect the franchisor from untrue or misleading representations made by salespeople and others, including the franchisee, about the company during the course of the initial negotiations. Another view is that the franchisee is an independent business owner and is selling his or her own business and may sell it without using a disclosure document.

As long as the franchisor has not been suspended from franchising or has not voluntarily suspended its franchise sales activities, the disclosure document should be available to a buyer interested in an existing franchise. If the seller fails to disclose material information, that failure can lead to a lawsuit, with or without the disclosure document. More will be said in succeeding chapters regarding a seller's legal obligations to disclose. (See Chapters 14 and 17.)

The buyer's best position is to insist on the disclosure document, if one is available. The information the disclosure contains is invaluable. The mere existence of the information will give the potential buyer a good start on the pre-purchase research. If no disclosure document is available, the buyer ought to question why not.

## Too Much Information

What kind of information should the buyer be looking for? The seller will probably not give you too much information. If that happens, however, you should be more careful. A seller who inundates you with information may be trying to obscure some of the simpler elements that would be more obvious if there were less information. If you are interested in the customer base, don't be satisfied with materials on the population growth or community development. If you are asking about the terms of the lease, don't be satisfied with the building and zoning regulations or new highways and airports that are on the municipal drawing boards. In other words, make sure that the information given to you is relevant to the information you've requested. If it is not, again, you should ask why not.

This subject will come up again. Chapter 7 will lead you through the specific requests for information you need to make to a seller.

## What the Seller Needs to Know

Remember that the sale of a business is not exactly like the sale of an automobile. When you are selling a car, you are usually uninvolved with the future of the car after the sale. With the sale of a business, on the other hand, the situation is different.

First, you may carry a purchase money promissory note for a large balance of the purchase price. You will, therefore, have a very substantial interest in the future of the business and how the buyer handles it. After all, if the buyer fails, you may end up taking back the business and finding little more than a skeleton of the full-bodied business you sold.

It is in your best interest to pick a good buyer, help him or her succeed, and watch the business for danger signals. A buyer may feel uncomfortable with the seller looking on, but if the buyer still owes the seller money after the sale, he or she must understand that this is the seller's prerogative, if not the seller's obligation.

Even if there is no purchase money promissory note, your reputation in the community that you have taken years to build could be ruined in a few weeks by the wrong kind of buyer. If this is important to you, then you must be careful of the quality of your buyer.

If you were selling your car, you might not be particularly interested in the ethics or moral stature of the person buying it. When selling a business, however, you might be very concerned about these qualities in the buyer. Knowing about his or her business experience is important, if only to decide whether or not the purchase is a good idea for the buyer. After all, you know all about your business and the frustrations, the intricacies, and the demands it puts on you and your family. Your buyer will not have so clear and informed a perspective.

It is a good idea to know the size and makeup of the buyer's family and the lifestyle to which the family is accustomed. You are foolish if you don't look, with your buyer, at what family necessities and amenities the cash flow of the business can afford. Unrealistic expectations that have no chance of being fulfilled are the biggest danger to both buyer and seller.

Certainly a careful analysis of the buyer's financial history and current status is mandatory. If you do not arrange an all-cash purchase, you want to know exactly what the buyer can convert to cash if the business requires more working capital than either of you anticipated. It is also important for you to take as much security as you can get for the balance owing on the purchase. You need to know what other assets the buyer is willing to put at risk. A complete financial statement will tell you just what the buyer has available. Then both you and the buyer will be equally knowledgeable about each other. For more information on your need to have access to the buyer's financial information, see Chapters 14 and 15 and the Sample Confidential Business Application in Chapter 15.

You need to know what role your buyer expects to take in operating the business. Most businesses don't do well with absentee ownership and, if the sale is not all-cash, you will have less to worry about if the buyer is involved on a day-to-day basis than if the buyer were merely an investor.

Find out how much down payment the buyer is willing to make, especially in terms of his or her available cash. If the buyer is willing to put a substantial amount of cash toward the purchase, that money often speaks more loudly than any words about his or her commitment to the negotiations and purchasing your business.

## Legal Aspects of the Transaction

The buyer wants to ensure that all the representations by the seller are true. The real protection the buyer has, unless he or she pays the full price in cash, is in owing the seller money. The buyer will honor this obligation to pay off the promissory note so long as the business is, in fact, the business he or she expected to buy. If it isn't, the buyer is well protected by being able to withhold payments.

On the other hand, the seller wants to collect the full price for the business. More than that, the seller wants to ensure that the business will maintain its integrity until he or she has collected that full price. In order to do this, the seller must monitor the situation in some way: he or she must be able to see that the bills are being paid, especially taxes of all kinds, and that salaries and costs do not exceed the appropriate ratio to sales and profit that is vital to the business.

The seller can insert certain protective devices into the purchase and sale agreement to ensure that the new owner is operating the business appropriately. Any seller that does not use these protective devices is making a big mistake. (See Chapter 14 to learn more about how to protect your sale.)

## Body Language

Sometimes the things we say are contradicted by the way we say them or even by the way we sit or stand while we are saying them. It is commonly assumed that people are lying, for example, when they blink a lot or when they look flushed. Sometimes, the physical aspects of conversation speak much louder than the words. Keep this in mind during the early discussions, when both parties are still getting to know one another.

Note who is at the table with the other party. Did the buyer bring a spouse or a child who expects to participate in the operation of the business? Do both parties have lawyers, accountants, or consultants? Does the buyer have a partner who will provide part or all of the financing for the purchase of the business? Each of these people represents another aspect of the buyer candidate. Some will be positives; others will not. Your professional advisors may be able to help you interpret the role of your counterpart's family, friends, or advisors in the future of the negotiations and sale. Of course, you should always rely on your own instincts, but getting a second opinion is often smart.

The following chapters will return to many of the concepts discussed in Part One. However, Parts Two, Three, and Four will also lead you step by step through much of the work necessary to prepare yourself and your family to buy or sell a way of life—business ownership.

## Key Points to Remember

- Sellers must recognize the difference between a serious buyer candidate and a casual business analyst.
- Sellers need to read and interpret a potential buyer's financial statement to decide whether he or she is financially strong enough to sustain the business in all times, good and bad.
- Buyers need to examine the internal elements (such as cost of product) and the external elements (such as competition) that affect the stability and future of the business.
- Buyers must be prepared to disclose their financial position in detail if they expect the seller to carry back a purchase money promissory note.
- In the case of a franchise, buyers should be able to get all the disclosure they need on which to base a decision to buy. That's the law.

# PART TWO

# The Buyer's Perspective

# CHAPTER 6

# Committing to a Market Niche

### Illustration 6-1. A Franchisor's Assessment

John Scott, former CEO of Fastframe USA, interviewed many people who wanted to buy a Fastframe franchise. He didn't look so much for people who were technically oriented or who had experience working with glass and wood and nails. Fastframe proprietors work with the public every day. He explained his approach: "I don't subscribe to the theory that salespeople are made, not born. You can teach someone how to use a bag of tools, but you can't teach them how to relate to people. And, at the end of the day, it is the relationship with the customer that is more important than anything else."

> During the initial interview process, Scott would look for the ability of the prospective buyer to deal with people. "If I find someone who is clearly a fish out of water when it comes to dealing with the public, I would rather tear up the contract than take a chance. If the venture fails, not only is the owner not successful, but our franchise family will feel the pain of that failure for a long time."

You can invest in a business in a variety of ways.

You can invest time, money, energy, and emotion. Picking a business is not like picking a horse at the track. In a horse race, when the race is over, win or lose, you can forget about it until your next visit to the track. Similarly, deciding on a business venture is not like buying stock. The management of that public company is out of your control; if you don't like it, you can usually sell the stock quickly and allow the aggravation to quickly fade. Betting at the track or buying stock is a calculated risk of a relatively minor nature. It is unlikely you would put your net worth at risk in either case.

An investment in a business, on the other hand, is a commitment involving the better part of your financial empire. The investment might not require all your cash upfront, but it usually requires a commitment of your entire financial portfolio. You cannot make this business decision casually.

You can research either a horse or a stock at great length and, in both cases, you can get quite emotional about the results of your investment. Yet both are passive investments and neither really puts the whole framework of your life's energies to the test. Investing in a business certainly can and usually does. It really converts the financial investment into an emotional commitment.

## Consider a Homebased Business

"Sure, I'd like to operate my own business, but I can't leave my invalid mother at home alone." This is one clear scenario for operating a business from your own home. It is not the perfect situation, which will be examined, but, since life is certainly not perfect, you will also see why it is the beginning, in many cases, of business ventures that might otherwise not have happened.

But do not be misled. Starting a business from your home is not always a product of necessity. It is often the most logical method of starting the operation at the lowest cost until the profit of the business can afford to pay for its own facility. In many cases, the move to another facility may never happen. If location is not a major factor for the success of the business you are considering, you may want to start out at home. Instead of taking on the expense and headaches of an additional site, you could buy a business without its real property or lease.

## A Changing World

Years ago, few businesses operated from home. Times have changed. Years ago, businesses that didn't have an in-town address lacked a certain legitimacy. Today, FedEx, DHL, and UPS trucks are stopping in the best residential neighborhoods more and more to pick up business packages and letters.

Many changes have led to this dramatic adjustment in the complexion of the business community. There is, of course, the fact that people are living longer. As a result, there is a substantial and growing society of elders, many of whom need attention during the day. Many others, on the other hand, are still capable of operating a business, but no longer able or willing to maintain a commute to the office. Many more single parents need to generate an income while caring for their children. And there are many two-parent families in which both parents want and/or need to have careers.

Along with these phenomena, also consider computer technology, which allows computer stations to be in contact with words, graphics, and sounds immediately. With e-mail, online facilities in every field, and the plethora of information sources, the entire society could conceivably operate without anyone leaving home. Add cell phones and fax machines and the circuits are complete.

The latest business change to contribute to the homebased enterprise is downsizing. Companies are realizing that part-time capability without the complications of health insurance, traffic delays, time off for holidays, sick days, coffee breaks, interpersonal conflicts, and the like can improve the corporate bottom line dramatically. Many companies are taking advantage of downsizing, allowing in some cases and insisting in other cases, that a certain percentage of their employees be employed from home. The computer allows this to take place with ease. No judgments need to be made about this phenomenon. It is merely a concept to be recognized as a reason for a new generation of at-home workers. Even city leaders are in favor of more of the same. After all, working from home reduces traffic, consumption of fossil fuels, and smog.

But this is not the heart of homebased entrepreneurship. This is the world of business necessity and dividends to shareholders.

## From the Boardroom to the Bedroom

The entrepreneur at home is a different story. It is really a bigger story, because it is not born of corporate America; it is born of the stuff of dreams. But be careful—homebased businesses are not all a bed of roses.

It is certainly true that you can save money on lunches. You can save money on office rent. You can take certain deductions on your annual taxes, including the following:

- Office supplies and equipment
- Employee wages—full- or part-time, including your spouse and your children, if properly documented
- Business phones and fax costs
- Magazines and other subscriptions
- Business travel
- Entertainment—but only a portion and only when carefully documented
- A vehicle used for business—consistent with the percentages allowed by the IRS
- Advertising done to grow the business

But, be careful to examine these possible deductions with your accountant. You should consider some negative aspects before you act, particularly if you decide to write off a portion of your home as the facility from which you operate your business.

Finally, you must be absolutely aware of one significant element—discipline!

Discipline works in various ways. The workaholic must be careful to take time out for lunch. The more casual person must be careful not to take too much time out for lunch. The serious entrepreneur must set a time to start and a time to finish. Those who start late and those who stop too early are equally as guilty.

There is a way of doing business at home. It is very much the same as with writers. One writer says that the typewriter keys will move when they are ready. It never happens. Another writer claims that, all other things aside, you must sit in the chair. Nothing happens near the typewriter unless and until you are sitting in the chair. The same is true for your homebased business: nothing will happen unless and until you create a business atmosphere within which you can function as a serious businessperson with the same goals as those who jump into their offices on Wall Street each morning.

There is no lack of dignity in operating a business from your home—if you operate it in a businesslike fashion. Yes, there will be times when the children may demand more of your time than you would prefer. There will certainly be times when your elderly parents will require a little more attention than your business day allows. You must make judgments. Adjustments will be necessary. But you are the decision maker. And the goal of a successful business will be the same whether you are answering the telephone in the bedroom or in the boardroom.

## Homebased Office Needs

The first order of business involves a legal question. Does your business violate the zoning restrictions of your residential neighborhood? The more practical question might be: Does your business create a visibility that would be offensive to your neighbors?

The visibility question revolves around these four factors:

- The number of employees you have coming to work daily and where they park
- The number and frequency of customers coming to the door for a product or a service

- The number of deliveries coming to and leaving from the premises via UPS, FedEx, DHL, the Postal Service, or other delivery service
- The amount of mail delivered to the premises

There are ways to avoid some of these visibility problems, including using a post office box and/or a warehouse and having your employees telecommute. However, the necessary or appropriate approach to the problem of visibility would best be discussed with your legal advisor.

In running a business from your home, you should be careful to note just what kind of protection your business receives under your homeowner's policy. In most cases, protection for liability, fire, and your business equipment will require at least a business rider, if not a separate policy. See your insurance professional for the best approach.

Starting with the basics, it is clear that you will need at least the following items. These, of course, are in addition to the myriad of minor items you will need, such as paper clips, a letter opener, stamps, tape, a stapler and a staple remover, pens, pencils, highlighters, and a checkbook.

**Computer.** A computer will give you the quick and easy means to type letters, revise draft documents, keep files, and maintain a reservoir of information from which you can easily retrieve items when you need them. Along with the computer comes a printer and whatever software is appropriate to operating your business properly. There are programs for keeping books and records, accounting and invoicing, preparing for tax time, pricing guides, and client records. Be sure that you are comfortable with handling any or all of these in-house. Be careful not to have so much sophisticated software that you end up in a nightmare with a dramatic learning curve.

You also should have an internet connection so you can use e-mail and access the web. Be sure that you have an appropriate need for whatever technology you acquire, so you don't lose time with things that get in the way of operating your business properly.

Caution—it is imperative, when using a computer, to have a backup system to protect against the loss of information in the event of a system breakdown. Some of the newest and more expensive software has built-in backup systems. If you have not yet reached this level of sophistication, be sure that you use a backup system appropriate to your needs. Using a backup disk or jump drive is the beginning of the protection. If you're going to be using the computer to build a substantial reservoir of information that your business needs to survive and continue, it may be wise to invest in a dedicated backup system—and use it!

**Fax machine.** You'll likely need a fax machine so you can transmit and receive documents. You can also use it as a copier if your copying needs are minimal; otherwise, you may also need a copy machine. You can also use your computer with internet connection to send or receive information without paper.

**Answering machine.** A telephone answering machine, voice mail, or equivalent service, backed up by your local telephone company, if possible, is essential. Whatever your business, you don't want to miss any calls. Some businesspeople feel that a "live voice" answering service is better than a machine, but the contrary argument is just as persuasive. One device that seems to offend many callers who just want to leave a message is the answering system that lists options—if callers have the patience to stay on the line long enough to listen to the litany.

**Additional phone lines.** Carefully examine your need for two or more separate telephone lines if your business gets busy. Most telephone services have a "call interrupt" feature, which allows you some flexibility, but if your fax is busy, you might want a better option. Cost is normally not prohibitive. If you connect to the internet through a phone line, you may want to install a dedicated line.

**Magazine subscriptions.** Subscribe to some magazines that are appropriate to your particular trade or industry, as well as magazines for small businesses. Check your local bookstore to get a good idea of what you'll need. The ideas you find in those magazines will serve you well. In addition to the normal creative ideas you may find in many generic business magazines, you will find in magazines about homebased businesses and home offices many ideas for setting up your office. Remember: if you get only one idea from a magazine, the subscription was probably a worthwhile investment. Reading business magazines will also give you many ideas about the most critical aspect of practically every business—marketing.

**Miscellaneous.** In addition to obvious items like a desk and a wastebasket, you will also need a calendar, a clock, a notebook, a calculator, a filing cabinet, a bookcase, and a desk file for telephone numbers and addresses for all your business numbers—clients, vendors, prospects, associates, and professionals. Everything that happens or should happen while you are in your office should be recorded in your notebook. All checks received or written should be recorded immediately. Copies of checks should be made before they're deposited.

The last item that must be mentioned, again and again, is that any business, at home or otherwise, should have a business plan. This will tell anyone, and remind you, what purposes the business is supposed to serve and what the dollar allocations are for launching the business and operating it successfully. Your business plan should also discuss the competition, the asset structure of the business, the need for additional capital, and the purpose for those expenditures. It should have a beginning, a middle, and an end. It should be a map that can be followed from the beginning, with signposts along the way to indicate alternative directions as the economy, the competition, and the future of the industry dictate.

## How to Make a Smart Business Investment

You will find it very difficult and statistically against the odds to survive, let alone succeed, in any business venture if you don't invest all your efforts. Some people say success relies on good fortune. But as Mark Twain wrote, "The harder I work, the luckier I get." There is no magic to success, but there is an attitude about those who succeed.

### The Right Attitude to Succeed

If you are going to buy a business, be prepared to invest everything, not only your money. You must invest time and energy and make the emotional commitment to succeed. If you are not sure about whether or not you will, don't do it. A positive frame of mind creates the motivation, generates the energy, and keeps the wheels moving, not only in the face of adverse circumstances, but on the smooth roads as well. A positive attitude of commitment makes success happen.

Thus, in examining the marketplace and choosing your business or market niche, you must consider the long haul and examine your personal and emotional commitment to the business you choose. If you don't consider yourself mechanically inclined, don't buy a business that is equipment-oriented or that constantly requires equipment repair or maintenance. If you are not financially oriented, don't get involved in a business that requires a high degree of financial sophistication, like tax advising. If you don't enjoy dealing with people, avoid any business that depends on the customer relationship to succeed, like a restaurant. If you are not quality-conscious, don't buy a business that depends on high-quality standards of performance, like a quick printing facility. And, for heaven's sake, if you don't like selling, don't buy a business that depends on outside sales.

## Emotional Containment

The other side of emotional involvement is emotional containment. Of course, your judgment will be based, in part, on your gut reaction to the business itself. This is natural. Some people, for example, might have a real problem cleaning clogged drains or getting rid of pests and rodents. Others might be very excited about dealing with domestic animals or taking trips to exotic places around the world. It is fine to become emotionally involved in a concept, but don't let your emotions make a business judgment on which the welfare of your family and your future might depend. In other words, be careful that your positive emotions don't dictate decisions in the face of a negative business analysis.

## Can You Make the Sale?

Finally, make sure the requirements of the day-to-day activities of the business match the capabilities of your background—not the capabilities you'd like to have, but the capabilities about which you feel comfortable. You will then be ready to examine some more serious questions, such as the industry, location, competition, and growth potential.

Deciding whether you will be successful at selling requires more research than it might at first appear. The key to any business is making the sale—marketing and selling your product or service to potential customers, whoever or wherever they are. You must find them, sell to them, and satisfy them. You must maintain appropriate prices, quality, inventory, equipment, and staff to make the sale. In fact, your goal is to develop the business such that you can hire people to do the day-to-day activities while you oversee the growth and future of your business.

Many people consider themselves good cooks, yet they should not own restaurants. If you like to cook, but don't like to shop for groceries or hire and supervise a staff of waiters and dishwashers, the restaurant business is not for you. If you are not willing to keep abreast of restaurant marketing techniques—ambiance and decor, discounts and specials—then, again, you should consider another industry.

How do you feel about customer contact? Some businesses require customer contact, but no selling. Some even allow you to avoid extensive conversations with customers and outside sales altogether. However, these businesses may require heavy inventory supervision and bookkeeping, much of which is now done on computers. Computer literacy may then be important for you.

As you research the market for the industry that interests you, look at the skills and interests other owners and proprietors possess. For example, Illustration 6.1 at the beginning of this chapter shows how important the ability to deal with people and sell can be to your success.

## Specific Research Strategies

You can follow certain basic strategies when you conduct a prepurchase research project. Here are some that will get you started.

**Develop your questions.** The information you get depends on the questions you ask. The more general the question, the more general the answer. So the more specific you make the question, the more likely you will get a specific answer. You need specific answers to make an informed decision, so take the time to develop your questions properly.

**Ask a competitor or franchisee.** Any prepurchase research project begins with asking a current competitor (who ought not to be in the immediate neighborhood of your intended location) or, if the business is a franchise, a franchisee about the business. The person who is in the business can give you much more specific information. He or she can speak about customer problems, profit, and cost factors—the real essence of the business.

**Consult your professional.** Analyze the business with your business consultant, attorney, or accountant. Let the professional give you an uninvolved, objective view from his or her experience in the business world. Your consultant, attorney, or accountant may also contribute relevant personal information regarding the particular trade or industry.

**Read trade magazines.** Most industries have trade associations that produce magazines to update their members on the latest technology, trends, and innovations in the industry. These trade magazines can be a valuable resource for you. However, be careful to balance the positive attitude expressed in most trade magazines with the obvious negative aspects of the industry, which are less likely to appear in the same publication.

**Speak to executives.** Contact the executives of the franchisor or the vendors from whom the seller buys goods or services. The franchisor will always try to maintain your interest in the franchise relationship by giving you the best possible picture of the industry and of the business you're considering buying. On the other hand, the vendors will give you a broader picture of the good and the bad of the industry and their reaction to the individual businesses they service. These two views may diverge or they may concur. In either case, it is a good way to look at more than one side of the industry.

**Look at the answers.** Examine the list of questions you've asked and the answers you've received during this process. As you become more knowledgeable about the particular trade or industry, you will find that you will be better able to construct good questions. Revise your list of questions.

**Ask a competitor or franchisee again.** By now you will be able to have a more in-depth discussion with a competitor or franchisee because your research has taught you so much about the business. You will likely have thought of more sophisticated questions and need to turn to the competitor or franchisee again for answers. Establishing this relationship with other owners of the type of business you're considering buying is a valuable process for your business future.

You will find as you proceed with your research that most businesses are not necessarily what they appear to be. Don't let a broker or a seller convince you of anything that you have not researched. Examine and read the selling materials carefully. If you are buying a franchise, look over the disclosure document carefully and trace the company, its concept, and its competitive position in the marketplace. If you are buying an existing business, review its financial history via the profit and loss statements and the balance sheets. Do a historical analysis of the business, examine the business community on which its success depends, and get a feeling for the impact of the business on its current customer base. See the worksheet on the accompanying CD for some more research strategies and sources.

## Money—the Common Denominator

Finally, you need to consider your funding resources and the potential of the business to pay off your promissory note and provide you with an income. You may have to pay back money you have borrowed or replace the interest income you lost when you converted or sold other investments to buy the business. You may simply need to make enough money to keep the business going and feed your family at the same time.

Every business must account for its sales, costs, and income to the IRS, state taxing authorities if applicable, and other bureaucratic agencies. You must consider your overhead, your equipment, and your personnel, on whose productivity the success of the business depends. In addition, you must consider your customers (current and prospective)—who they are, where they are, and how to market to them. Existing customers are the best source of new sales.

Don't ignore these issues until after you have bought the business. Begin your research early. As mentioned earlier, picking a business is not like picking a horse at the track. You can't walk away from a loss as easily.

Chapter 7 will lead you through some important specifics you should request from a seller. The research strategies presented in this chapter, combined with the appropriate information supplied by the seller, should get you well on your way to making an informed decision about a business.

## Key Points to Remember

- Before you buy a business, make sure you have the right attitude and commitment to make the investment a success.
- The business you buy will require certain skills and abilities. Look objectively at the talents and experience you bring to the business before you commit any money to it.
- Doing research and asking questions may be embarrassing, time-consuming, and tedious, but these activities are absolutely necessary to making the right decision.
- Your funding resources must be equal to the business's financial demands. No amount of skill or commitment will make a business a success unless you also have the necessary working capital.
- The ability to sell is a key factor to many business enterprises. If you need that skill to succeed in the business, be sure you have it before you sign the papers.

# The Asset Variables

**Illustration 7-1. Asset Sale vs. Stock Sale**

Ali Markson decided to buy John Lehigh's business. He decided to buy the entire corporation by acquiring the seller's 100 percent share holdings instead of just buying the assets. He also decided to pay all cash instead of making payments. It seemed like the fastest, easiest way to acquire the company. Shortly after the purchase, Ali was hit with three lawsuits against the company. He told the people bringing the lawsuits that he was a new owner and not responsible for any of those past infractions. His plea fell on deaf ears, since the old company was responsible and he now owned the old company, lock, stock, and lawsuits. Had Ali sought professional advice before the acquisition, he would have been told that when you buy a company through its stock, you buy it all. Ali should have made this an asset sale: he would have been responsible for his company's new obligations and not any obligations from its past. The alternative would have been to hold some part of the purchase price in escrow in order to handle whatever insects he might have found in the woodpile after the sale.

An existing business offers many types of assets, and each asset's value will eventually be figured into the selling price in one way or another. To determine the value of the asset variables, you will have to do some research, consult professionals (appraisers, accountants, or attorneys), and request specific information from your seller. This chapter will help you isolate many of the variables, lead you in the right direction to determine their value, and give you some specific questions you can ask your seller to get all the answers you need.

Much of this book deals with what businesses have in common, such as operating profit, debt, and even the commitment of the owner to make the business a success. However, the differences among businesses, particularly as they relate to the value of the assets for sale, are equally important to the buy-sell process.

Service, soft goods, food, manufacturing, wholesaling, and retail businesses make up only a small portion of the business complex in a marketplace. To understand exactly what your business represents, you need to look at its components. This chapter will help you identify the more subtle elements to examine as you research your business purchase.

As you read through the following sections, consider how the various assets apply to your business and how you will research their value and ultimate effect on the selling price.

## Just What Is for Sale?

Businesses do not have the same assets to sell. For instance, mail order businesses don't need to worry as much about location as retail outlets. A legal practice may not have as large an investment in equipment as a medical practice. Consider what the seller has included in the business package and how valuable each element is to operating the business.

## Equipment

Every modern business relies on equipment. Sometimes people improve a concept without making the original equipment obsolete. In that case, buying a business with old equipment is perfectly appropriate. In other cases, old equipment can seriously dull your competitive edge. You must assess the value of the equipment for every potential business purchase.

The cost of the equipment or of equipment replacement is, in some cases, a significant factor. In some businesses, on the other hand, the equipment is hardly a factor at all. Careful analysis by experts in the industry will help you make this assessment.

Be careful to check on equipment innovations on the horizon in the specific industry. What might be appropriate today could easily be obsolete tomorrow—and tomorrow might come more quickly than you anticipate. Equipment innovations could include new ways to heat with less energy, to move heavy or bulky items with smaller and/or more powerful motors, to eliminate waste more expeditiously, to freeze more quickly, or to use machinery of all kinds with fewer replacement parts required over the life of the equipment. The scope of equipment activity is endless. Be sure to make an appropriate assessment for the business in question.

Check with the appropriate state authorities involved in maintaining ownership records and ensure that there is not a lien or encumbrance on the equipment. This can sometimes happen at the time when the equipment is sold or leased to protect the seller or lessor until the entire purchase price is paid or the lease term expires. It can also happen later, when a lender or a creditor wants to have some security in an item of value to protect a loan or an extension of credit. These security situations are normally found under the personal property laws of the state in which the personal property is located or under the Uniform Commercial Code, which covers most states.

## Inventory

From manufacturing businesses to retail outlets, inventory is always a factor. Inventory can be significant if the seller has allowed levels to get too high or too low. Sometimes, the inventory is totally obsolete and not worth the space it occupies; sometimes, it is so valuable that it needs to be safeguarded. Perishable foodstuffs have a limited shelf life and need to be disposed of rapidly. Certain chemicals need supervision or they may deteriorate. Certain items of inventory become obsolete because customer tastes change. Others retain their value and even outlive the business. Indeed, some items may have such utility that they can effectively be used by many people and industries.

As the buyer, you make this initial assessment. Then, based on market value, wholesale cost, replacement cost, and depreciated value, you decide on the dollar amount you place on the product and the amount you are willing to pay for it as part of the purchase price. In some cases, inventory represents a modest percentage of the entire business package; in other cases, the inventory may represent the entire business package.

Make sure that you physically see, handle, count, and otherwise examine the inventory for yourself. Make sure the seller actually owns the inventory and has paid for it and that it has not been pledged or otherwise used for security. If the inventory has been used for security, you may not be able to obtain title to the property without having to face interference from some party who claims an interest in it for one reason or another.

## Real Estate

If a seller owns the real estate on which the business is located, it may not necessarily be part of the package for sale. Many owners have confidence in the business they are selling, which means the business is a good tenant: it can pay the lease. In that case, they will want to lease the location to you, rather than selling it, because they know they can collect the rent consistently. They will be able to pay any mortgage on the property and, if the area is growing, the property will be worth more with time.

You can operate the equipment, count the inventory, and stand on the real estate, but assessing the value of the lease is a little different. Consider whether the business depends on the location, whether the rent figures significantly in the overall business picture, and whether the growth of the business may require additional space in the future. The lease and its terms are essential to the welfare, maintenance, and continuity of most businesses.

You need to understand all the terms and conditions of the lease. Some are more complicated than others and some are so obscure that only a carefully trained eye will catch the nuances. Have your professional take a close look at the lease. Here are some things to which you want to pay particular attention.

- How long is the lease?
- Is there an option to renew?
- Is the option defined in terms of the rent and other obligations?
- Is it a percentage lease, entitling the lessor to a percentage of your profit if your gross sales exceed a certain amount?
- Are you obliged to pay a portion of the property taxes or common area maintenance?

Then you may also need to consider some of the more subtle issues not in the lease.

- Are there any adjoining areas that you might be able to acquire if you need additional space?
- Is the lessor renting to any other businesses that could compete with or jeopardize the business you are acquiring? Does your lease protect you against such competition?

If you are not used to examining leases with a fine-tooth comb, consult your professional advisors before you make any commitment to the business.

On the other hand, if you buy the property as part of the transaction and later need to move the business, the real estate could become a problem. The property may have an independent value, but if its value is overly dependent on the business, you may be making a big mistake by purchasing it along with the business.

An analysis of the business is quite different from an analysis of the real estate. You must do a separate analysis to be sure of the value. Needless to say, if you purchase the property, make sure that it is free and clear of all liens and encumbrances. Note also the possibility that previous use of the property has resulted in an environmental infraction for which you may ultimately be responsible for paying for cleanup and/or damages.

## Building

In some cases, the real estate is not part of the sale of the business, but the building is. Paying for a building when you don't control the property on which it is located is almost always undesirable.

On the other hand, if you owned the building, the rent you would pay for the bare property would probably be much less than if you were renting the building as well as the land. It is simple enough to create an equation to approximate the value of the building based on the differential of the rent, with or without a building. Then, of course, you have the question of the age, utility, and condition of the building.

- Is there space to expand?
- Is the land lease long enough to ensure that you will not have to move the building?
- Does the area lend itself to a different use of the building in the event you decide to move the business?
- Do you have the right to sublet the building in the event you decide to move the business?

Here again, apart from doing an analysis of the business, you certainly need to have the building appraised and carefully examined. A serious roof repair, for example, could wipe out a lot of the profit of the business. A defect in the building could lead to an expensive insurance policy or an accident and a lawsuit. If the building is for sale with the business, you are really buying two properties and you need to examine each carefully.

## Highly Qualified Employees

When you buy a business, the employee question may be one of the trickiest issues of all. A good employee certainly appears to be a real benefit to a business. Is it possible for this same employee to be a detriment as well? Yes.

First of all, what happens when a good general manager in a particularly intricate manufacturing business, on whose capabilities the business has been dependent, moves to another state? How do you replace such a valuable employee? How much would it cost? Is any suitable replacement available? How long would it take to find such a person?

Companies have pension and profit-sharing plans that make it worthwhile for long-term employees to stay with the company. If they leave before a vesting, they normally cannot enjoy their full benefit package. Make sure you examine any insurance or program the current owner has in place to protect the business from losing its most important employees.

Many highly qualified employees are also on the front line of the business. They are in the sales department or in constant touch with the customers at the counter or on the telephone. These people actually control your customer base. In many instances, customers will buy the product exclusively because they trust the person selling it. Most markets are so competitive now that you rarely find a product for which there is no comparable replacement or competitor. All too often, the customer buys the salesperson, not the product.

If any employees control your customer base in this sense and decide to change jobs or work for the competition, the move could devastate your business. No legal language can guarantee total protection from the defection of a key employee in this type of situation. Make sure the business you are buying is not vulnerable to this kind of predicament. When the seller is putting a value on his or her personnel, be careful that you don't discuss this value without also considering the possibilities of losing those employees and the potential damage.

## Customer Base

You cannot overemphasize the value of customers. Many businesses follow the philosophy that it is easier to increase your business by cultivating current customers than by finding new customers. Your current customers already know the value of your product or service, how to get to your location, where to park, your basic price structure, and many subtle and personal things that affect buying behavior.

Many businesses train their counter people to call the customers by their names. Some businesses have their counter people wear nametags so the customers can know the names of the people with whom they are doing business. This personal touch can cause customers to stay with you despite discounts and other incentives offered by your competitors. As one entrepreneur said, "We have the same goods as everyone else. That's true. But the customers keep coming back because our people treat them with dignity. It really does make a difference."

The relationship between employees and customers is often the core of the business, regardless of the product or service. Customer loyalty can be a significant asset. If you are good to your customers, a time will come when they can be good to you.

## Customer Contracts

Some businesses are so dependent on certain large customers that they have written contracts with them. One reason is that if a business has to build up a strong inventory, purchase new equipment, or hire additional personnel to accommodate the needs of a particular customer, the business owner must have some security that he or she will be able to move that inventory off the shelf and not have to let employees go. If the current owner of the business has a special relationship with a substantial customer because of family or personal ties, the customer may no longer be loyal to the business under a new owner. If that customer leaves, sales could drop significantly. As you examine any business, define the large clients and satisfy yourself that they will continue to buy from that business.

If you buy a business that depends, even in part, on customer contracts or, for that matter, manufacturing contracts (for example, to take all the goods that a particular manufacturer can produce or to produce all the goods that a particular customer will buy), you must be careful to examine the contracts. More importantly, examine the relationship between the parties and make sure it has been and will continue to be successful for both parties.

## Location

Some people say that the three most important elements to consider when buying a business are location, location, and location. You may find it difficult to sell thermal underwear in Hawaii or bathing suits in Alaska. It is important that the business you buy be located in the middle of its largest potential customer base.

Your location may need to offer some or all of the following:

- Good signage opportunity so that traffic can recognize your location from both or all directions
- Good parking if your customers depend on it for shopping convenience
- A window to display impulse items if you have any
- The ability to maximize space efficiency if your business is not based on customer convenience

## Logo and Trade Name

Some businesses have the advantage of longevity in the marketplace, which goes a long way to establish name recognition. Some businesses are geared to high-visibility advertising, which not only generates sales but creates corporate name recognition in a relatively short time. These businesses can be selling anything from fast food to underwear. Sometimes, name recognition can be a strong wedge for your salespeople in the marketplace, just as Microsoft is in the computer field. A logo can also be a big drawing card for consumers, like the famous golden arches of McDonald's.

If you are buying a business that has a recognizable logo or an established trade name as part of the package, you must be prepared to pay for this market advantage. You may feel that this single business element makes the price exorbitant and that you can sell an equivalent product or service without the use of the logo or recognizable mark. In some cases, you may be correct. What you save on the purchase price may be enough to enable you to fight the advantage enjoyed by your competitors with powerful logos or trade names. In other cases, fighting the established and accepted brand may be like tilting at windmills.

Make this assessment early on. A marketing survey could help you determine the importance of the logo or trade name. In some case, it is virtually impossible to beat out a product that has been active in the marketplace for years and spent millions of dollars in advertising. The value of a logo deserves careful and objective analysis. If franchise logos dominate the marketplace, your best option may be to buy a franchise instead of an independent business.

## Reputation

Following closely behind the logo and trade name question is their logical successor, reputation. Although the logo and trade name are the face of the building, the reputation of a business is represented by the activity that goes on inside and the people who work with the customers.

Part of the franchise concept, for example, is that a customer can expect to find the same product, service, and even the same cosmetic environment whether he or she is in Maine, Oregon, Florida, or California. The reputation of a franchise business for cleanliness, professionalism, quality of product, and consistency brings customers back to the business wherever individual franchises are located. The same can also be true of an independent. Customers expect a certain level of service and quality every time they turn to the business because of its reputation.

If you are considering buying a franchise, you may be asked to pay a higher price than you might for a comparable independent operation because the franchise offers a nationally recognized reputation for quality. However, because of the quantity discount available to franchise companies, you may save enough on the equipment package to make up for any initial premium you will be asked to pay for the franchise reputation.

The question of paying a continuing royalty on sales to the franchise company is quite another question. See Chapter 9 for cost comparisons between franchises and independents.

## A Secret Formula

Each business is unique to some degree. Some are different because of their unusual inventory, some because of their location, and still others because they have a product based on a secret formula. Many formulas exist in the food business, ranging from pancake batter to the flavoring in carbonated sodas. Other less obvious formulas consist of chemicals and other additives to increase product longevity and strength or to improve smell, looks, and palatability.

If the business you are buying uses a secret formula of some kind, be careful that the essence of the product is properly protected under the appropriate laws. Determine the longevity of that protection, whether the formula is necessary to compete in the marketplace, and whether the price you are paying is commensurate with the advantages you expect to enjoy.

## Computer Hardware

In the 1960s, businesses started taking advantage of computer technology to eliminate many of the manual bookkeeping aspects of the business. If you had taken a tour of one of those businesses back then, you might have been shown a room that had wall-to-wall computers, a separate air conditioning system, and a special generator that would go on automatically in case of a power failure, and even then you wouldn't be allowed to see the room because of equipment sensitivity and confidentiality.

Computers now exist that are the size of a notebook with as much power and memory as the whole complex of computers in that room. You can protect your material by access codes and move the equipment from one room to another as easily as a cup of coffee. You can send and receive texts, pictures, and videos to and from computers all over the world at the press of a key.

The problem is that you must understand the nature of the equipment you are buying and the part it plays in the business. In most cases, the computer is your friend and ally. Be careful, however, of those situations in which the computer is so important that anything less than perfect could jeopardize the business.

## Computer Software

While the computer hardware is often fundamental to a business, without the right software for your business needs, it's just chips and cables and other components in cases. It is your obligation to either understand each program or have someone by your side who understands it and whether or not it serves the purpose for which it was intended. Just as the software needs to be designed or adapted to meet your needs, you must understand it so that you are not held hostage by a system that only a few people can handle.

## Computer Capability

Finally, you must examine whether the computer technology is really a benefit to the business. Some businesses have simple needs for computers, while others need a lot of computer power to function optimally.

Some people are convinced they should get very sophisticated and expensive computers to accommodate the potential growth of the business. They argue that it is less expensive to buy all the equipment now than to build up their capability incrementally as they need it. Some businesses have spent so much money on computer equipment that they have used up the working capital needed to capture their customer base in the marketplace. Look at both the positive and the negative sides of the computer system you are purchasing with the business and value it appropriately.

## Latest Technology

Whatever business you are considering, you will invariably find working aids of one sort or another. Ask yourself whether you need to pay for state-of-the-art equipment or whether you can get along with something more basic and less expensive.

Some of the latest technology may save some time but might be much more difficult to learn or teach. It may be much less expensive and less time-consuming to repair an older, simpler piece of equipment than a highly technical state-of-the-art machine. And the more complex machine may not prove to be nearly as cost-effective as the old standby. Look carefully and don't be fooled by appearances. Examine what is there and determine what would best serve your interests in the short term and the long term. You may be able to work well with the original equipment until either your profit allows an upgrade or your business demands it.

## Absence of Competition

Competition or the lack of it can be either a positive or a negative. Give it careful attention. The absence of competition can be as much a sign of danger as too much competition. Perhaps competitors haven't arrived yet—or maybe they have already left. Competition can be devastating or it can be tremendously important.

For example, you will very often find a proliferation of nightclubs or restaurants in a single area of the city. This cluster of shops and clubs allows customers to come to the general area, park their vehicles, and then choose where to go. Making this scheme work is, of course, a delicate balance. Seven restaurants in one place could be very successful. The eighth could throw off the competitive balance and drive them all into bankruptcy. You have to know your business and the market to recognize the balance.

If you are the only coffee shop in the neighborhood, for example, you might ask if others were there before. Why are they not there now? What is happening to the area? Why is rental space so readily available and inexpensive? You may buy a business that has no visible competition because all the knowledgeable people in the industry know a certain innovation is going to obsolete all current activity. Consider the silk stocking and its nylon replacement, the cloth diaper and its disposable replacement, or the metal container and its plastic replacement.

# What to Request from Your Seller

You found some research strategies in Chapter 6 and will undoubtedly have to turn to professional consultants for real estate appraisals or other more complicated valuations. However, your seller is required to give you as much relevant information as he or she is able. Below are some basic disclosures you can request from your seller early in the negotiation process.

## Money In and Money Out

Always start with the simplest elements. You should be looking for two things: money in and money out. What are the sources of the income to the business?

What are the costs necessary to generate that income? These basic items are found on a profit and loss statement, which, together with a balance sheet and a cash-flow analysis, will give you a good idea of the finances.

You need to see more than one year's P&L; after all, different years will involve different elements—different competitors, employees, market factors, and cost factors. You will certainly need at least one full year to allow for seasonality and vacation scheduling.

Look at other barometers of the business, including the aging of receivables, how long it takes to collect for the goods or services sold by the business. Collection times will tell you how large a working capital account you need. A working capital reservoir will support your operating costs while you wait the 30, 60, or 90 days it may take customers to pay their bills. As always, have a good accountant working along with you right from the beginning of the buying process. He or she will know about which figures to check and where to find them.

## Accrual vs. Cash

Keep in mind that the profit and loss statement should be on an accrual basis, to show the dollars owed at the end of the month, whether paid or not, such as rent. A cash basis presentation, in contrast, can be very deceptive: it will show what has been paid, not necessarily what is owed. Having both will give you a much clearer picture. If you are not familiar with reading financial documents and understanding how they work together, make sure you have your professional go over these with you.

## The Balance Sheet

You will need more than one balance sheet. A balance sheet shows certain elements as of the moment when it was prepared. The only way you can make judgments about long-term debt, large equipment purchases, and other substantial dollar obligations is to compare one balance sheet with another. Here again you want to be sure you understand how the financial picture is painted. If you are not sure about any of it, don't pretend you are. If you are going to operate a business, you must understand the basics. Speak with your accountant.

Some other specific questions need to be answered:

- What are the key accounts?
- Who are the key employees?
- How are relationships with key vendors established and what terms are available with each?
- What is the history of the company?
- Does the business have any current or potential litigation?
- What are the reasons for the good months and the bad months?
- What are general problems in the industry?
- What are competitors doing?

Remember: each industry is a little bit different; the smart buyer will do a complete analysis before making a judgment.

## The Lease—an Asset or a Liability?

Perhaps the biggest single key of all in the retail business is the lease. With rare exception, most retail businesses fundamentally depend on location. In the case of a business that depends on local traffic for its existence and success, location is clearly a top priority. It would be frivolous to consider buying a retail business that has only a short time left on its lease. Examine whether the lease has an option to renew; if not, you must consider the problem of moving and finding comparable space at a comparable price in the same marketing area. Examine the lease to ensure that the cost of the premises falls within the appropriate ratio parameters relative to the cash flow of the business, the customer base, and the growth potential. Moving the business might mean leaving and losing customers that it has taken years to cultivate and on whom the business is relying for its survival and growth.

## Questions, Strategies, and Results

By now you have probably developed a good list of research questions and strategies. As you continue to explore the possibilities for buying a business, consult that list of questions and strategies, revise it, and make sure you get the specific and accurate results you need.

## Key Points to Remember

- A business is composed of many parts. Make sure you understand what each part represents and how it contributes to the success of the business.
- One of the most significant elements to the retail business is the premises lease. Go over it with your professional advisors so that you understand its terms completely. A surprise in your lease after a sale can be devastating.
- Your customer base is your business. Know who your customers are and how to sell to them.
- A business's financial statements provide the history of the business and insight into its current value and future growth. Go over the profit and loss statement, balance sheet, cash flow analysis, and general ledger carefully with your professional advisors.

# CHAPTER 8

# Investors and Partners

## Illustration 8-1. Learning Experience

When Iris Norton decided to start a magazine, she knew that she would need working capital at various stages along the way—getting the first issue to press, waiting for the first issue's advertising dollars to come in—but the bank wasn't eager to fund a new business. When Bill Lawrence said he'd fund the magazine for half the revenues, Iris knew it was the only way to get her first venture off the ground. Bill decided to invest the money "a little at a time" so he could control some of the decision making. When the advertising dollars weren't coming in as quickly as anticipated, Bill decided to stop the funding and Iris was essentially left out in the cold. She didn't realize that an incremental investment program could kill the dream she had. Iris will likely dream again, but she will certainly have a better grasp of reality.

Some business sales can occur in one simple transaction—the papers are signed, money changes hands, and the seller goes on to begin his or her new life. Most sales of businesses, however, require a transition period, ranging from something as relatively simple as repayment of a promissory note to something more complicated, such as the seller acting as a paid consultant, an investor, or a partner.

Not all investors or partners are former owners of the business, though such an arrangement is one way to creatively finance a sale, as discussed in Chapter 3. Buyers often need the participation of other people for money, guidance, or actual labor.

If you are considering taking on an investor or a partner, the guidelines in this chapter will alert you to some of the issues related to sharing control of your business. The checklist toward the end of the chapter will help you focus on the issues involved.

Keep in mind that investors differ. The investor who buys stock in a public company is not involved in the day-to-day activity of the business. The investor in a small, privately held company normally serves on the board of directors, both to protect the investment and to help direct the financial affairs of the company. This chapter, as with this book as a whole, is directed toward the small, often family-run companies that make up the great bulk of the small business community.

## The Investor Profile

Investors come in all shapes and sizes, with different motivations and funding. Some are interested in getting a return on their investment because the business is a start-up expected to produce income after it gets on its feet. Other investors are interested in a business that is doing well and has strong potential for future growth, possibly leading to going public. Still others may recognize the possibility of duplicating the business in other markets, potentially leading to the formation of a franchise.

At a meeting of friends to consider investing in a radio station, one potential investor said, "It might not make any money, but it will at least give us all an excuse to get together once in a while." These people have a somewhat different motivation for investing, as do people who invest occasionally because they think they are supporting a worthwhile community project. Investing for camaraderie or for a charitable purpose is not just for those with a big purse. Many people do it at one time or another. This kind of investment bears a very different return, however—a return not measured in dollars.

The investor types in this chapter are those who seek a financial return— a multiple of the money invested or an interest in the growth potential of the business. While friends or benefactors may make good investors, you should always find out at the very outset of your relationship with an investor exactly what the purpose of the investment is and what the investor or the investor group expects from it. A lack of this kind of understanding can create chaos, whether the business succeeds or not.

## The Control Factor

Money speaks loudly at the conference table. Ask yourself whether the size of an investor's dollar interest in the business speaks so loudly as to interfere with proper operation of the business. Investors would like to make sure their money is serving the business purpose for which it was intended and not being rerouted or diverted to someone's pocket for personal use. Two ways to do that are to sit on the board of directors and to attend periodic management meetings where the expenditures of money and the future of the company and its activities are decided.

Management must be in the hands of those who can make the appropriate business decisions. Investors tend to protect their dollars by acting in the short term and lose sight of the long-term picture, although the long-term result is often why they invested.

The securities laws work to protect investors who are not in a position to gamble with their dollars. The laws prescribe extensive disclosure documents for anyone seeking investors in a publicly held company. This disclosure normally explains that the investment is not secure and that the probability of the business's success is highly conjectural. Investors whose loss would put their families in jeopardy are certainly not the ideal investors. They tend to second-guess every business decision, looking for any misstep by management. This kind of short-term, over-the-shoulder supervision can inhibit advantageous long-term planning. Be careful about your investors and the size of their investments relative to their net worth.

## The Time Factor

Every investor expects a return of investment within a particular period. You need to clearly define the length of this period when you begin the relationship with your investor. Often, this will be implicit in the document representing the investment.

For example, one investor may receive a promissory note in return for the dollars invested; this note may call for the periodic payment of interest, with the principal to be paid at the end of a certain time. Other notes may call for the obligation to be fully amortized: the principal and interest are paid periodically until the entire investment is repaid. In still other cases, the investor may receive common stock in the corporation, which will not entitle him or her to any return on investment until the corporation declares a dividend, is sold or otherwise liquidated, or has a public offering. Often, the investor participates in the company by having some combination of the above. A portion of the investment is returned and another portion remains in the company as the investor's equity participation.

In some cases, an investor may take a different class of stock that allows him or her to participate in a periodic return, depending on the conditions of the obligation or of the company. An investment of this type also may provide the investor with some voting privileges or veto power over management with regard to certain kinds of decisions.

When posturing the company for an investment that gives the investor a periodic return and voting privileges inside the management team, whether before or after you purchase the business, make arrangements to accommodate whatever return the investor expects. If an investor holds security of some kind to protect the investment, this security position may jeopardize the future of the company if the company needs to borrow money.

The best approach, if you must pledge assets to an investor, is to have the investor agree to subordinate his or her interest in the security to a lending institution if it becomes appropriate to seek new money for growth purposes. This approach makes the investor's security interest junior to the new interest of the bank, a senior security holder. Without this subordination agreement, the company would not be able to borrow additional money because the bank will not be satisfied with a second position in the security.

Make sure that time is always on your side and that you understand the rights and obligations of the parties. As you can see, a decision to handle a short-term problem can be a serious detriment to long-term goals. Have your professionals examine any pledge of the company's assets to ensure that the loss of that asset for security purposes, however temporary, will not hinder the company's ability to borrow elsewhere.

## The Dollar Involvement

Unfortunately, the dollar speaks with a loud voice. If the investment is large enough to be the basis for the company's existence, you, as management, may actually be working for the investor. If the investor controls 51 percent or more of the participating stock in the company, he or she may hold veto power over your long-term judgments, even though you are responsible for the managing the company's activities day to day. You need to be aware of the ground rules before your investor exercises the right to overrule your management decisions. You can protect against an investor's excessive control of management, particularly if you act early in the relationship. Set priorities, anticipate the contingencies, and agree on who is responsible for which decisions.

## Value to the Company

The next important factor in determining an investor's power in the company is the value of the investment to the company. If the investment is essential to maintaining the company's activities, you may have to give up some control for the privilege of going forward. If you give up too much control, the investment will undoubtedly prove inimical to the best interests of management. Remember: the investor, no matter how excited he or she may be about the business or its potential, will not normally be the best person to make decisions about the business. The investor's judgment may be skewed to making decisions that affect the investment in the short term, which is often the worst perspective for making business decisions.

For every financial investment, you want to create a quid pro quo relationship—everyone gets something for giving something. You may want an investor so you can acquire additional inventory, property, personnel, equipment, or locations. Your desire to do something more quickly or efficiently may propel your search for investors. You may even want particular investors to participate not for their money but for their ability to enhance the reputation of the company in the community or the marketplace. For example, many companies ask famous athletes to lend their names to products or advertising to promote the company image or its visibility.

You have to pay for the privilege of growing more or doing more with your business. The question is whether the value to the business and its future is worth the shackles an investor may put on the business. Be careful when you make this decision, because it is not an easy one to retract. If the business succeeds, the investor will expect to reap the rewards. If the business becomes problematic, the investor will still want something in return for the risk he or she took. Be prepared to pay the price in either case.

## The Partner Mystique

Partners, like investors, come in all shapes and sizes. You must examine not only the motivation of your potential partner, but also your own motivation. Occasions arise when you would like to have someone by your side who has extensive experience in a particular industry. You can retain and pay a consultant, you can hire somebody appropriate, or you can create a partnership. Much will depend on the nature of the business. You may start up or purchase a business because you have good ideas and creativity. However, your lack of expertise or experience in the industry could prevent the business from realizing its full potential.

For example, if you have an idea for a magazine because you understand the needs or the desires of your potential readers, you may be extremely wise to partner with someone who understands the magazine business in general. A partner who understands subscriptions, advertising, list maintenance, printing price structures, and other areas in which your knowledge is limited can be very valuable. You may need a money partner because the magazine venture will likely not break even until it publishes a number of issues and builds a reputation that earns the respect of advertisers.

If you are looking for a money partner, you should get advice from an investor, not an expert. The two are very different. An expert makes sure you attend to the details of the business. An investor makes sure you don't make business decisions that could outpace the dollars you have available for growth. Three participants in a business—an expert, an investor, and the creator or founder—may be a much better balance for the future and success of any business than the singular and biased view of any one participant.

## The Partner Contribution

Partners and investors are not the only way to obtain money or expertise. You can buy expertise from paid consultants or hired staff. You can borrow money. On the other hand, money that the company doesn't need to pay back leaves management with less weight on its shoulders, and the expertise of a partner who occupies the next office is much better than the expertise of a consultant with whom you must schedule an appointment.

Whether you choose to take on a partner or an investor or to seek other sources of money and advice, be sure that the help you get meets the needs of the business. If you give up shares in the business for an expert's help in a minor aspect of the business, you may no longer have enough shares to entice an expert when you need additional help. If you agree to share management control for a small amount of capital from an investor or partner, you may create problems for yourself later, when you need additional capital. You may have to dilute the interests of the current investors by taking on more investors. You may decide to dilute your ownership of the business by taking on more partners. This approach is very undesirable if it causes your share participation in the company to fall below 50 percent, a controlling interest.

The most difficult question is what to do when you take on a partner who will contribute to both management and financial strength. You want to be sure you have the full attention of your partner and that he or she is willing to participate completely. One way to help ensure that a partner participates completely in a business is to gear the partner's ownership to the time, energy, and success he or she contributes during successive periods of business growth. Any partner who says that his or her primary goal is to build the business should find this arrangement fair and reasonable. If, on the other hand, the partner just wants to invest and not participate, you should find out early so you don't depend on someone who isn't available.

What do you do when someone who could be a great partner doesn't have enough money to make a significant contribution to the financial strength of the company? One philosophy is that it doesn't matter how much a partner can afford as long as the investment is at least 80 percent of whatever the partner has. In other words, the partner must contribute enough money so that he or she has something at risk it would hurt to lose! The amount at risk must be significant to the contributing partner.

If your partner doesn't have any dollars available for investment, you could still structure a partnership by having a portion of the partner's income allocated to a fund that would eventually purchase a designated partnership interest. In other words, you can always find creative ways to achieve your goal. Don't decline to proceed without first exploring all the possible alternatives.

In many cases, two people want to start a business because they have had a mutual experience. Strangely enough, these kinds of partnerships tend to lack strength because neither partner has the background to contribute what the other cannot. Make sure that each partner can make a complementary contribution, such that all contributions together cover the essentials.

## The Partner's Return

One last issue is the percentage of the partnership to which each partner is entitled. The ideal situation gives each partner a percentage based on his or her contribution of time, energy, expertise, and dollars. This ideal is rarely achieved. The key is to examine the contribution of each partner and make some hard decisions early on that will prevent any partner from feeling down the road that he or she was taken advantage of and that there should be a redistribution of investment or return.

## Diamonds Are Forever

It is hard to conceive of a perfect partnership, because "perfect" suggests not only equal work for equal pay, but also that the partnership's longevity is beyond question. You may experience perfection in your partnership for short periods, but partners will eventually disagree on something. Each of you brings at least a slightly different experience and perspective to everything you do. The nature of your personality will cause you either to adjust to your partner or to expect your partner to adjust to you. Lack of immediate adjustment could lead to conflict; conflict, without appropriate compromise, could lead to confrontation and dispute; and dispute, without resolution, could lead to a breakup of the partnership or even litigation. The last frontier of litigation in business is the destruction of the business itself. Diamonds may be forever, but partnerships are not, and you should not expect them to be.

The most significant lesson of all, therefore, is the need to build into your partnership agreement a method for any partner to withdraw in the event of serious and irresolvable conflict. Do this in such a way that you allow the business to continue to function. In most partnerships, you will undoubtedly have *key person insurance* (also called *key man insurance*) to replace an important partner in the event of his or her death. This eliminates the problem of "inheriting" a partner you didn't intend to have and about whom you may know nothing. Take the same care to ensure that the business continues in the event of a disagreement. After all, whatever the differences between partners, no partner wants to see his or her investment of time, energy, creativity, or money go down the drain. It is in the best interests of all partners to ensure the integrity and continuity of the business.

## Forms of Participation

The joint venture concept—the collaboration of people participating equally or unequally in a business operation—has many alternative forms.

**Sole proprietorship**—The simplest form of business ownership is the sole proprietorship: only one person owns the business and any collateral participation is by way of dollar investment, commission on sales, or bonus based on extraordinary contribution to the success of the business activity.

**General partnership**—In a general partnership, two or more people participate equally or in designated percentages. The problem with the general partnership is its inequality, regardless of distribution of profit. The joint and several liability of the general partnership makes any partner 100 percent responsible for any partnership obligation. This type of liability is a big danger, particularly to the partner with the deepest pocket—the most money. The wealthiest partner is usually the one who is sued. The court can render judgment against this deep pocket for all the damages even though he or she was only partly responsible. The party who pays is entitled to sue the others for their share of the obligation, but the process is tedious and expensive and the others may not have the money to reimburse their partner.

**Limited partnership**—The limited partnership affords most of the partners very much the same protection as they would have as shareholders in a corporation. The limited partnership usually has a general partner who is completely responsible for all the activities and, in turn, for all the obligations of the partnership. The limited partners are liable for the full amount of their investment, but not for any obligation incurred during or as a result of the business activity. However, this limited liability applies only if the limited partners do not actively participate in the daily operation of the business.

**Corporation**—One way to protect yourself from personal liability is the corporation, which operates the business as a separate entity and is responsible for all business debts, but only to the extent of the financial capability of the corporation. The officers and directors of the corporation have no personal liability except if any of them signs personally or guarantees an obligation of the corporation or if they engage in fraud, misrepresentation, or other criminal activity. Otherwise, they are insulated against having their personal finances at risk. The shareholders are, of course, liable for the full amount of their investment. If the corporation files a bankruptcy, the shareholders are not entitled to any of their investment until all the creditors are satisfied.

**Limited liability company**—A relatively new form of doing business, the limited liability company (LLC) closely resembles and is taxed as a partnership and it offers the benefit of limited liability like a corporation. Because of the newness of LLCs and the potential tax advantages and disadvantages of this entity, ask your accountant or attorney how to investigate its potential for your business.

Many variations exist for each of the above structures: you should examine them carefully before making any decision on the format you will use. Base your final judgment on both the short-term and long-term goals of the business. You will have to do part of your analysis according to the number of people involved and the extent of their financial participation, in addition to their actual involvement in the day-to-day activities of the business. Go over the alternatives carefully with your professionals.

## Key Points to Remember

- If you accept investments in your business, find out how much control over the business you may have to relinquish.
- Know the goals of your investor(s) or partner(s) and whether they are consistent with your goals.
- The long-term value of an investment must be consistent with the needs of the business and its ability to function in the future.
- If you take on a partner, make sure your partner's goals are clearly defined and that you both agree on a plan to dissolve the partnership if it becomes necessary.
- A business can take many legal forms. Examine them with your professional advisers and choose the best form for your short-term and long-term goals.

For additional information on partnerships and partnership relationships, see *Forming a Partnership and Making It Work*, by Ira Nottonson, Entrepreneur Press, 2007.

# CHAPTER 9

# The Franchise Decision

## Illustration 9-1. The Starting Point

The excitement was extraordinary in 1998 when the entire Formatta family got involved in purchasing and operating their Yogurt/Cinnamon Factory franchise. Over the first five years, they actually opened up six locations and each member of the family ended up owning and operating a franchise. It was a family dream fulfilled. They recognized that they were paying a constant royalty of 10 percent of all sales, but they were willing to wait the ten years until the franchise contract expired. Then, the 10 percent would drop right into their pockets when they replaced the name "Yogurt/Cinnamon Factory" with their own "Formatta Yogurt/ Cinnamon Co. Kitchen." But they were wrong.

Their franchise contract actually precluded them from remaining in the business unless they retained the franchise name and continued to pay the 10 percent royalty to the franchise company. The shock devastated the family! They should have read the franchise agreement more carefully when they signed it ten years earlier.

If you are new to entrepreneurship, a franchise can offer you a comfort zone you may not experience with a nonfranchise business. The franchise company may serve as a kind of silent partner to whom you can turn for advice and assistance. Franchise companies can offer training, expert help, advertising assistance, market analysis, equipment research and development, and trade name and logo recognition.

However, none of these services are free. You will have to commit to paying an initial fee to the franchise company and ongoing royalties for many years. Furthermore, you need to know how helpful and reliable the franchise company will be during your long-term relationship. The decision to buy a franchise cannot be taken lightly.

Whether you decide to purchase an existing franchise operation or start up a new franchise, think carefully before you make your decision. Compile a list of questions to ask—and make sure the questions are specific. Ask for advice from professionals, franchise owners, and owners of nonfranchise businesses.

The task is not simple. You will need to look at several issues, among them:

- The strength of the franchise company
- The dominance of the franchise logo
- The effectiveness of the franchise advertising in your marketplace
- The talent that you as a businessperson bring to the business
- The talents you lack and for which you need support
- The kind of business
- The competitive element involved

Some of the guesswork is eliminated if you buy an existing franchise. Any existing operation will have a record you can examine, including the relationship between the franchisee and the franchisor.

This chapter will lead you through some of the factors involved in the franchise decision. It will show how franchising has changed since its dramatic growth in the 1960s and how its evolution may affect your decision to buy into a franchise company. You will learn about some of the legislation that regulates franchising and how it affects buyers and sellers. Finally, you will find a checklist in the worksheet for this chapter on the accompanying CD that will help you ask the right questions and structure your ultimate decision.

## Franchising—Past and Present

When franchising started to hit its stride, around 1968, businesspeople perceived that franchise companies knew their industries well. Franchisees bought into the franchise concept knowing they would be totally dependent on the parent companies for survival, growth, and success.

In those days, before computers, microchips, and satellites, the franchise concept was a good one and it worked. A person with few skills in a particular trade could be trained in a matter of weeks to operate a business. The training used proven methods to create confident and competent business owners. A franchise company was normally started by a man or woman who had taken a business concept and made it a success. This successful businessperson understood and could empathize with the day-to-day problems the franchisee faced. A certain respect and synergy existed between the franchisor and the franchisee.

### The Change in Profit Distribution

As time went on, many franchisees became extremely successful and knew more about the business, certainly in their own geographic areas, than the young and sometimes inexperienced men and women whom the franchisor hired to visit and supervise franchisees.

Despite having mastered the basics of the business, the franchisee still needed someone to help deal with new and more sophisticated questions—how to expand in the marketplace and maximize growth and profit potential. Unfortunately, many franchise companies believed the franchise concept was designed to deal with the lowest common denominator, people who knew nothing about the business. Some franchise companies did not invest in support services for their more successful franchisees, because they thought the franchisees could buy the help they needed with the profits from their success. The franchisees, on the other hand, felt that because they paid a higher royalty on their large gross revenues, they deserved more than the basics in return.

## Franchising as Big Business

Matters between franchisor and franchisee really began to deteriorate when franchising became a business of its own. Rather than a distribution method that employed the energy and investment of small business owners to mutual advantage, franchising became a numbers game. Some franchise companies were more interested in how many locations they could open than in how much support they could offer their current owners.

The appearance of the public company in the franchise industry, new management, and the leveraged buyout changed the face of franchising. A new generation of executives entered the game. Instead of working with another person toward a mutual goal, the individual franchisee had to turn to a corporate bureaucracy for assistance and advice. The original relationship of mutual trust and support disintegrated.

Even the basic concept was lost in the confusion. One chief executive officer of a franchise giant remarked, "If the franchisee won't cooperate, I'll fire him." This executive certainly had no understanding of the synergistic relationship between franchisor and franchisee. Further, this person didn't even understand the basic premise that the franchisee is an entrepreneur. A franchisee can't be fired!

Some franchise companies gave up doing market research on sites because they were more interested in getting new locations open. They did not update their training programs or maintain research on new equipment. They focused more on national advertising, which in some industries was not as effective for individual franchisees as local advertising.

## Legislation to Protect the Franchisee

You need to be assured that any franchise company you join has worked through the corporate greed to which some fell victim in the 1980s. The economic and political trend today is toward small business, and specific legislation has been enacted to protect the individual franchise owner. The requirement for complete franchise disclosure before offering a franchise for sale essentially keeps the franchise company from making promises that it can't or won't keep. Today, this legislation is effective in all 50 states. If you're buying a franchise, you can now depend on receiving full disclosure about the business you are buying and the company from which you are buying it.

While franchising has undergone many changes in the last decade, franchising as a whole has been a successful part of the American marketplace and one of the cornerstones of small business. One bad franchise company does not necessarily represent the whole industry. Franchising will continue to play a significant role in America's economy for many years.

## The Variables Involved in Your Decision

While disclosure documents are very helpful to a potential franchise buyer, you will also need to do some primary research on your own—research into what a franchise company will provide for you in return for your royalty payments.

Anyone who has ever operated a business will recognize that the daily activities of the business become so consuming that there is very little time to do research on new equipment in your industry, evaluate the directions your competitors are taking, follow up with your customers to increase their orders, develop a current marketing program, analyze your labor force to maintain a fair compensation package, or think about new directions your business can take.

The strength of the franchise comes from its ability to maintain its support services—services that the individual businessperson has neither the time nor, in many cases, the inclination or expertise to get elsewhere. A national franchise can also give quantity discounts on supplies, offer training seminars, and, of course, provide national name recognition. The availability or unavailability of these services can represent a significant factor in the success or failure of a business.

You can expect help from the franchise company with some of the various issues involved in buying a business. As you have read in previous chapters, you need to know about the necessary working capital reservoir, the competition, and the value of the business location to assess the potential for success. A franchise company can help you research these issues, but, as with any business investment, your success or failure depends ultimately on your own efforts.

## Working Capital

Lack of adequate working capital, particularly in a new business, is a key reason for serious problems and even failure. In some cases, a franchise company will paint a success scenario that gives the franchise buyer a less than realistic estimate of the working capital requirements. A responsible franchise company will be too concerned with the long-term relationship to let this happen. However, many franchise buyers, to qualify for the franchise purchase, may exaggerate their own financial resources. Don't be tempted to engage in such deception.

## Competition

"Competition" is a word that can generate fear among more naive business owners. The more sophisticated businessperson accepts competition as a positive element that exposes a product or service to a wider consumer audience. In most instances, the success of a franchise in battling the competition depends primarily on the initiative of the franchise owner. However, the purpose of buying a franchise is to benefit from the franchisor's experience in the marketplace. The franchisor should have developed marketing concepts that are proven to be effective in generating a competitive advantage. The franchise company should certainly make these techniques available to the franchisee.

## Location

How many times have you heard that in most businesses, the three most important elements are location, location, and location? Although you certainly don't have to subscribe to this somewhat simplistic philosophy all the time, you cannot deny its validity in certain instances, particularly in businesses where substantial customer traffic is an absolute necessity. When an area has many vacant sites available, the goal in locating a site is simply to find the best for the business. Unfortunately, when there are not many vacant sites available, the goal is to find the best location available. You cannot expect magic from a franchise company when you look for a location for your business. Usually, all the franchisor can do is lend its experience and expertise to find you the best location available.

## Future Success

The purpose of affiliating with a franchise company, whether you open a new franchise or buy an existing one, is to have an experienced partner on whom you can rely for business advice. However, the responsibility for succeeding with the business does not rest on the franchisor, but rather squarely on the franchisee.

On the other hand, the franchise relationship is based on the entrepreneurial initiative of the franchisee and the extensive industry experience of the franchisor. Successful franchisors recognize this relationship and offer help in every way. If the business is in trouble, the franchisee must work to fix the problem. However, the franchisor should at least participate in an analysis of the problem in order for the franchisee to work in the most appropriate direction and with the best tools to correct the problems.

Nonetheless, the law does not allow a franchisor to tell a franchisee how good a living he or she can make. The success of a small business enterprise is very much in the hands of the franchisees—their initiative, creativity, personality, work ethic, and energy.

# A Franchisor's Marketing and Advertising Capabilities

One of the most important factors in a successful business is finding and selling to customers. In the early days, active selling by the franchisee was not the most significant factor in the stability and growth of the business. Most competitors were independents who didn't have the national buying power or name recognition of franchise companies or the allocation of dollars for local advertising. Now, most competitors are other franchises that all have similar benefits. It is now extremely important, not only for success but simply for survival, for owners to be sales-oriented, particularly in those fields where outside selling is appropriate. Franchise companies used to say that you didn't have to be sales-oriented to succeed. Some franchise companies are still saying this. In great part, it is no longer true. You need to assess how your franchise company will help you sell. Look especially at its training program.

## The Franchisor Does Your Market Research for You

One of the services many franchise companies provide is market research. To assess your franchisor's marketing capabilities, you need to examine and evaluate:

- Your market environment
- Your customer base
- Your marketing priorities
- Your maximum marketing impact and the approach best suited to achieve it

These concepts may seem a little complex, but they are the focus of most franchise marketing departments. Having someone develop and constantly reevaluate these concepts when you don't have the time, experience, or inclination to do it yourself has a dollar value.

Consider, for example, a retail ice cream company that failed to recognize the following facts:

- The competition was getting stronger in the marketplace.
- Yogurt was impacting the ice cream market.
- Low-calorie substitutes were appealing to diet-conscious consumers.
- Exotic flavors were becoming popular.
- Supermarket freezers were becoming subtle but serious competitors in sales to on-the-street-consumption customers.

A shop owner who is involved with the daily problems of refrigeration breakdowns, tardy or absent employees, delivery times, shop hygiene, and customer complaints might find it difficult to address the long-term, but ever-important demands of market research. Having a parent company there to help has a dollar value.

The ice cream shop's franchisor monitors changes in the marketplace, plans ahead with new test flavors in a few stores, and recommends changes in décor to attract new customers or draw old customers back out of their homes and into the shop. Obviously, this kind of analysis could go on and on without even addressing each industry's particular dynamics.

## Is Purchasing a Franchise an Advertising Investment?

The advertising services provided by the franchise company are also at the core of many franchise relationships. Many businesspeople consider advertising an expense of doing business rather than an investment in the future. Survival, let alone success, requires good advertising. You must tell people that you have a product or service for sale.

You could save money by not advertising if you weren't obligated to do so by a franchise contract. You shouldn't buy a franchise just for the discipline of making certain advertising commitments. Advertising is mandatory whether you are a franchise owner or an independent. Your only consideration ought to be whether the franchise company can do a more effective job locally than you can. Who will impact your customer base more? The effectiveness of a national advertising campaign depends on the type of business and the size and financial strength of the franchise company.

Some franchise companies actually develop focus group studies that tell them about the customers' interests and tastes in a given geographical marketplace. They then develop materials to make their national or local advertising most effective. The independent just doesn't have the dollars or the resources to develop this kind of program.

In advertising, frequency is often the key to success. An isolated ten-second spot on national television may not be as effective as ten 30-second spots on a local radio station, but the cost may be exactly the same. The quantity purchasing power of the big-dollar franchise to buy multiples of advertising space in all media makes it very difficult for the independent to appear as often or take as much space in any medium with his or her spending limits.

In many industries, the franchise system ensures noncompetitive situations within its own franchise family by designating exclusive geographical areas. Keep in mind, however, that this offers only the protection of preventing another member of that particular franchise from *opening* a location within that territory. It does not prevent any businesses from advertising anywhere they choose! And websites on the internet have made this even more problematic.

## Making the Decision

You now know some of the many variables that will go into your decision to buy a franchise. One method you can use to structure your ultimate decision is a line-by-line analysis of what a franchise company offers and how much it would cost to obtain those services elsewhere. You also need to consider whether buying an existing franchise is a better option for you than opening a new franchise or buying a nonfranchise business. The remainder of this chapter will prepare you to make those decisions and the worksheet for this chapter on the accompanying CD will give you some specific questions you should answer before you decide.

### A Line-by-Line Analysis

As you research the prospect of buying a franchise, try to objectively weigh the pros and cons of joining a franchise family. You will need to look at several aspects of the franchise relationship, find out what services the franchisor provides, and assess the value of those services to you.

- Examine the royalty and advertising commitments of the franchise contract and relate these costs to the actual cost savings and other dollar advantages offered by the franchise.
- Compute the amount of equipment replacement for obsolescence during the average year and equipment purchases needed to remain com-

petitive in the industry. Compare the savings offered by the franchisor's national discount price with the cost of the same or similar equipment without the franchise price break.

- Consider the research and development capability of the franchise and give it a fair and thoroughly negotiated value. Many franchise companies ease the burden of equipment research by testing, analyzing, and reporting on equipment innovations to its franchisees.

- Assess the value of equipment service contracts you would receive through the franchise. An independent who may never buy another piece of equipment from a vendor is not going to get the same kind of service from a vendor as a franchisee whose parent company acquires thousands of dollars' worth of equipment from that same vendor every year.

- Calculate the value of financial coordinators and analysts whose services the franchise company offers its franchisees to go over their financial paperwork and cost-profit percentages. Independents who hire outsiders to do this face high costs for the service.

- Factor in the value of periodic seminars, an annual convention, or the periodic visits of company personnel that the franchisor may offer to help franchisees with marketing, equipment, vendors, maintenance questions, advertising, and industry updates.

- You may want to develop a cost-per-item accounting of the franchise company's services and compare it with the royalty and advertising commitment mandated by the franchise contract. The worksheet on the accompanying CD can help you get started.

## How New and Existing Franchises Compare

If you buy an existing franchise, you will have the benefit of knowing the specific history of your franchisee-seller's relationship with the franchise company. A good, solid working relationship may be one of the most valuable assets of an existing franchise.

You will, of course, want to consider several other issues:

- Working capital is still a primary concern, but you will have an immediate cash flow from the business, so the working capital requirement will be more clearly defined and therefore much less disquieting.
- The competition is no longer an unknown, because the questions about where competitors are, what they do, and how they affect the future of the business are a basic part of analyzing the purchase.
- The question of location is eliminated, because the record of the business eliminates any conjecture about the viability of the site.
- The question of the franchisor's cooperative attitude is answered by the experience of the seller. (You can, of course, find out about the franchisor's attitude by questioning franchisees, whether you decide to purchase a new or an existing franchise.)
- The question of the profit potential of the business is no longer a mystery. It is merely a question of carefully examining the books and records of the business to understand its actual performance. In other words, much of the guesswork is taken out of the picture!

Does this mean you should definitely buy an existing franchise rather than a new one? Not necessarily.

In a new franchise, you have the opportunity to find the following:

- A dynamic location in a growing area, as opposed to a current location that might be in a stagnant or declining market area
- An expandable business facility, as opposed to one whose growth potential is restricted by other buildings or zoning regulations
- A wide-open market potential in a growing community, as opposed to a restricted business environment where all the competitors have to fight for part of a static or shrinking customer base
- A fresh start with an opportunity to use your own personality as the basis for the relationship with your customers, as opposed to taking on a customer base that might not be consistent with your own business attitudes
- Many other advantages, depending on the particular industry involved

Is it possible to find a definitive answer? Yes, though it requires a good deal of research and self-analysis.

## Consider Your Needs

The franchising community today is adding different kinds of new buyers. Fewer new franchisees are gamblers and more are prudent businesspeople than was the case ten years ago. Most are less interested in big profits than in a consistent and lasting growth pattern.

Changes in the U.S. economy during the past decade have fueled this shift. Insecurity over jobs and pensions has focused the small business buyer's attention on a secure position with retirement potential. In addition, the average franchise candidate is probably ten years older than the average candidate ten years ago.

You should now be getting closer to deciding between a new and an existing franchise.

If you are a gambler hoping to make a good deal of money from buying a new franchise, you still have an opportunity as franchising moves from its adolescence to maturity. You must only keep in mind that the stakes are a little higher and the road a little more dangerous.

If you are more conservative, landing in the franchise field with a golden parachute and wanting to ensure that your retirement is relatively safe, then purchasing an existing franchise business is wiser. It gives you the benefit of the proven record and the opportunity to improve it. Buying a franchise that has already gone through the "whether or nots"—whether or not the location is good, whether or not the competition is manageable—will prove more prudent in the short term.

The only question left is, if you buy an existing franchise, how much should you pay for it? Remember the two basic priorities. An existing business ought to provide a living wage and be able to service the purchase price of the business out of operating profit. Any payment schedule to handle the balance of the purchase price after the down payment by the buyer should not come from the buyer's pocket. It should come from the business.

Follow this philosophy and you won't have to worry much about location, competition, or breaking even. You can concentrate on other things like maintaining state-of-the-art marketing techniques and cutting costs—looking toward building the business for the future and your family.

You will need to assess your own personal strengths and weaknesses as a businessperson to make the decision. Some people are very adept at taking advantage of the services offered by a franchisor and some are not. Some people have family members involved in their business organization who have good business sense. Others are not so fortunate: they have only competent but not so dedicated employees and are therefore more vulnerable to fluctuations in the marketplace, particularly with respect to personnel problems. Consider your situation thoroughly before making the franchise decision. A worksheet for this chapter on the accompanying CD will help lead you through the process.

## Some Legal Fine Print

If you are still wondering whether to buy an existing franchise or a nonfranchise business, consider one last item. If you decide on a franchise, the franchisor needs to consent to the transfer, making the transaction a three-party contract. You are taking the seller's place in the all-important franchisor-franchisee relationship. It is the seller's obligation to explain to you thoroughly and positively what this relationship represents. The seller will tell you about royalty payments, the right of the franchisor to challenge the accuracy of these royalty payments, and the many services and advantages offered by the franchisor.

You should recognize certain basic issues involved in this process:

- The franchisor doesn't want to be in a less secure position after the sale than before the sale. When the original franchisee applied to the franchise company to buy a franchise, he or she filled out a financial application detailing his or her assets. The franchise company sold the franchise based, at least in part, on this financial strength.
- The franchisor doesn't want to give up good financial security; it wants to replace it with security of equal or greater value. The franchisor will look at your application to see if your assets and monies represent the same relative financial strength that it is giving up by releasing the seller from any further obligations under the franchise contract. Your asset strength ensures that the financial obligations to the franchisor are paid

whether the business can afford to pay them or not. However, you should note that the continuing obligation of the seller after a sale is not the same in different jurisdictions. Ask your professional about this.

- Of course, the franchisor primarily wants to know that the cash flow of the business can support a successful transfer and that the buyer can meet the obligations. The franchisor will certainly be concerned, for example, with your ability to meet the payment schedule of the purchase money promissory note to the seller and any notes the franchisee might still owe to the franchise company. If you are unable to meet the payments on these obligations, it is unlikely the franchisor will be able to collect the periodic royalty payments in timely fashion. The franchisor is then facing potential costly litigation to collect on its debts. The franchisor may then try to go after the other assets listed on your application.

- The franchisor wants to ensure that its reputation in the business community will not be depreciated in any way with regard, for example, to trademarks or logos.

- The franchisor wants an acceptable buyer under the terms of the franchise contract from the beginning. For example, the buyer normally cannot already have an ownership interest in a competing business.

- The franchisor wants all the details in all parts of the selling agreement pertaining to the franchise company properly and clearly stated. This will afford the franchisor protection in the event of litigation between the buyer and the seller later.

Even though the franchisee is selling his or her own business, it is always appropriate for the seller to comply with the disclosure law in the particular jurisdiction. If a disclosure document is available from the franchise company, you should receive one. If you are buying a new franchise, the franchise company is mandated to give you a disclosure document. See the Sample Introduction to a California Offering Circular in Chapter 14.

## Franchisor's Right to Refuse or Reject a Buyer

Another legal issue to consider with regard to buying an existing franchise is the right of the franchisor to purchase the franchise for sale. Most franchise contracts contain a clause that gives the franchisor a right of first refusal. The company has the right to buy the business on the same terms and conditions as the actual offer of the prospective buyer. It cannot change the terms if it exercises this option.

If it waives this option or fails to exercise this prerogative within the option period, it is still possible that the franchisor could refuse to consent to the sale. Although this could be a dangerous position for a franchisor to take— it could lead to a lawsuit by the seller—it has a right to do so if it feels that the business will not be able to support the purchase price or will not be operated properly. Any legitimate reason that may put the franchisor at substantially more risk than currently exists is cause for the franchisor to exercise the right to reject the prospective buyer.

## Key Points to Remember

- Positive and negative aspects exist in a franchise relationship; you must look at a franchise opportunity with an eye to both.
- Your first priority in examining a franchise opportunity is to ask for the franchise disclosure document. It contains a good deal of the information you need to know about the company.
- Have your attorney and accountant explain all the elements of your relationship with the franchise company. You need to know your obligations and your prerogatives.
- Determine all the services or programs the franchisor offers, whether you need them, and if you can acquire them from another source and at what price.
- If you feel the franchise offers you the comfort zone you need as a new entrepreneur, don't be afraid to make the commitment.
- Once you commit to joining a franchise family, take advantage of all the benefits and services available to you.

# CHAPTER 10

# Finding the Help You Need

**Illustration 10-1. When Greg Met Maria**

Maria's Italian Restaurant closed two years ago after she lost her lease at a location that had been very successful for the previous ten years. Maria moved on and began operating a yarn shop. Greg had wanted to open a restaurant for years, but he didn't have the experience to do this. As serendipity would have it, Maria and Greg met at a church function and got involved in a serious business conversation. Maria's restaurant had a solid reputation for good food and had developed a pretty good following. Greg wanted to take advantage of both Maria's expertise and her reputation. Although Maria was now in a different business, she was willing to help Greg get started and would allow him to use the name of her former restaurant for 20 percent of the business. Greg wanted to know if this was fair. Is there a formula to follow in such a case?

The fairness of any business relationship depends, in great part, on what each of the parties brings to the table. If Maria works with Greg and gets paid in cash for her time as a restaurant consultant, she would be entitled to a smaller share of the business, if any. If, on the other hand, Maria works with Greg without being paid in cash, then the value of her time in dollars can be equated to a share of the business. If the investors are putting up $200,000 and if Maria's time is worth $20,000, then she would be entitled to about 10 percent of the business. *But Maria needs to earn this share by being there and being involved. Promises don't equate to dollars or equity.*

The question of using the name "Maria's Italian Restaurant" might deserve a separate examination. If the restaurant had closed recently, Maria's position would be stronger. Still, even after being closed for two years, the restaurant no doubt developed some loyalty among many of her customers over the ten years in business. Much will also depend on how close the new restaurant will be to the old location. These things must be considered. Whatever the assessed value of this somewhat conjectural participation, it can represent a license fee (a percentage of gross income; e.g., 1 percent to 2 percent) or be converted to an equity position in the business.

What benefit would you attribute to Greg's use of Maria's former restaurant name? Would your answer be different if the new location were 50 miles from the old one?

What percentage of the business do you think Greg should be entitled to if he had no actual money invested? Do you think he should have some right to "earn" a portion of the equity of the company? What do you think Maria's consulting fee should be per hour? Would it be better to give Maria a license fee for using the name or give her a piece of the business?

Many people have a similar dream—to build a successful business with an income for their family and a retirement potential for their future. The problem is that each of those people carries a different set of tools with which to do the job. Some entrepreneurs have a substantial education in accounting or engineering; others have substantial capital or access to financial support. Nevertheless, if you buy an independent business instead of a franchise, you will need help with areas of the business in which you lack expertise. Chapter 8 discussed how investors and partners can support you and Chapter 9 described some of the support services franchises offer. But what if neither of these options is for you?

In this chapter, you will learn how to find, employ, and pay for the services of experts. The concept of starting and building a business has been fine-tuned by franchise companies for the past 30 years. However, you can enjoy the benefits of their experience even if you do not choose to invest in a franchise.

You will always come across people who prefer to pay the ongoing franchise royalty fees for the satisfaction of having someone to turn to in the event of a problem. These people feel much more comfortable as part of a franchise family. Others are willing to pay for the experience necessary to start the project, but have the confidence to handle the day-to-day problems by themselves. These people hire an expert to aim the business at the appropriate target and then depend on their own talents and tenacity to achieve and maintain success. The choice is yours.

Starting, building, and maintaining a successful business involve constant activity. If you have never embarked on such an adventure, keep in mind that it is attention to detail, constant supervision, and flexible creativity that make the difference between success and failure. Family and other activities will, of course, divert your attention, but it is a rare moment when the business does not occupy a part of your thinking. Having someone available on whose judgment you can depend for backup is important—sometimes essential. If you can find that player early in the game, you will be many steps ahead in your search for success.

## The Franchise Option
### Saving Time and Money

If you have heard about the franchise concept and like the idea that a company has already tested the consumer market for its particular product or service, understand that if you join a franchise you will pay for that experience. This kind of experience can have a very definite value. As you continue to examine the franchise concept, you may be convinced that it is worth the money to use the company's experience to find a good location, negotiate a fair lease, buy initial equipment, acquire inventory, hire and train personnel, learn the best computer technology, and understand the best media for advertising. Then you find out about the continuing royalties.

## Paying the Royalty

You may be perfectly willing to pay for the expertise and knowledge of the franchise company to get started. However, owning a franchise means paying the franchise company a royalty on your gross sales every month for the life of the franchise. The continuing royalties essentially turn the franchise company into a lifelong partner, which may not be your intention.

Some franchise salespeople explain that you should think of the royalty as merely a way of paying the franchise company back for the initial training and all the extraordinary things that it does for you during the early days of the relationship. This is a pretty good argument—until you start to add up the dollars. If you are going to pay 5 percent of your gross sales every month for ten years and your gross sales average about $50,000 per month, the continuing royalties will cost you $300,000 by the end of that period. That is a lot of money to pay for the expertise that the company gave you during the early days of your relationship. What if your gross sales were $100,000 per month and your royalty was 10 percent?

## Earning the Royalty

Franchise salespeople would make a more convincing argument by telling you that the franchise company continually earns the royalties you pay over the course of the franchise relationship. The company is constantly researching the best products and services for your customers, the best way to advertise the concept to new customers, and the continual upgrades of all equipment, inventory, and state-of-the-art concepts to keep you ahead of, or at least even with, the best of your competitors.

However, after a while, you will know as much about your customer base as any franchise executive. Furthermore, the trade organizations in nearly every industry can help you to keep up with the same things as the franchise, without the fee—changing customer demands, equipment innovations, advertising philosophies, and marketing techniques.

If you need additional help from attorneys, accountants, or advertising agencies, the $300,000 that you would be paying in royalties over the ten-year period could buy a good deal of independent and professional assistance. Weigh these trade-offs carefully. Maybe you will prefer the franchise support system and maybe you will want to try to save money by hiring independent consultants.

Some franchise systems actively generate the customer activity on which your business depends. For example, some use toll-free numbers in the Yellow Pages under their logos to entice potential customers to purchase from the franchise rather than an independent business. These extraordinary types of services are yet another reason you may want to consider joining a franchise.

The one substantial element that has no equal is the trade name or logo that a franchise has promoted over many years. A familiar sign or trademark can cause an immediate and positive reaction in customers all over the country. You may want to join a franchise if a recognizable logo or trade name will give you a significant edge in the market. Note the story of Maria's Restaurant at the beginning of this chapter.

## The Dilemma

The decision between getting the services a franchise offers for a relatively fixed fee and going it alone can be difficult for the average entrepreneur. You would like to have the experience of the franchise at the beginning, but don't want to continue to pay for it during your entire business life. You would like to think that you can do it alone, but you recognize the number of failures of those who also thought they could—and then couldn't.

A good franchisor will explain to you that buying a franchise is not a guarantee of success, but rather a good insurance policy against failure. The help you get at the beginning of any venture will invariably save you time, money, and aggravation down the road. But is there any way to have the best of both worlds?

Franchise companies are particularly interested in you, as an entrepreneur, because you bring to the table all the things they need for success. You bring energy, creativity, various valuable experiences, and money to get started. Perhaps more than anything else, you bring the fear of failure and the hunger for success. The assets and characteristics you bring to the business relationship could prove successful for both you and the franchise company. However, maybe you do not need the franchise company. You have other options that offer you the benefits of insider experience in your industry.

## Insider Experience

A franchisor may have experience at opening your kind of business. But are there any other people with similar experience? Yes.

Some people have worked for franchise companies and left for one reason or another. Some have worked with vendors or equipment manufacturers that deal with franchise companies and independents. They gain an understanding of how each business works. Some of the former employees of franchises and vendors decide to open up shops of their own. Some are successful and some are not. The reason for their success or failure usually goes back to the tools they brought to the business. Remember: knowing how to cook does not necessarily qualify you to build a successful restaurant or a successful restaurant franchise.

If you speak with former employees of equipment manufacturers, they will be quick to tell you what they know, but it is what they do not know that is worrisome. If you speak with former employees of franchise companies, it is likely that they will know the details of running the business but will not have experienced the frustrations when things don't go according to plan. Without knowing about the frustrations, you really get only a part of the picture. No one can know everything about the business. You need to consult several sources to find the most reliable information.

## How Do You Find the Right Expert?

As you examine the spectrum of business activity in the marketplace, you will start to narrow down the kind of activity that is most appealing to you. You will ask many people questions about the marketplace until you eventually learn who is most successful in your industry. As you develop relationships with those people, you can begin to build a reservoir of names, hold conferences, and narrow your list to those who are most excited about working with you. The ideal situation is to find an individual with talents and experience that complement your own. If both of you are deficient in the same areas, you may enjoy working together, but you may not achieve the success you wish for the company.

Make sure the expert you find is the expert you need. Find out about his or her expertise and decide whether it represents what you need to fill the gaps in your knowledge and experience to build a successful business.

## What Do the Experts Cost?

People who tell you what to do are the least expensive. Those who show you what to do are more expensive. Those who do the job with you are the most expensive; however, they are also the most cost-effective.

You will save money on the seminars and workshops—the people who tell you what to do—by going to the library or the local bookstore and browsing in the business section. The people who show you what to do are sometimes more helpful, but they may be unable to relay some subtle details, such as the difference between a good location and a bad one. If you are going to rely on the expertise of someone else, be prepared to pay for it. Remember: you will certainly be paying less than the royalties to the franchise over a ten-year period.

The most qualified experts help others find their niche and put together a business program, and they expect to be paid for their expertise. You may be quoted a package price, but this is normally an approximation of the time it will take to do the job, properly calculated at an hourly fee. Sit down with your prospective expert and discuss in detail exactly what each of you is expected to do and the time each item will take.

Most experts want to be paid for their time and expertise but are not interested in becoming your partners. If they wanted to build a business of their own, they could presumably do it without your help. Don't be discouraged or offended if experts reject your partnership offer. It is, of course, helpful to find someone willing to participate as a partner for a portion of his or her fee. A partnership makes the upfront costs of the venture more manageable. On the other hand, be careful of the expert who wants to control as well as participate.

Whatever the arrangement, make sure you can buy out your expert partner after the business gets going. Set the buyout amount at roughly the level of the deferred fees. You should, of course, determine a certain percentage increase for the time your partner has waited for his or her money. And you should certainly arrange a compensation package for the time your partner spent orchestrating the business with you after it opened, unless your partner has already been compensated for this participation. Sometimes, it is a good idea to make the expert your partner, even if only for a short time. It is not a guarantee of success, but it is a solid hedge against failure. For additional information on partnership relationships, see *Forming a Partnership and Making It Work* (Entrepreneur Press, 2007) by Ira Nottonson

## Has the Concept Been Successful?

One of the questions you might be curious about is whether the expert is the right person. An expert who depends on reputation for the continuity of his or her consulting business will probably not allow you to fail after taking a fee because it would put that reputation at risk. However, you need to decide if the expert's experience is limited to one portion of the industry or wide enough in scope to cover all bases. Your best option is to hire someone who currently is or has recently been the owner of a business similar to the one you intend to operate.

## The Expert Looking for a Job

In today's marketplace, many people with extensive experience in a particular industry are, for one reason or another, out of work. By advertising in the right media and using your own good sense about people, you might very easily find the right candidate who can be your employee and get your business started successfully. If this person turns out to be extraordinary, he or she could eventually become your partner. Be sure to read Chapter 8, which sets out the guidelines for sharing control of your business.

## Key Points to Remember

- Be prepared to pay for the training and education necessary to properly understand and operate your business, whether you pay a franchise company or an independent advisor.
- You can resolve the question of paying a franchise royalty by comparing the services and benefits you receive from the franchise with the cost of those same services if you remain independent.
- If you decide to use independent experts, make sure they are indeed experts in their fields and the experts you need.
- When you use an independent consultant, make sure the money you pay is consistent with your needs and the quality of the advice.
- Don't discount the possibility of finding the help you need by hiring an expert as your employee; many experts are looking for employment.

# Don't Let Your First Mistake Be Your Last

**Illustration 11-1. Franchise: Proceed with Caution**

Kathy Dixon was enjoying a cup of coffee and a cinnamon bun at a local shopping mall. In a discussion with the owner, who was retiring due to illness, Kathy indicated an interest in the business. The pursuit was on. As the conversation got more serious, Kathy was wise enough to discuss the matter with her professionals. Several facts came up during negotiations that should have been danger signals to any buyer.

- The business was a franchise and the franchise company wanted Kathy's mother's and father's signatures on the final documents to ensure payment of the franchise royalties for the next ten years.

- The franchise company wanted a $3,000 transfer fee for changing ownership on its books and records.
- A competitor—a donut shop—was opening right across the walkway, a fact the landlord and seller neglected to mention.
- The landlord wanted a higher rent to sign a new lease.
- The income of the business had fallen in the last 12 months.

By the time these items were factored into the financial paperwork that the seller gave to Kathy, it became very clear that the business was not profitable and its future was doubtful. If it were not for her accountant, who pointed all these things out to her, she would have bought. She was so enamored of the business concept that she was temporarily blinded to the realities of the bottom line.

Buyers face many decisions as they research and search for a suitable business. The chapters in Part II are intended to point out some of the important issues you, as a buyer, need to consider, such as choosing your market niche, valuing the various parts of a business, and possibly sharing control with investors, partners, or a franchise company. If you are like many Americans whose job security has evaporated, you may be looking at business ownership to replace the uncertainty of your employment future. You may think that you don't have the time to research a new business venture carefully. Don't ever allow yourself to make that mistake!

This chapter is largely devoted to cautioning those buyers who may be excited or otherwise emotional about buying a business. Beginning such a venture without proper forethought, research, and professional counsel is dangerous. In this chapter, you will find horror stories and success stories—and more than one word of caution.

## Feeling the Pressure

Many people look for a business because they can't find a job. Most people don't want to talk about it and are embarrassed to disclose their plight to others. They don't want to face the reality of being another statistic. If you are ready to face that reality, this chapter is for you.

People may say to you, "I know how you feel," when in fact they don't know how you feel at all. They try to empathize with your traumatic situation and it is comforting because it is an expression of caring. However, they really don't know how you feel. Nobody does!

In today's economy, you are not alone in experiencing these types of hardships. Many people are in line at the unemployment office. Some people are forced to walk away from lengthy careers because their jobs are eliminated. Maybe the jobs went to other countries, to younger workers, or to computers. If you have faced a similar situation, you know that the most difficult part of the problem is going home to break the news to your family with the prospect of no longer being able to meet their expectations and fulfill their dreams. It can be devastating.

The experience of losing your job can be so devastating that you may want to take more control of your employment future by going into business for yourself. You may be reading this book for that reason. However, you need to be careful that your fears and anxieties about being unemployed do not cloud your good business sense. Take the story of John Rayburn, for example.

---

### Illustration 11-2. Latching onto the First Good-Sounding Idea

John Rayburn was out of a job. One day he took his son out for batting practice at a baseball center. They had a good time. Afterwards, he was convinced that this was the business opportunity of a lifetime.

He immediately got in touch with the owner and asked him if he would be interested in opening a baseball center in another state, 3,000 miles away. The owner would participate with John in some way in the new venture. The owner was delighted to be of service. He understood just how to open a center and was eager to participate.

John asked to see the owner's books and records to get an idea of the profit potential. The owner said he would be happy to share this information with him—for a fee of $2,000. "After all," he said, "I wouldn't want to share this information with just anyone who was merely curious." John called his attorney for advice and his attorney advised him not to look at the books and records for $2,000. It would not take John very far toward understanding the business and, if he paid $2,000 for every peek at financial records, he would be broke before he found the business that suited him best.

---

After John had done some initial research on his own and considered more seriously the prospect of purchasing a business, he contacted a franchise company selling a similar business. They had a good deal of financial and other important information in their disclosure document. He then discussed the matter with vendors who serviced baseball centers. They shared some cost and profit factors and solicited John to become a customer of theirs when he opened his business.

John asked the baseball center owner if he would be interested in helping John set up the business in the distant state for a fee. The owner was very interested and told John that he would do it for $10,000, as soon as John found the appropriate location and signed a lease. $10,000 might be a perfectly appropriate figure for the consulting service; however, one of the keys to most businesses of this type is location. For John, a newcomer to the business, to pick the location without the more experienced owner's help is foolhardy. John needed more expert advice than he could get from the baseball center owner.

Fortunately, John asked some competitors for advice and found out how important location is to a baseball center. He did not pay the owner the consultation fee, but rather sought an independent consultant for help in choosing the site for his center.

## A Potential Partner or Consultant

A potential partner or consultant should understand the importance of his or her input at every stage of the buying process. If the potential partner or consultant doesn't understand the importance of choosing something like a good location, you definitely need to find a new consultant.

### Listen to Good Advice

If you are so involved with a business idea that you cannot make an objective decision, find someone who can lend some objectivity to your decision-making process or you will regret your haste and lack of caution. Getting involved in a business about which you know nothing may seem like an exciting idea, but it's likely a disaster waiting to happen—and the worst part is that you may never know why the disaster happened.

Listening to a good friend who merely wants to be encouraging can be a big mistake. It's your money at risk, not your friend's. Someone who pats you on the back and tells you what a great salesperson you are, when you are not a great salesperson, is not doing you any favors. Your insincere friend is, in fact, doing you a great disservice.

Business owners who tell you what a joy it is to relax in your own shop and wait for the customers to come through the door, but do not tell you of the terrible frustration when they don't, are also not doing you any favors. These people may have the best motives and they may, in their particular businesses, enjoy waiting for the customers to roll through the door. But every business is different, every location is different, and every year is different. Don't be taken in by a singular description of success. You cannot afford to be wrong.

Talk with a number of people in the industry in which you are interested. Read some trade journals and find out what the success-failure ratio is and why. Find out how locating in different areas around the country can mean different results for a business.

For example, a fast-food company had substantial success in operating in malls and on well-trafficked streets. The company decided to open up in drive-in movie theaters. It seemed like a good idea at the time, but it turned out to be a disaster. Even businesses with successful experience behind them can be wrong.

Be careful about the advice you receive and the motives behind the advice. Be especially careful about your own analysis and judgment. Your knowledge about a particular industry may be sorely deficient, but you can study the industry and become familiar enough to develop a basic understanding. Your instincts as a consumer are probably as good as anyone else's—providing you don't let yourself be swayed by an overdose of either self-indulgence or self-doubt.

## Take the Time to Think It Over

Time can be very persuasive. Some people will claim that if you don't take advantage of a given opportunity immediately, you will lose it forever. Sometimes it is true that if you don't catch a wave at its crest, you will miss a singular chance. However, you can make an equally convincing argument that if an idea is good today, it will be good tomorrow. And you may add that if it isn't good tomorrow, then it wasn't meant to be.

Those who insist that a business transaction must be done today often have suspect motives. For example, a franchise salesperson might like to make a quota by month's end and an owner may want to get out of a dying industry before losing any more money.

Good judgments are not made under time pressure. Yes, it is often a good idea to expedite your decision making and not waste time. But gathering the information to make a carefully calculated judgment is much more important than making the decision today just because someone says you should. Let the opportunity go rather than find out after it is too late that the investment was a bad one. You can afford to let many good opportunities go by, but you can't afford the bad one you chose to take.

## Check on Your Available Tools

Before you jump into owning a business, capitalize on the talents, experience, and dollars you have available. You may find it very difficult to recognize the talents you have, but it is often more difficult to recognize the talents you don't have. If you have never operated your own business, don't make the assumption that managing all the daily details is easy. It is not, particularly for someone who has never done it. However, don't base your decision to buy a business on whether you can manage every aspect of it yourself. You can find people to perform the tasks you cannot, providing you recognize the need for them and have the dollars to pay for them. Keep this analysis in mind.

As you discuss with your accountant or attorney the possibility of buying a business, he or she will invariably ask you questions about your abilities and inclinations. Many businesses require a substantial selling effort to keep up with the competition. If you are not experienced in sales and, worse yet, if you don't really like this kind of customer interrelationship, don't pretend to yourself or anyone else that you can do it. Deception of others is bad; self-deception is much worse.

To find out which skills you have and which you lack, speak with those who know you best and who will give you an honest perspective. Remember: this may be the most important decision you make for many years. Don't let anything stand in the way of putting together your best information about the venture and about your talent and experience.

## Educate Yourself First

Most businesses do not have anything unique about them. If you can duplicate some of the basic concepts of a business after careful examination, you may also be able to duplicate the success of that business. This learning process involves a good deal of self-education. People go through it all the time, particularly entrepreneurs. Many aspects of owning a business cannot be learned in school, but only through experience and observation.

For example, many businesses are transported to other countries by foreign businesspeople. They copy what they see in the United States and duplicate equipment configurations in their own countries without the permission or involvement of the original businesses, despite international copyright laws to protect certain designs, logos, trade names, and formats. You can consider copying what you see—aside from the privileged protections just mentioned—to learn about the methodology of any given business. It is all part of the entrepreneurial exercise.

A businessperson learns every day from his or her competitors. Anyone who doesn't recognize what competitors are doing or what the innovations in a given industry represent is not doing his or her job. You have an obligation to examine every aspect of the business you intend to enter before you accept the challenge. Ask questions, take pictures, examine marketing materials, and interview personnel when possible—these tasks are all part of the process necessary for you to make an educated decision.

Getting an education through firsthand research and observation has costs—the biggest of which is the time it takes. However, you cannot decide to go into business for yourself without investing the necessary time. That's called paying for the education!

## When Your Money Won't Buy the Dream You Want

You may look at a car because the advertising suggests that it's within your price range. When you get to the dealership, the dealer tells you about all the extras that you thought were standard and the price rises well beyond your original intentions. The dealer then tells you how you can fit the payment schedule within your family budget and you end up buying the car. If you are in the market for a house and give your budget parameters to your real estate broker, you will invariably be looking at homes just beyond your original intentions. Once you have seen the upgrades, it is difficult to accept something less for your family. Besides, the broker will tell you that you can meet the payments because they will stay the same as your income rises. This might have been true years ago, but it is less so today.

You cannot allow yourself to be tempted beyond your means when you are buying a business. You cannot fit the purchase of a business within your budget. *The business is your budget!* You will be taking whatever reservoir of cash you have and investing in a business for the very purpose of generating a family income. You must have enough for the investment required by the seller and to establish a working capital fund to sustain the business during its formative stages. You must have enough for emergency purposes based on the nature of the business. Your emergency fund must accommodate the loss of big customers or seasonal lapses in business. You must also have enough to handle family emergencies. You are not buying a material thing; you are buying a life source. You cannot stretch it beyond the maximum capabilities of your financial portfolio.

When your money won't buy the dream you want, change the dream! Put a little reality into your life. Buy a business that fits. You can always piggyback on success. If the business works, you can expand it or buy another. You can sell it at a profit and buy something else, perhaps even the one you couldn't afford at first. Failure, on the other hand, doesn't afford you those prerogatives. Don't be taken in by the promise of a dream. Start with your reality and build the dream from there.

## Full Disclosure for Both Husband and Wife

Why should a business book be discussing the relationship between husband and wife? Indeed, in certain cultures, such a discussion would be offensive. In modern American society, however, where both spouses are involved in family expenditures and where, in many cases, both spouses are responsible for generating the family income, any discussion that excludes the subject of husband and wife would surely be lacking in reality. Whether it is the husband, wife, or significant other who decides to become an entrepreneur, the decision will certainly affect the entire family in both the short term and the long term.

One spouse may find it difficult to candidly discuss the personality deficiencies of the other, yet this type of candid discussion is essential to making an informed business decision. You may find it problematic to compare what the individual prefers with what the family needs. Some businesses can easily be operated by an individual. More likely, however, the business will require the attention of both husband and wife. It will require actual time involvement and constant analysis and decision making. In all cases, you can be sure the business venture will not be completely separate from the daily routine and involvement of the family.

Franchisors usually insist on meeting both spouses, even when the stated intention is that only one will be involved in the business. They know that the purchase of the business will invariably affect the family unit. It is normal for any seller of a business to be interested in meeting the buyer's spouse. This is particularly true if the seller is taking back a note for a portion of the purchase price. In the case of a franchise, you may be sure that the franchisor expects to get the signatures of both husband and wife on the franchise contract.

You must set aside many of the communication problems that may exist in your marriage and create a new communication that allows the involvement, to some degree, of your spouse. In many cases, the necessary documents on leases and loans require the signature of both spouses. Certainly, the signatory will be interested in the significance of signing and the potential impact, both good and bad, of the new involvement. You might not come to a perfect agreement, but make sure that both of you at least understand the basic issues involved in buying a business.

## Making the Hard Comparisons and the Harder Judgments

Buying a business at age 25 is not the same as buying one at 65. A car wash or a chimney-sweeping business requires more physical energy than a tax consultancy. One of the interesting parts of growing older is that the mind still thinks the body can handle tasks that it really can't. Make sure you understand the physical requirements and are capable of fulfilling them. Self-deception in this area can be devastating.

Before you embark on your adventure, you will have to make several decisions—whether to buy a business or to start a similar venture from scratch, whether to buy a franchise or an independent business, and how much money you can really afford to invest while still keeping an emergency fund available. While deciding on the most appropriate business venture for yourself and your family, make a list of all the questions that need answers. Ask yourself questions about dollars you have available and talents you bring to the business. Most importantly, put on the list those things that frighten you—all the unknowns that generate your biggest concerns.

## Key Points to Remember

- Don't let someone who has an ulterior motive—like a commission—talk you into a business venture..
- Don't let your emotions lead you toward an investment that does not use your particular talents and experience. It can be fun, but it can also be dangerous.
- Examine the obvious and not-so-obvious elements of the business as you do your preliminary examination.
- Meet with your spouse and family members to ensure that everyone knows the implications of time, energy, and money required for your new business venture.
- When you can't afford to buy your dream business, change your dream!

# PART THREE

# The Seller's Perspective

# CHAPTER 12

# Your Retail Business and How to Package It

**Illustration 12-1. Fake Flowers, Real Business**

Georgia Baker had been involved in the artificial flower business for some years, operating a shop for her friend. When she was ready to go into business for herself, she started examining franchises in the industry, because she had heard that they really knew their business and that they could give a business owner a good start on how to operate profitably.

Looking at the paperwork, she recognized some positives and negatives. The initial franchise fee would help her to find a location and help her design her build-out in the most appropriate way. The ongoing royalty would be 10 percent of all gross sales and would continue until the end of the ten-year contract. When she read the franchise agreement, she recognized that she would not be able to stay in the business under *any* name unless she continued her contract and continued to pay the royalty every month … forever. This was the sticking point.

At this juncture, she started asking herself a bunch of questions. Since she had already been operating an independent flower shop, why did she need a franchisor to tell her how to do it? Since she already knew where to buy the products wholesale, why would she need someone to do it for her? And, since she already knew what kind of business environment the customers liked, why did she need any advice on that score? In other words, why did she need to pay a franchisor to tell her these things that she already knew? She didn't.

She started her own independent business and now has a very successful operation. And she keeps all the profit! What's more, she can sell the business without the buyer being obliged to pay a royalty.

As you prepare your business for sale, you need to look at the components of a small business, as your buyer will, and learn to stress what is most appealing to a potential buyer. To do this, you need to know your business and know your buyer.

Part Two discussed a buyer's motivations, financing options, and negotiating postures. This chapter teaches you to look at your business objectively and to be prepared with the right answers to buyer questions—the answers that help you procure a successful sale right up to the last payment on the note. An extensive worksheet for this chapter on the accompanying CD will help you analyze your business, competition, location, and growth potential, and prepare you to answer buyer questions.

The most successful sellers make every effort to make their business show a strong operating profit, right up to the last minute. Remember: your asking price will depend in large part on the profit your business shows. Anything you can do to maximize your profit, within legitimate parameters, is a must.

Packaging your business to make the most effective presentation requires that you compare your business with other businesses and franchises. You need to look at your customers, competition, location, lease, and growth potential. Finally, you need to know how your business looks on paper and at the negotiating table.

## The Franchise Comparison
### Speak Well of Your Franchise

If your business is a franchise, talk about the positive aspects of the franchise relationship. Describe the various services the franchisor provides, such as the following:

- Initial training
- Ongoing support—equipment maintenance, financial help, marketing techniques
- Local or national advertising
- Research and development
- National pricing for equipment and products
- Competitive guidelines, including pricing guides and product recommendations

Although there are some rare exceptions to the general rule, most franchise contracts allow you to sell your business, but only as a franchise. Because you cannot convert your franchise to an independent business, your buyer will have to take over your relationship with the franchisor; therefore, you want to speak well of your franchisor and extol the virtues of the franchise relationship, even if your particular franchise falls somewhat short of the ideal parent company. Most unhappy situations are due to the personalities involved and not to the concept of the franchise system itself. Whether this is true in your case or not, market reality dictates that you sell the franchise system along with the franchise. Legal realities, however, also dictate that you not misrepresent the facts. For example, if the franchise company is bankrupt or no longer serving the franchisees, you need to disclose that information.

### Offset the Franchise Advantages

If your business is not a franchise, then offset some of the franchise advantages. Tell potential buyers about alternative ways to obtain the same benefits as a franchisee without the franchise. If the franchisor knows how to market and advertise, then why can't you? Franchises do not possess any magic formulas for successful advertising. Your buyer can access plenty of independent services, such as maintenance, financial, and marketing services. They provide the same security as a franchise and, because they are local, they will likely be more easily accessible and better oriented to your particular customer base.

Franchises do not have a monopoly on successful pricing guides either. You can easily compare the pricing guides prepared by the franchises because franchises often distribute their price lists to customers as advertising material. You can also determine a franchise's standard price markup by making a random price sampling of wholesale prices from vendors and retail prices from competitors. Why spend the time, money, and energy to develop the same formula the franchise companies use? The pricing guides are normally not copyrighted and, if they are, the basic content can usually be changed sufficiently to avoid any legal problems and still maintain their utility and purpose. You will know if something is copyrighted if the copyright legend appears on the first page of the material. The real value is in the numbers, not the format, and computations cannot be protected.

Always suggest that your buyer consult the trade organization in your particular industry. Trade organizations are geared to help newcomers to the industry. They would like to contribute to your success, and they usually have access to all the information sources you need.

## A Good Customer Mix

Discuss your customer base with your buyer. What kinds of customers constitute a good mix for your business? Which are more profitable? What kind of mix do you have? You know all about your customers, but does your buyer? You do not need to go through your invoices one by one and explain the nature of every sale, but you may want to give potential buyers a general view of four or five basic customer groups.

You can, of course, isolate a myriad of customer categories, from hospitals to universities, poets and songwriters to apartment property managers, from doctors, lawyers, and real estate brokers to city employees, travelers, and retirees. See how these types of customers fit into your particular industry.

Categories may change dramatically as you move from an urban marketplace to a suburban marketplace. When selling, you need to explain your particular customer complex to interested buyers. Tell them about your customers in the most favorable light to the future of the business. Providing a general view of your customers will help the sale, whether you are dealing with a knowledgeable buyer or a novice. Your buyer needs to know how to advertise to your customers, serve them, and get them to return to buy your services or products.

## What Is Your Competition?

Defining your competition is always an interesting process. To begin with, examine the question in its simplest form.

Question: "What is your competition like?"

Answer: "Well, there are a lot of people in my industry, but I don't really consider any of them competitors. My product/service is so much better/different that I am really in a different class than the others in the marketplace."

How many times has this been the answer from the entrepreneur? Nearly always—and it is nearly always wrong.

For example, if you are selling tacos, you are in competition, to some extent, with anyone who is selling food. You are clearly in competition with another shop that also sells tacos. Yet, some taco sellers deny even this. If you sell primarily tacos, and someone else merely includes tacos as an item on a diverse menu, are you in competition? This question is difficult to answer without some further analysis.

To say two shops selling primarily tacos are in competition is basic. The better taco will put the other taco out of business. Or will it? If it is a good taco in a dirty restaurant, will it? If it is a good taco in a location that is difficult to find or impossible to park near, will it? If it is a taco served by an ill-groomed or impolite counterperson, will it? If the ambiance is unappealing to the customer, will it? How can such a simple marketing question turn out to be such a strangling competitive analysis? And you are not nearly through with the problem.

If you are selling primarily tacos and you are near a shop that has tacos on its menu as one item among many other food choices, you may actually have a competitive advantage rather than a problem with competition. After all, the shop that deals with a specialty item might have a market advantage in many ways. The specialty shop is not trying to be all things to all people. It is looking for a market niche. It can afford to offer a variety of tacos that meet the taste of a large number of taco connoisseurs as well as those who like to reach out for a new taco flavor. It can target its advertising and marketing dollars to a more specific group of consumers. A focused product can more easily generate more cost-effective advertising.

Now, what if tacos were tennis shoes? You can see that the question is not about food at all. The question is about business! Potential buyers of your business will want to know what kind of competition you have and how they can carve a niche to become the unique product or service in the marketplace.

## Location and Lease

You will need to discuss your lease with potential buyers, particularly its terms and options to renew, if any. You may encounter so many buyer questions relating to lease and location that it is possible to expose you to only a few here.

## Rent

For example, your buyer will want to know the terms for any rent increase. Are rent increases for any option period subject to a formula or merely to negotiation at the time the option is exercised? What if the landlord sells the building and the business must deal with a new landlord? How relevant are prices per square foot of comparable rental space within the same market area? Are you prepared to discuss this with your buyer? You should be.

You should also be prepared to discuss whether there will be rent increases during the term and what effect, if any, an increase is likely to have on your profit picture. Is there a percentage rent of any kind involved? How does this relate to gross sales or net profit? Do you understand the Consumer Price Index (CPI), how it affects your annual rental obligation, and the concept of putting a cap (maximum) on the CPI if it is pertinent to your lease and option terms? Are you familiar with expressions such as triple net lease? If it applies to your lease, you ought to be prepared to discuss it with your buyer.

What about the buyer who says: "I have a ten-year purchase money promissory note to pay to you for the business, but I have a lease (including options) for only six years. What happens if I lose the premises?" This is not a particularly unique scenario, and you must be prepared to handle this type of concern. The answer is that a business venture is not normally designed to terminate at the expiration date of its initial lease term. The termination of a lease is a business problem your buyer should expect to deal with at some point in the life of the business. Franchises, for example, are often for a period of ten years or more. Leases, on the other hand, are often for a period of five years or less.

## Protective Clauses in the Lease

Are there any protective clauses that preclude certain types of business in the lessor's business complex? The buyer is certainly entitled to know, for example, if the landlord can rent to a similar business in the same complex in which your business is located. How much harm would your quick printing business suffer if a landlord allowed a nearby tenant to sell photocopies? How much harm would your hamburger business suffer if a nearby tenant was allowed to sell tacos? What kind of protection is afforded?

Are there any clauses that allow the lessor to terminate the lease due to a pending sale or for other reasons unilaterally? It is not unusual to see leases where the landlord has a right to cancel on six months' notice for any reason or without any reason. The landlord's right to cancel on short notice does not give the buyer very much security and could conceivably end your sale negotiations. Here are some other questions you need to be prepared to answer:

- Is the facility expandable for increased business over the years?
- Is it possible for the business to acquire the building?

- Do you have an option to buy or a right of first refusal? Do you understand the difference between the two?

An *option* is a contract that specifies the time and terms by which a person may purchase property. It must be supported by consideration.

A *right of first refusal* gives a person the right to buy property providing that he or she is willing to meet, without change, the offer of a third person to do so.

# Parking

You will also need to address the parking situation around your business. For instance, what kind of parking is available, and what is the demand for parking in your particular business and by your particular customer? Be prepared to explain how parking is handled in your particular case.

Negotiating your lease and location may bring up hundreds of issues. Which issues become points of contention depend on your particular lease and how it could affect your buyer over the years. You must, realistically, be prepared to discuss all these aspects with the buyer. Lease and location are key factors involved in the purchase of a retail business.

## Growth Potential

You may want to research your business's growth potential to make the buyer feel more secure about your knowledge of the business marketplace and to give the buyer a better, more knowledgeable, and more positive perspective from which to examine your business. You can obtain market information from a variety of sources: the local chamber of commerce, building and zoning departments of your city or town, national statistics put out by the U.S. government, magazines or pamphlets published by your city, and trade publications carrying all kinds of statistical evaluations of the industry, the competition, and prospects for future growth.

## Create a Selling Portfolio

Finally, put the information you have researched and prepared into a selling portfolio or business plan to give to each buying candidate.

If you are able, you may also want to look at the sales presentations the more professional franchise sales departments create. They have some interesting approaches you can use in your selling portfolio. You never really know which little piece of the presentation will prompt the buyer or his or her spouse to make the purchase. Remember: small businesses are often family businesses, and spouses, children, or parents are likely to be involved in the purchase negotiations. Be prepared to tailor your presentations and negotiations to involve familial members of the buyer's negotiating team.

Husband and wife represent the tightest partnership of all. The opinion of the spouse is often a significant factor in any decision-making process. Sometimes, the location or customer base may be unimportant to one spouse, but of particular significance to the other. With the participating spouse in mind, it is essential that you use every selling concept you can think of in presenting your business. Make sure, if you can, that you are speaking at some point with both husband and wife. After all, if you were selling to a partnership, you would certainly want to speak to all the partners to ensure that you did not leave important questions unanswered or have the decision maker absent.

Remember: the purpose of the exercise is to find a buyer who wants to take this business opportunity as his or her new way of life—with the best equity realization for the seller.

## Key Points to Remember

- If your business is a franchise, make sure the buyer understands the advantages the franchise family offers.
- If your business is not a franchise, explain to the buyer the many sources in the business community from which the buyer may duplicate the franchise benefits and services.

- Create a selling portfolio that extols the benefits of the business and explains to the buyer about the growth potential he or she can anticipate.
- Your buyer will be very interested in your premises lease. Be sure you understand all its intricacies so that you can answer the buyer's questions.
- Your buyer knows the importance of the business's customer base. Be prepared to discuss this aspect of your business in great detail if the buyer inquires about it.

CHAPTER 13

# Selling the Bottom Line

**Illustration 13-1. When to Sell Your Business**

The best time to sell is not when you must. Unfortunately, this is all too often the case. It's probably a good reason to be prepared all the time. By examining your equity position periodically and by doing a "fast business valuation" every year, you will at least have a sense of your company's value, should the need arise to make that decision to sell.

## Buy Low, Sell High

Conventional wisdom is always happy to give you the ultimate platitudes. "Always sell when you can get the best price; always buy when you can pay the lowest price." Duh!

The problem is that most of the time you don't have control over the circumstances that dictate the time frame. Certainly, it is a good idea to sell your business when it has achieved a peak of success. But even this represents certain problems. Since most businesses are not sold for cash, the seller must be careful to properly secure the balance of the purchase price after the down payment. The seller must be sure that the buyer and the business can continue to make payments on schedule for the balance of the purchase price. Otherwise, as is sometimes the case, the seller ends up with the down payment and little else. It is interesting that with the sale of a business at its zenith, the problems may be bigger than with the sale of a business that has not yet reached its potential.

## Be Careful Not to Overreach

Whatever the value of the business, the seller must keep in mind that the business itself is usually the basis for the purchase. It is the profit of the business from which the buyer will feed his or her family and likely make the payments to the seller. If the price of the business goes beyond this framework, the payment of the purchase price can become problematic for both buyer and seller. This is the reason why the basic logic of any purchase is said to be right when it's good for both the buyer and the seller. Any good professional will try to put you on this road to success, whether you are buying or selling.

## The Selling Parameters

There is no "one price" for a business. Much depends on the needs of the buyer, the circumstances of the sale, and the expectations of the seller in both the short term and the long term. All businesses have a certain risk factor. It is this risk factor that will dictate the reasonableness of the time frame for pay-out of the business. When the seller expects the buyer to pay forever, something is wrong, whatever the business may be worth. On the other hand, when the buyer expects to pick up the business for peanuts because the seller is in unfortunate circumstances, business ethics must come into play. There is usually a particular value, within a certain set of parameters, that will basically fulfill the expectations of both buyer and seller. The seller wants to convert his or her earned equity to a dollar value and the buyer wants to be able to maintain the continuity of the business and take care of his or her family. Think about it. It is the essence of negotiating.

## The Key to Preparation

All sellers must keep in mind that there are things that ought to be done in preparation for selling. These things are not necessarily consistent with the things that need to be done for growing the business. And, above all, sellers must recognize that neither plan will work overnight. There must be an appropriate time frame in terms of preparation. This is why you must always have a sense of your business's value and the time required to "convert" from one "preparation posture" to the other. As one young professional said to her father, "Your lack of planning should not turn into my emergency." It's a good thing to remember in terms of the most important asset you may have.

# Your Operating Profit

Your operating profit is the key to determining an asking or selling price. To present the best view of the operating profit to potential buyers, you need to reconstitute your profit and loss statement, also known as your income statement. This chapter focuses on the variables that affect your bottom line, compares different profit and loss statements, and leads you through checklists to help you with your own profit and loss statement. By the end of this chapter, you should have a good idea of the most defensible asking price for your business (notwithstanding your buyer's situation), the areas where you may need to streamline your business or eliminate excess costs, and the way to present all the figures to the buyer in the best light.

## Operating Profit Leads to an Asking Price

Chapters 1, 2, and 3 discussed how important operating profit is to developing an asking price for your business. The business must pay for itself: the operating profit must be able to support payments on the promissory note (full amortization of buyer's investment over a reasonable period of time) and leave the buyer with a respectable income. When you sell your business, you are really selling the bottom line, a stable operating profit from which the buyer can pay the business's debts, including the note to you or to whomever the purchase money was obtained from.

You may adjust the price up or down depending on many factors—the length of the note, the value of the business assets, or the stability or instability of the operating profit. The buyer must be able to see consistency in the cost factors that create your operating profit. Seasonality and other business fluctuations aside, the operating profit should represent a reasonably dependable bank deposit for the buyer through the year.

In fact, the buyer will look at the dependability of the profit to assess the risk involved. As discussed in Chapter 2, if purchasing the business represents a higher-risk investment—because the operating profit is not stable or dependable—the buyer will want you to lower the price.

Returning to the basic premise, if the business is operated properly and your costs are within normal parameters, you should be able to formulate a basic asking price by using a multiple of the operating profit. If the price you get is too low, examine the cost factors of the business. Keep in mind that each percentage category may vary because each accountant has his or her own method of allocating items (chart of accounts) on the profit and loss statement. It might be necessary to make adjustments in these categories. Review Chapter 3 and on the accompanying CD, Worksheet 3-2.

## Pie Charts and the Business of Percentages

Your first priority in determining operating profit and selling price is to examine the profit picture of businesses in your market, how the percentages are supposed to work, and how the percentages can be increased by cutting costs and instituting better marketing techniques. Do a financial analysis of your business, if you haven't already.

To do a financial analysis, do not use the profit and loss statement used for tax purposes. You need to look at the real percentages involved, taken from a particularly conservative standpoint and without any consideration of the tax advantages you can use. You can analyze most businesses by looking at the percentages with which they operate. Consider that a 1 percent savings on the cost of product or labor can drop quickly to the bottom line, operating profit, right into your pocket!

"The business is going out the back door" is a phrase applicable to many businesses, particularly the restaurant business. In restaurants, it means that employees are taking food home, a loss of inventory that increases costs and decreases the operating profit of the business. Obviously, a correction in this type of cost inflation will help to increase the profit margins. This kind of savings in turn increases the operating profit of the business. As already stated, the greater the operating profit, the higher the potential asking price the business can command.

A good place to start is a simple pie chart. Although each business has its own peculiarities, you can normally represent the percentages of your business by cutting a pie into four basic parts. A pie chart can be especially interesting to those of you who are statistically oriented, but it can also help you prepare a mental skeleton of the percentage parameters within which any business should properly function.

The ideal ratios for some businesses are 25 percent for cost of product, 25 percent for cost of labor, 25 percent for standard monthly obligations (fixed expenses, such as rent, electricity, and insurance), and 25 percent for operating profit (see Figure 13-1).

For a good comparison of how the percentages can work for and against your business, look at the profit and loss statements for Bob's Printing and Spry Print Shop on the following pages. As with any business, you want to ensure the following:

- Products or services are priced to properly reflect costs of product and labor

- The number and kind of products or services offered for sale are within appropriate ratios to maximize profit
- Wastage caused by poor management is kept to a minimum

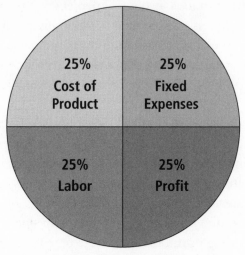

**Figure 13-1.** Pie chart showing ideal allocation business ratios

| | BOB'S PRINTING | | SPRY PRINT SHOP | |
|---|---|---|---|---|
| Sales | $ | YTD % | $ | YTD % |
| Printing | $191,917 | 50.60% | $188,899 | 51.92% |
| Bindery | $26,264 | 7.72% | $21,197 | 5.83% |
| Outside Services | $52,409 | 13.82% | $64,811 | 17.82% |
| Self-Service Copiers | $8,648 | 2.28% | $27,846 | 7.65% |
| Automated Copiers | $97,108 | 25.60% | $65,201 | 17.92% |
| Merchandise | $143 | 0.04% | ($2,622) | −0.72% |
| Discounts | ($200) | −0.05% | ($1,535) | −0.42% |
| Total Sales | $379.289 | 100.00% | $363,797 | 100.00% |

**Table 13-1.** Sample profit and loss statements with different percentages (continued on next page)

|  | BOB'S PRINTING | | SPRY PRINT SHOP | |
|---|---|---|---|---|
| Cost of Sales* | $ | YTD % | $ | YTD % |
| Beginning Inventory | $3,721 | 0.98% | $7,186 | 1.98% |
| Purchases—Paper | $26,073 | 6.87% | $37,149 | 10.21% |
| Purchases—Supplies | $2,668 | 0.70% | $9,828 | 2.70% |
| Outside Services | $27,964 | 7.37% | $37,131 | 10.21% |
| Self-Service Copiers | $6,491 | 1.71% | $23,022 | 6.33% |
| Automated Copiers | $19,516 | 5.15% | $8,376 | 2.30% |
| Allocated Sales Cost | $16,556 | 4.37% | $12,047 | 3.31% |
| Less Ending Inventory | ($2,703) | −0.71% | ($6,748) | −1.85% |
| **Total Cost of Sales** | $100,286 | 26.44% | $127,991 | 35.18% |
| **Gross Profit** | $279,003 | 73.56% | $235,806 | 64.82% |

*To get a true picture of the operating profit, the principal payments on the automated copiers, which appear on the balance sheet, should be added to the monthly Cost of Sales.

| **Operating Expenses**\*\* | | | | |
|---|---|---|---|---|
| **Labor Costs** | $ | YTD % | $ | YTD % |
| Salaries—Printing | $58,756 | 15.49% | $77,535 | 21.31% |
| Payroll Taxes | $4,788 | 1.26% | $7,125 | 1.96% |
| Casual Labor | $1,022 | 0.27% | $304 | 0.08% |
| Workers' Comp Ins. | $1,938 | 0.51% | $2,538 | 0.70% |
| Group Insurance | $1,839 | 0.48% | $2,613 | 0.72% |
| Allocated Labor Costs | $27,569 | 7.27% | $20,556 | 5.65% |
| **Total Labor Costs** | **$95,912** | **25.29%** | **$110,681** | **30.42%** |

\*\*These shops send a share of printing and bindery work to a central plant and are assessed a share of central plant costs, reflected in Allocated Labor and Sales Costs.

**Table 13-1.** Sample profit and loss statements with different percentages
(continued on next page)

|  | BOB'S PRINTING | | SPRY PRINT SHOP | |
|---|---|---|---|---|
| **Advertising\*\*\*** | $ | YTD % | $ | YTD % |
| Yellow Pages | $1,309 | 0.35% | $1,783 | 0.49% |
| 1% National | $3,793 | 1.00% | $3,691 | 1.01% |
| Other | $2,720 | 0.72% | $3,714 | 1.02% |
| **Total Advertising** | **$7,822** | **2.06%** | **$9,188** | **2.53%** |

\*\*\*These shops contribute to a national advertising program mandated by the franchisor.

| **Operating Expenses** | | | | |
|---|---|---|---|---|
| **Other** | $ | YTD % | $ | YTD % |
| Automobile Expenses | $333 | 0.09% | $1,206 | 0.33% |
| Cash Over/Short | $97 | 0.03% | $349 | 0.10% |
| Employee Benefits | $881 | 0.23% | $806 | 0.22% |
| Entertainment & Promo | $1,081 | 0.27% | $1,314 | 0.36% |
| Insurance—General | $923 | 0.24% | $923 | 0.25% |
| Meetings | $252 | 0.07% | $326 | 0.09% |
| Office Supp. and Exp. | $1,250 | 0.33% | $1,803 | 0.50% |
| Operating Supplies | $1,873 | 0.49% | $2,682 | 0.74% |
| Postage | $358 | 0.09% | $756 | 0.21% |
| Allocated Overhead—CP | $10,103 | 2.66% | $7,362 | 2.02% |
| Parking | $11 | 0.00% | $90 | 0.03% |
| Rent | $26,939 | 7.10% | $27,953 | 7.68% |
| Repairs—Equipment | $3,807 | 1.01% | $4,120 | 1.13% |
| Repairs—Shop | $458 | 0.12% | $3,563 | 0.98% |
| Royalties | $29,384 | 7.75% | $28,567 | 7.85% |
| Taxes and Licenses | $2,097 | 0.55% | $2,447 | 0.67% |

**Table 13-1.** Sample profit and loss statements with different percentages
(continued on next page)

| | BOB'S PRINTING | | SPRY PRINT SHOP | |
|---|---|---|---|---|
| Telephone | $1,723 | 0.46% | $3,454 | 0.95% |
| Travel—Mtgs/Conv. | $289 | 0.08% | $1,157 | 0.32% |
| Total Operating Exp. | $185,529 | 48.91% | $208,747 | 48.91% |
| Total Operating Profit | $93,473 | 24.64% | $27,059 | 7.44% |

**Table 13-1.** Sample profit and loss statements with different percentages (concluded)

For Bob's Printing, the cost of sales is 26.44 percent, the cost of labor is 25.29 percent, and fixed expenses are 23.62 percent (total operating expenses minus the labor costs: 48.91 percent minus 25.29 percent). This leaves operating profit (income from operations) at 24.64 percent. These figures are not far from the hypothetical figure of 25 percent for each category of the sample pie chart. This operation is run well from the standpoint of industry standards and the operating profit is good.

Now look at Spry Print Shop. The cost of sales is 35.18 percent, the cost of labor is 30.42 percent, and fixed expenses are 26.96 percent (total operating expenses minus labor costs: 57.38 percent minus 30.42 percent). This leaves operating profit (income from operations) at 7.44 percent. These figures are not at all close to the ideal. This operation is not run well and the operating profit is small.

You will notice that Bob's and Spry are generating almost equal sales. However, Bob's cost of product is 8.74 percent lower than Spry's. Bob's is spending 5.34 percent less for paper and supplies than Spry. Spry is spending a good deal of money on paper, which represents serious waste. Print jobs at Spry are probably being done more than once to get them right, driving up the cost of product.

You will also notice that Bob's cost of labor is 5.13 percent lower than Spry's. Bob's personnel are functioning better than Spry's and are more productive.

As you compare each profit and loss statement, look for other differences in the way the owner operates Spry Print Shop. Bob has less income from outside services, but his markup is almost 100 percent. (Compare costs for outside services with sales from outside services.) Spry has more income from outside services, but the markup at Spry is much less than 100 percent.

Notice that there are various ways to account for equipment contracts. Bob's and Spry both make payments on automated copiers. When they sell their businesses, they will have to work out with the buyers, their accountants, and the buyers' accountants how payments on the copiers will be absorbed. The size of an equipment contract and the time until it is fully repaid are differentials that can dramatically affect your price structure—differentials you need your accountant to work out. If very few payments are left on a contract, it could be paid off at closing without negatively affecting the profit on which the value is predicated. A longer contract will obviously have a negative effect on the profit picture.

Not all businesses will fit the 25-percent quarters of the sample pie chart. In some businesses, certain factors will be much different. For example, in a service-oriented business, the cost of labor might be 45 percent and the cost of product 10 percent. In an inventory-heavy business, the cost of product might be 60 percent and the cost of labor only 5 percent. The pie chart graphic is intended to give you a hypothetical picture of the four basic elements. Let the real figures in any business flow into the chart and create a larger or smaller percentage in any one or more of the categories. Whatever the percentages, you should be able to compare any given business in that industry with the industry standards.

## The Costs of Absentee Ownership

Another priority in examining your operating profit is represented by those places where profit is lost due to poor management. Whenever a potential buyer speaks of wanting to be an absentee owner, you must take the time to explain the potential disaster in that approach. In unsupervised restaurants, the steaks (and therefore the profits) go out the back door. But restaurants are not the only type of business that experiences this problem. There are many places where profits can disappear in any business. Consider the quick-print shop discussed in Illustration 13-2.

### Illustration 13-2. A Print Shop Example

The quick-printing business is a convenient example of how quickly profits can disappear if an owner fails to manage the business carefully and effectively. As you read, try to correlate these examples with comparable ones in your business.

At the counter two things can happen that directly affect your percentages:

The counterperson isn't properly trained in sales and marketing techniques. If someone asks for stationery, it is certainly appropriate to ask if he or she needs business cards and envelopes as well.

If your personnel do not handle the pricing of the entire job request carefully from the beginning, the profit margin will shrink. Remember: the customer normally will not tell you when you've forgotten to figure in collating or stapling.

If a printing job needs to be "done over" due to carelessness, profit goes out the window.

Choice of equipment also affects the bottom line. For example, certain print jobs should be done on a copier and others on a press. The customer probably won't care which equipment you use. The manager may decide on the copier based on convenience. The owner will decide on the press based on profit—but only if he or she is present when the decision is made.

The execution of the job order also reveals potential excess cost. Sloppy camera work can force the use of duplicate plates. Sloppy press work or bindery work can lead to extra paper purchases. Bad quality can cause the customer to reject a job and require that the whole job be done again. A supervising owner can eliminate much of this waste.

The purchase of supplies is an obvious area for cost fluctuation. Buying paper in anticipation of monthly requirements is wise because it can lead to quantity purchase discounts. Buying by the day is terribly expensive and cuts into the bottom line. You will experience further waste when your employees have to go to the paper house every day for purchases that you could have and should have anticipated.

Finally, when work is done for cash and an invoice is never written or when the press operator or the manager decides to do a favor for a friend, it also creates the potential for abuse under an absentee owner who does not anticipate such cost factors.

This example shows how easy it is to lose a percentage point on the bottom line merely by not paying attention to detail. The same types of problems apply to almost any business involved in retail, manufacturing, or service—whether it's food, shoes, car repair, or any other product or service.

However well or poorly you fared with these percentages, you must be completely aware of them to have a knowledgeable conversation with a prospective buyer—especially if he or she knows anything about the business. Keep in mind that you can use these percentages as a selling tool, whether they're good or bad. If a percentage is good, you can convince the buyer that he or she is buying a well-operated business. If a percentage is bad, you can suggest where the buyer might easily improve his or her bottom-line profit with a little attention to detail. Make sure you can explain why you haven't done it yourself.

## Labor Cost: A Product of Efficiency

Cost of labor also varies, depending on efficiency. In the printing business, spending 45 minutes at the counter working with one customer to find the right type style, color, and quality of paper for the customer's wedding invitation is not the most effective time and cost combination. Neither is doing a printing job two or three times because the pressperson didn't pay attention to the instructions on the invoice or because the instructions on the invoice were ambiguous or misleading. People who understand the print shop business can never understand why the counterperson is often the poorest paid and least respected member of the quick-print team. If your business also relies on your staff to relate well with the public, you should learn to pay for that skill. Your people behind the counter may be the only people whom your customers remember and, therefore, the people who represent your business.

An inefficient staff can lead to a cost of labor substantially higher than the norm. There is no reason why you shouldn't maintain an appropriate percentage for labor. Whatever your business, you can find out the labor cost standard.

In the quick-printing business, for example, three people might operate a shop doing $15,000 per month in sales or a shop doing $25,000 per month in sales and the cost factor is entirely different. If those three people receive $5,000 per month in salaries, for example, that's 33 percent for labor in a shop doing $15,000 per month and 20 percent for labor in a shop doing $25,000 per month.

Also, keep in mind that each marketplace may have a different customer complex and that some businesses will be able to do larger volumes with fewer customers and thus fewer personnel. Another fluctuating factor might be if you offer your people a bonus incentive for work done, invoices written, or monies deposited. Staff incentives will, of course, change the percentage to some degree, although you should always factor in good, planned incentive programs to avoid unnecessary distortions. Bonuses for exemplary work usually produce higher profits for the business—and this kind of upward distortion is always acceptable.

Again, keep in mind that you don't have to give a seminar about your business in all its detail each time you discuss it with a prospective buyer. But the percentages, the lease, and the customer base must always be at your fingertips to answer questions from the buyer and/or his or her professional representative, questions that they are certainly entitled to ask.

## Fixed Expenses

Your standard monthly obligations, or fixed expenses, will also represent some variables, even though theoretically they should be the same each month—rent, telephone, electricity, and other utilities. On the one hand, if they stay relatively the same in actual dollars, they will change in terms of percentages of your growing gross sales. For example, a rental obligation of $5,000 per month when you are doing $10,000 per month equals 50 percent; that same $5,000 per month when you are doing $50,000 per month equals only 10 percent. Certain items, of course, will change to some degree with volume, such as telephone, electricity, and auto delivery.

On the other hand, you must also be careful to include only those items that would be germane to the operation of the business from the buyer's perspective and exclude those things that are for tax purposes, such as your personal car, spouse insurance, and other personal benefits. Including these items would obviously cause your cost factors to be less realistic and throw off your profit picture. Refer to Chapter 2 and the section "Reconstituting the P&L" for advice on adjusting your cost percentages.

With the appropriate cautions about costs of product and costs of labor and an awareness of the obvious fluctuations in percentages depending on business volume, you can now understand the pie chart concept as a graphic picture of your business. The pie chart is a selling tool and will make it easier for the buyer to relate to costs and profit. Continue to refer to "operating profit," as opposed to "net profit," because you are not including such non-cash items as depreciation and amortization and you are not concerned about the tax consequences to the buyer, since his or her financial portfolio could conceivably represent an entirely different tax obligation than yours.

## Key Points to Remember

- The business must pay for itself. Be prepared to show how you arrived at your bottom-line profit and how stable and dependable that profit is, so that the buyer knows the business can pay the purchase money promissory note.
- Labor costs and labor stability are important to the buyer. Be prepared to discuss the status of your employees and any contract personnel on whom your business depends.
- When you discuss the bottom-line profit, be careful to discuss any collateral elements, such as equipment contracts that will expire shortly and leave additional money for the buyer's pocket.
- If your buyer is considering owning the business without being personally involved in the daily business activity, you need to alert him or her to the negative implications of absentee ownership.

# CHAPTER 14

# Finding the Right Buyer and Protecting the Sale

## Business Valuation

For those entrepreneurs who are ready to sell their businesses, there are big surprises in store. The first surprise is that the business may not be worth what the seller thinks it is. After all, it is the buyer's expectations that need to be fulfilled, not the seller's dream of retiring on a desert island … a dream bought with the proceeds from the sale. The buyer is expecting to pay off the price and still have an income sufficient to take care of his or her needs and wants. Otherwise, why buy the business?!

## Selling Your Business with a Down Payment and a Promise to Pay the Balance

The second big surprise is that the buyer is not likely to have the money available to pay cash. The third surprise is that the bank is not interested in taking a chance on the buyer's lack of expertise or the seller's grandiose representations of the future. Banks are usually interested in bricks and mortar, not creativity, imagination, and growth potential. The next surprise should be expected. If the buyer can't pay all cash and the bank doesn't want to lend the balance of the purchase price beyond the down payment, then *the seller becomes the bank*. The seller has to wait for the buyer to pay the balance of the purchase price, usually over a period of years.

## The Business Valuation Process

The method used to determine the price, the down payment, the balance of the purchase price, the length of time for it to be paid, the interest rate, and the protective devices for the seller are some of the essentials of a proper business valuation. Although there are myriad ways that a business can be valued, anyone who loses sight of the buyer's expectations of receiving an adequate income and being able to pay off the balance of the purchase price from the profit of the business is losing sight of the point of acquiring a small business.

## Finding the Buyer

And that's after you've found a buyer who is capable of operating the business properly. After all, there's no advantage to waiting for payment if the buyer is not capable of continuing the business. Finding the right buyer is important because, until the buyer has completed paying you for the business, both of you have things at risk in the event the business does not succeed.

## The Selling Finality

Be careful with the buyer who has plenty of cash to make a big down payment and absolutely no expertise in the trade or industry of which your business is a part. As exciting as this prospect may appear, the buyer might be unable to continue the business as a profitable venture. Then, the only money you would get for your business would be the down payment and any payments he or she makes before the money stops. Also, be very careful about believing that "I can take the business back if the buyer can't make the payments." If that business is not doing well enough to support the payment schedule, what you'll be taking back may be a mere skeleton of the business you sold. And all the effort in the world to put the business back on track could turn out to be fruitless. This is good reason to monitor the business until the new owner makes the final payment. Remember that your relationships with customers, vendors, and bankers are essential to build and maintain a successful business. You can't afford to lose any of those relationships.

## Be Careful What You Sell

In many cases, the seller is so enamored of his or her business that he or she will set the asking price to cover not only the seller's equity at the time of sale, but also a part of the future of the business. This is a no-no.

Someone selling a business is entitled to convert to dollars what he or she has achieved, but only the buyer should be entitled to reap the rewards of what he or she will be earning as the new owner. There are exceptions to this rule, but they are fairly easy to recognize. So, if you're buying a business, be careful, and if you're selling a business, don't be greedy. Remember: if the business can't be maintained, then the buyer will lose his or her investment and the seller won't get paid!

Even though you must do many things to properly prepare your business for sale, you should not lose sight of a few basics. Where to look for the buyer and how to get his or her attention are two basics that this chapter examines. Whether you advertise by word-of-mouth or on television, you need to screen your candidates and narrow them down to the most serious and most qualified. To get from initial negotiations to an understanding that the sale is ready to take place requires care and sensitivity, especially as you want to bind the buyer, even though the final papers may be weeks or even months away. In this chapter, you will learn how to maintain the delicate balance between protecting the stability of your business and aggressively pursuing the sale.

## Finding the Buyer

The number of ways to put your business up for sale is almost limitless, from responding to a subtle comment at a Rotary Club dinner to using the most dramatic media of all, television and the internet. Neither of these extremes is as crazy as it might sound.

Advertising your business on radio, television, or the internet may seem quite exotic, but in the right circumstances it can be very effective. If your business is large enough to warrant broadcast media or the internet, you should consider working with a small advertising agency. You may also want to consider using a business broker, as discussed in Chapters 4 and 21.

## Social and Business Circles

Many sellers will find interested potential buyers in their social and business circles, such as someone retiring after a long time from a corporate position, government, or the military. Candidates in these groups may vary in age, experience, and resources, but owning a business is a very viable and much discussed option in these circles.

Some potential buyers have not decided whether to buy an existing business or open a new one. Many do not realize that the start-up period for a new store can be quite expensive and that they could exhaust their working capital base before reaching a breakeven point. These more naive buyers may be persuaded to buy a business that is actually at breakeven on the date of purchase. Bypassing the period a start-up takes to reach breakeven makes buying a business an interesting proposition, even when the business is not showing a substantial profit.

## Print Media

The print media and the internet are flexible and useful tools for advertising your business. You do not need to limit your advertising to trade magazines in your particular trade. Consider the franchise magazines as well, because the franchise companies are looking for the same candidates as you are. In addition, consider local, regional, and national newspapers and mailing lists.

Once you choose your medium of advertising, you must then consider the size of the ad, placement, length and frequency, and, most important, content.

Advertising experts say that too much copy puts off potential readers. This is usually true; however, the ad must keep readers from turning the page. Once the reader passes the page without seeing your ad, it is unlikely he or she will go back for a second pass.

You have probably admired billboards that are simple but effective, like "Kahlúa and milk. Ahh!" or "Things go better with Coke." However, advertising a business is a little more complex. For one thing, your ad is in the middle of other ads for "businesses for sale." How can yours be different? Keep it simple. Surround your copy with plenty of empty space. Use magic words. Best suggestion: "Widget Shop for Sale by Owner. Santa Clara County. Good Income, Low Down, Creative Financing, Full Training: (555) 815-2390."

Local newspapers can also be an effective and relatively inexpensive medium. They allow you to increase your frequency, the number of times your ad can appear. Papers with national circulation offer even greater frequency. Many sellers find *The Wall Street Journal* very effective. Business-oriented people all over the country read it.

And the appeal of different regions may also be important: e.g., Florida, California, and Arizona. These states tend to draw buying candidates from all over the country—particularly in the winter when people in the North are reminded how difficult it can be to survive in the snow and the cold. The ability to draw buying candidates from all over the country is particularly valuable if you are part of a franchise company in which franchise owners occasionally sell their franchises in order to move to a different climate. An open letter to other franchise owners can be very effective. See the sample letter at the end of this chapter.

## Mentioning Money

Although mentioning a dollar requirement will prequalify your candidates to some degree, it can also eliminate some good candidates. To give a dollar figure that includes a working capital requirement can intimidate a potential buyer, because it seems like a very high down payment. It is also difficult to explain the purpose of working capital in a short ad, since people who are not familiar with owning a business will probably not understand.

For example, would the average buying candidates understand if you told them that the working capital account in a particular business is usually used to accommodate the receivable turnover period? (See Chapter 2.) Unfortunately, most buyers don't understand these terms without some further explanation. If you want to use a dollar figure to qualify, make sure to include the working capital in the ad or mention that working capital is required. If you don't, you may have a lot of explaining to do when potential buyers respond to the ad—and then find that they need another $40,000, $50,000, or $60,000 even though it's only temporary.

> **Note:** Working capital is required until collections catch up with sales. As time goes on, the capital account will "fill itself" from operating profit.
>
> Keep in mind, however, that if you find a good candidate who is interested in this business opportunity, there are ways to stretch the dollar—from minimizing the down payment to arranging a working partnership buyout. (See Chapter 3 for more on creative financing methods.) Don't be too quick to dismiss potential buyers—they are not that easy to find!
>
> Although you can consummate a sale with a handshake at a first meeting of the parties, it is much more appropriate to expect six to 12 months to find the right buyer and finalize the sale. Remember: you're not selling a pair of shoes—you're selling a way of life.

## The Disclosure, the Memorandum, and the Agreement

If you are selling a franchise, one of your first tasks is to ensure that the buyer is properly informed by presenting the franchise disclosure document. (See the language in a typical offering circular at the end of this chapter.)

After you have made full disclosure, whether you are a franchisee or not, and you and the potential buyer have agreed to the basic elements of sale, your next step is to prepare a letter of intent. (See the sample at the end of this chapter.) The purpose of this document is to separate the buyers from the lookers. A potential buyer's signature on this letter of intent is not necessarily an agreement to consummate, particularly since many buyers will not agree to the letter representing an actual purchase contract, but it will definitely intimidate less serious individuals and secure a deposit. In some cases, the deposit is refundable if the sale fails to consummate, no fault on the part of the buyer. In other cases, the deposit represents the fact that the seller will withhold the business from the market and is not refundable: in other words, the seller will not use the offer as leverage to get other potential buyers to raise their offers. In the letter of intent, the parties agree that their attorneys will prepare a formal contract of purchase and sale. The formal agreement can take a variety of forms and can be a 10- to 12-page agreement or a 20- to 30-page agreement. Its size and form depend on the personal preference of legal counsel and the kinds of protection the buyer's or seller's asset portfolio requires.

## Protecting the Sale

Both buyer and seller have a number of devices at their disposal with which to protect the sale.

### Buyer Protections

The buyer's best protection is the very fact of owing the seller money. A down payment entitles the buyer to begin operating the business, but if the buyer finances the purchase with a promissory note, he or she will owe the seller a substantial amount of money—money the buyer can withhold if he or she finds that the seller misrepresented anything of a material nature during the disclosure and negotiations.

A buyer may also seek a certain level of protection from the type of legal form the company adopts after the purchase. That form could be a C corporation, an S corporation, a limited partnership, a general partnership, a sole proprietorship, or a limited liability company.

> ### Debt Responsibility
> The buyer should keep in mind that, with a sole proprietorship, a general partnership, or a limited partnership, the buyer, as the moving force in the company, is completely liable for all debts and obligations of the company. On the other hand, the buyer is protected from

all debts and obligations, other than the buyer's actual investment, when the legal entity chosen is a corporation or a limited liability company.

To a great extent, tax and liability considerations will determine the particular form. These are buyer prerogatives and the buyer should discuss them with his or her legal and accounting professionals.

## Seller Protections

What do these buyer protections mean to you, the seller, and how can you protect yourself and the business you sold from post-sale trauma? The seller is entitled to protective devices if the buyer takes over the business before paying the entire purchase price. You could include many kinds of protections, particularly if the buyer makes no down payment or a small down payment. These protections can prevent the buyer from depleting the cash or valuable assets of the business. Some of these protections are negotiable, but some of them are absolutely necessary to protect you, the seller, from losing control of the business and its viability.

As a seller, always keep in mind that a business entity with limited personal liability (C corporation, S corporation, or limited liability company) is only as good as its pocketbook: if that pocketbook is empty, you have no way of getting your note paid. You can, however, protect yourself in the following ways.

- Get a personal signature or guarantee on the purchase money promissory note. If the business is a franchise, the franchisor will normally require this personal signature to ensure that the post-term, noncompete covenant is respected. If it's an independent business, you want the buyer to be personally responsible for payment whether the company has depleted its cash or not.

**Note:** A *post-term, noncompete covenant* is designed to prevent the individual buyers and other signatories from operating a business in competition with the franchise after the franchise contract expires or is terminated.

- Get an acceleration-upon-default clause in the note. If the buyer falls behind on promissory note payments, this clause will enable you to sue for the entire balance, as opposed to just the payments the buyer has missed.
- Hold the business as security for the note, so you can take back the business in the event the buyer either refuses or is unable to make payments on the note. Keep in mind, as noted throughout this text, that it is always preferable to have security in addition to the business.
- Insist on the right to examine the books and records of the business if the buyer falls behind on promissory note payments, to ensure that he or she is not draining the business in anticipation of running off.

It is also a good idea, under any circumstances, to have the buyer obtain a life insurance policy for the amount of the purchase money promissory note, to protect you in case the buyer dies before paying off the note. In some cases, the buyer might not be critical to the proper operation and continuity of the business. In other cases, the buyer might be the key factor.

Another protection the seller may mandate is that the buyer maintain certain maximum percentages on cost of product and cost of labor, for example, to ensure that he or she doesn't drain the business and then walk away after essentially stealing back the down payment.

The financial tests listed at the end of this chapter are some of the devices recommended by attorneys and accountants to protect against either intentional or inadvertent dissipation of the business. The sampling is not intended to be exhaustive but merely representative of the kinds of protections that you can use.

The protection devices suggested here are just some of the things that should be part of a seller protection plan. They should also allow you to better understand some legal concepts to discuss with your legal counsel.

In addition, you may wish to review Worksheet 14 on the accompanying CD. It will help you review ways to protect the sale of your business.

WARNING!

As always, do not use this book in the place of competent legal counsel! This book only introduces you to some general concepts involved in a business sale. Always seek professional advice concerning the issues involved in your particular transaction. (Please see Chapters 4, 19, and 20 regarding the use of legal and financial professionals.)

## Disclosing the Sale to Your Employees

One other question about seller protection you ought to address is how you can protect your business from employees who may either leave or slack off while you look for an appropriate buyer. How and when should you tell your employees that you are going to sell the business? Please note that I say, "you are going to sell," not "you have sold." You should address employee disclosure in the early stages of your thinking.

Sharing this information with your employees is not just a basic courtesy, but good business sense. You may find a potential buyer among your employees. It is not unusual that an employee who seems the least likely prospect will approach a relative, a friend, or a customer and generate the money necessary to qualify as a buyer. If that happens, of course, you would then need to share the basic dollar amounts with that individual—asking price, working capital requirement, down payment, and purchase money promissory note variables such as the number of payment years and monthly payment schedule. You would need to relate to that employee on a different level. The employee would already know the basics of the business and have some knowledge of your customers, which would give him or her quite an advantage in owning the business.

By informing employees of a potential sale, you will also be telling them that you are mindful of the effect selling the business will have on their personal lives. They will want to know what will happen to their jobs if you sell the business. Explain that most people who buy a business are interested in the employees who contributed to its success and eager to examine the possibility of keeping as many of these employees as possible.

You may need to arrange some sort of termination pay bonus for your key people, in the event the new buyer does not choose to retain their services. Keep in mind that if the business does not sell, you want to keep your employees and give them an incentive to stay as long as possible. If the business sells, you want your key employees to stay with the new owner at least until he or she is able to replace them. Most buyers are not able to fill key positions immediately following a takeover because they do not yet know all the nuances of the customer base, the equipment, the vendor relationships, or even the basic operation of the business.

You don't want employees to leave and take customers with them or to leave the business without adequate personnel to maintain its stability. Either of these scenarios could devastate the business and seriously jeopardize your purchase money promissory note. In all likelihood, you will have enough cash from the sale to pay the key employees something that will keep them with the business for at least a minimum period. Offering your employees some kind of bonus to stay with the new owner during the transition period might be the best insurance policy you ever bought. Consider, for example, how Tony Martinez handled this situation when he was selling his business.

---

### Illustration 14-1. Contract with a Key Employee

Tony Martinez wanted to protect the continuity of his business by ensuring that his key employee stayed with the business until the takeover was complete and the buyer could stand on his or her own. Toward that end, he made a contract with his top manager.

"As a result of your satisfactory employment and our need to assure any potential buyer that you will continue to give the business your best efforts after a sale is consummated, I have agreed to the following:

1. You will receive a bonus of $5,000 under the following conditions:
   a) You remain with the buyer, after the sale is consummated, for a period of no less than six months;
   b) In the event the buyer chooses not to retain your services for the entire six-month period, you shall obtain a letter from the buyer indicating that you are not being terminated for cause; and
   c) If the buyer is unwilling to give you such a letter, then you shall keep narrative notes as to any problems you incur with the buyer during your tenure, so as to satisfy me that your termination was not a fault of yours."

---

Interestingly, the contract also served to keep the manager with the business under even more trying circumstances. Tony passed away before he sold the business. His widow took over the business and, because of the letter, which she was happy to honor, the manager stayed with the business during a very difficult transition period. The letter served not only the needs of the pending sale, but also the needs of the family. It turned out to be a bonus letter in more ways than one.

In most cases, disclosing the sale to employees early on is the best course of action. The only exceptions to this rule are situations in which the details of sale are worked out quickly and quietly and the buyer intends to replace all personnel. These situations do not normally involve trade secrets or customer relationships, either of which could prove seriously problematic, regardless of the buyer's ultimate intentions. Remember: if key employees have developed a personal loyalty with a few large customers, termination of those employees could cut deeply into the company's cash flow and profit. Protecting trade secrets from competitors is another reason to be cautious about the relationships with key employees. Angry ex-employees can be hard to control, even in court.

Disclosing plans to sell can be particularly tricky if you have a manager or long-term employee who has taken on some owner-type responsibilities and shows a personal concern over the success or failure of the business. In that case, your relationship with the employee will dictate how to handle such a situation.

The reason for the sale—health, insolvency, retirement—and the nature of the purchase—single purchaser, acquisition by a larger company, merger with a company of equal size—will all bear on the employee's reaction. How will the employee's reaction affect the success or failure of the sale? If you are going to take back a note from the buyer, what effect will the employee's action and reaction have on the future of the business after the sale? Look at the following examples for insights that may help in your particular situation.

### Illustration 14-2. A Positive Employee Reaction

As the result of some bad expansion decisions, Lori Jamison had a serious financial problem and could not continue to operate a multi-store complex. It became clear that she had to sell some of the stores to stabilize the business.

She had a very good working relationship with all her managers and, as the result of her multi-unit activities, had left many of the daily responsibilities to the manager in charge of each store. Lori's managers took their jobs seriously and each was a stable and significant factor in the success of his or her store.

Although management had made some bad decisions, the industry was strong and most of the stores were doing well. Lori's professionals suggested that she afford each manager and each administrative person the courtesy of a personal meeting to make a relatively full disclosure regarding the general situation and the possibility of selling some of the stores.

Although Lori didn't know the extent of her managers' interest or the financial wherewithal of their families and friends, she indicated that she would first offer each of them the opportunity to buy the store that he or she was managing. After all, if the operating profit is big enough for the business to pay for itself, then any employee with working capital and a down payment can become a potential buyer.

Lori was delighted to find that eight managers and two administrative people were interested in the opportunity to buy. In fact, as time went on and the news spread among employees generally, additional interest came to the surface.

Two administrative people bought three stores. Lori sold the other four stores to people who responded to advertising and in every case the new owners retained the manager. The concept of disclosure was, in this case, a good idea.

### Illustration 14-3. Beware of Disgruntled Employees During a Sale

Linda McCain had hired an inexperienced general manager who, after two years of operation, had devastated her multi-shop operation. She terminated the general manager and proceeded to position many of the shops for sale. Because she had semi-retired during the general manager's two-year tenure, she did not have a close relationship with her remaining managers. The industry was good, but the shops were doing badly.

Although she offered the managers and the administrative people the opportunity to purchase, the situation was dramatically different from Lori Jamison's experience. Their perspectives had already been poisoned by the negative attitude of the terminated general manager. In this case, most of the managers were new, the shops were doing badly, there was no loyalty or even a friendly relationship between the owner and the employees, and the terminated manager had left a negative impression on all the managers about the business, the industry, and its future.

Two stores were consistently losing money and Linda closed them. Three managers left the organization. When Linda completed the reorganization at the end of a year and a half, the franchisor bought back three locations, a manager bought one location, Linda sold two locations to insiders, and she retained two locations herself. Linda was able to survive. However, because the terminated manager had left the business in an unhealthy condition, Linda had her hands full with a very difficult rehabilitation process.

In both Illustrations 14-2 and 14-3, disclosing the troubles of the business and its possible sale to employees was not a serious problem. With Lori Jamison, employee reaction was very positive. Linda McCain got help with her reorganization from a manager and two insiders who purchased locations. Although the two situations were significantly different, disclosure to employees is clearly the best approach when preparing to sell your business.

## Sweat Equity vs. Absentee Ownership

If an employee, particularly a manager, buys the location in which he or she is working, you should keep something else in mind. Even the most dedicated employee will recognize that, as an owner, he or she would probably arrive at work earlier, work harder, examine the details of the day's activities more closely, and leave work later. Even the most zealous manager recognizes the difference between sweat equity and absentee ownership. Allowing employees as potential owners to examine the growth potential of the business they could own gives them a much different perspective.

A business sale in which you collect the balance of the purchase price over time requires you to have some faith in the ability of the buyer to operate the business successfully. Most buyers, however experienced they may be in the business or industry, are unknowns in many ways. Although you may be very diligent in examining the buyer and his or her history in business, you have no way to really assess his or her personality, attitude, and ability to get along with customers, employees, and vendors. It is difficult to know whether the buyer will be straightforward and honest in his or her relationships or deceptive and underhanded. The advantage to dealing with an employee as a potential buyer is that you probably know more about his or her personality and business sense. This comfort zone cannot be equaled with a buyer about whom you know little. In this context, it is often a big advantage to sell to an employee, even though the dollars may be short upfront and you may have to anticipate waiting longer for full payment for the business. Often, the longer wait is the smarter method of collection.

## Key Points to Remember

- You can advertise for a qualified buyer in many ways. Make sure the method you choose will maximize the effect of your advertising dollars.
- The disclosure, the letter of intent, and the purchase and sale agreement must be properly orchestratedby your professionals to afford you the maximum protection after the sale.
- Do not use this book in place of the appropriate legal and financial professionals.
- Discuss with your professional advisors the best way to disclose the sale of your business to your employees. Remember: you may find an ideal buying candidate within your walls.
- Make sure your attorney builds the appropriate protective devices into the buy-sell agreement if the sale is not all cash.

**Corporation Logo**
**SPRY PRINT—La Mesa/El Cajon**

Dear Spry Print Owner:

THIS is a REAL opportunity!!!!! Where have you heard that one before?

My SP locations in El Cajon and La Mesa are for sale, one or both. They are located in East County, San Diego—with the greatest climate anywhere, 70 to 80 degrees year round—in a business atmosphere of growth but with the relaxed California business pace. A perfect combination for semi-retirement.

As many of you know, my center of operations is in Northern California. I purchased these Southern California locations with my son, who has now expressed an interest in returning home to Northern California.

Attached are some financials for your perusal. The trend—positive!!!!

Price and payment schedule subject to negotiations.

Call Artie Target at (408) 111-3456 (days) or (408) 111-6543 (home, evenings) or, better yet, come down to San Diego and we'll kick the tires and kiss the bricks together.

Thanks for your consideration.

Artie Target

P.S. If you are too tied down to home, pass this on to somebody you feel may be interested in this REAL opportunity.

P.P.S. For those of you who understand SP growth potential, there is room for another SP location in the territory.

**Figure 14-1.** Sample Sale Announcement to Fellow Franchisees (letter to the current franchisees of the Spry Print Franchise)

### Franchise Offering Circular

A number of states have legislated requirements to protect their citizens from people who are selling franchises without full disclosure or, worse yet, by virtue of deceptive practices or misleading statements about the company's worth or the buyer's prospects. To protect

**Figure 14-2.** Sample Introduction to a California (continued on next page)

all citizens of the United States, whether in states with such legislation or not, the Federal Trade Commission has its own requirements. If you are selling a franchise, you are mandated to observe these laws or your sale may be rescinded (canceled) long after you execute the final papers. It is also possible that you could be subject to criminal penalties.

*(Although the language of the disclosure is currently undergoing legislative scrutiny and change, the import of the disclosure remains the same. Check with your local authority to note any change that may have taken place.)*

To give you an idea of the language, the following is a typical offering circular used in California.

THIS OFFERING CIRCULAR IS PROVIDED FOR YOUR OWN PROTECTION AND CONTAINS A SUMMARY ONLY OF CERTAIN MATERIAL PROVISIONS OF THE FRANCHISE AGREEMENT. THIS OFFERING CIRCULAR AND ALL CONTRACTS AND AGREEMENTS SHOULD BE READ CAREFULLY IN THEIR ENTIRETY FOR AN UNDERSTANDING OF ALL RIGHTS AND OBLIGATIONS OF BOTH THE FRANCHISOR AND THE FRANCHISEE.

A FEDERAL TRADE COMMISSION RULE MAKES IT UNLAWFUL TO OFFER OR SELL ANY FRANCHISE WITHOUT FIRST PROVIDING THIS OFFERING CIRCULAR TO THE PROSPECTIVE FRANCHISEE AT THE EARLIER OF (1) THE FIRST PERSONAL MEETING; OR (2) TEN BUSINESS DAYS BEFORE THE SIGNING OF ANY FRANCHISE OR RELATED AGREEMENT; OR (3) TEN BUSINESS DAYS BEFORE ANY PAYMENT. THE CALIFORNIA FRANCHISE INVESTMENT LAW REQUIRES THAT A COPY OF ALL PROPOSED AGREEMENTS RELATING TO THE SALE OF THE FRANCHISE BE DELIVERED TOGETHER WITH THE OFFERING CIRCULAR.

IF THIS OFFERING CIRCULAR IS NOT DELIVERED ON TIME, OR IF IT CONTAINS A FALSE, INCOMPLETE, INACCURATE OR MISLEADING STATEMENT, A VIOLATION OF FEDERAL AND STATE LAW MAY HAVE OCCURRED AND SHOULD BE REPORTED TO THE FEDERAL TRADE COMMISSION, WASHINGTON, D.C. 20580, AND THE CALIFORNIA DEPARTMENT OF CORPORATIONS AT ANY OF ITS OFFICES.

THESE FRANCHISES HAVE BEEN REGISTERED UNDER THE FRANCHISE INVESTMENT LAW OF THE STATE OF CALIFORNIA. SUCH REGISTRATION DOES NOT CONSTITUTE APPROVAL, RECOMMENDATION OR ENDORSEMENT BY THE COMMISSIONER OF CORPORATIONS NOR A FINDING BY THE COMMISSIONER THAT THE INFORMATION PROVIDED HEREIN IS TRUE, COMPLETE AND NOT MISLEADING.

*The following language in the sale agreement is recommended to a seller who takes a purchase money promissory note as part of the sale.*

So long as any of buyer's obligations under the Note remain unsatisfied, buyer's operation of the business shall be subject to the following tests:

**Working Capital:** During each month of the calendar year 200_, the business shall maintain a ratio of current assets to current liabilities (as determined in accordance with generally accepted accounting practices, uniformly applied) of at least 1:1.

**Payroll:** The monthly aggregate total of all sums paid to or for the benefit of the employees of the business, including draws taken by buyer, including but not limited to salaries, payroll taxes, workers' compensation insurance payments, group insurance premiums, and other benefits, shall not exceed 30% of the monthly gross sales of the business.

**Cost of Goods:** The monthly cost of goods sold by the business, as determined in accordance with standards and guidelines established by the previous practice of the business and of the industry, shall not exceed 27% of the monthly gross sales of the business. This shall be in accordance with the particular chart of accounts used by the business at the time of sale.

*Additionally, if the seller wants to keep an even tighter rein on the business, particularly when the down payment has been small (or nonexistent), a clause regarding financial reporting may also be inserted.*

**Financial Reports:** Buyer shall permit seller (and its agents) full and complete access to the books and records of the business and shall supply seller with the following documents and information in a timely fashion:

(a) Quarterly or monthly financial statements

(b) Sales tax returns and proof of corresponding deposits

(c) Payroll tax returns and proof of corresponding deposits

(d) Royalty statements

(e) A monthly schedule of the business accounts payable showing the age of each item in months to accompany the financial statements

(f) A monthly summary of the business accounts receivable, broken down according to the age of such accounts to accompany the financial statements

**Figure 14-3.** Sample Financial Tests

*The language "Memorandum of Sale" is used to suggest a more formal arrangement than merely an intent of the parties. This is often followed by the language in paragraph one of the letter below: "this language will then represent a purchase contract." Whether this language is "enforceable" is seriously conjectural but, if allowed to stand, represents an intimidation factor to the buyer.*

January 5, 2008

David Money
120 Promissory Lane
Sunnymead, California 94105

Re: Sale of Instant Printing Location referred to as (Spry Print) SP 303, located at Post and Palm in the City of Sunnymead

Dear David:

This letter will serve as a memorandum of sale with respect to the above SP location. If you sign where indicated and return it to me with the deposit noted below, this letter will then represent a purchase contract. A more formal Purchase and Sale Agreement will then be drafted consistent with the terms of this letter.

Seller is Absolute Corporation, a California Corporation, represented by Michael Dance, its President.

Buyer is a General Partnership whose partners are David and Della Money.

The price is $210,000, and the business is to be sold free and clear of all encumbrances, with the exception of the Promissory Note and Security Agreement on the Kodak 200AF, which is to be assumed by the partnership and payable to Kodak; the actual balance to be determined at the time of closing.

*[Note: You may designate the buyer to assume the debt on certain pieces of equipment. See Chapters 3 and 13.]*

It is anticipated that the transfer of the business will take place at the close of business, Wednesday, August 31, 2008. There will be no adjustment for inventory, with the understanding that "normal" levels of inventory will be maintained until the time of sale.

**Figure 14-4.** Sample Memorandum of Sale, sometimes referred to as a "Letter of Intent" (continued on next pages)

(Alternatively, there can be an adjustment for inventory at the close of business on 8/31/05, with the amount in excess of $_____ being a credit to the seller, the value of the inventory to be based on the Unisource price book then in use.)

Attorneys' costs in preparing the necessary documents will be apportioned equally between buyer and seller.

*[Note: Apportioning attorneys' costs tends to ensure fairness and prevent negotiations from becoming protracted and costly.]*

The transfer fee to SP Corporate (if any) will be allocated one-half each to the buyer and the seller.

The down payment shall be $40,000 and shall be held in your (our) attorney's trust account (or in an escrow to be opened at Wells Fargo Bank) until the closing.

Sales tax will be the responsibility of the buyer.

*[Note: Making sales taxes the buyer's responsibility prevents the buyer from insisting on a large allocation to equipment for depreciation. Alternatively, the sales tax can be apportioned between buyer and seller.]*

The balance of the purchase price shall be represented by a promissory note of $170,000, which will reflect monthly payments of $2,245.70 to fully amortize the balance over a ten-year period with the unpaid principal balance bearing interest at 10%.

The Purchase Money Promissory Note shall be secured by the business itself, the exact form of which will be discussed between buyer and seller. There shall be a $70 late charge should any payment be made more than two weeks after the due date and an acceleration clause upon a default in payment not cured within the appropriate time periods.

*[Note: The late charge ensures that payment dates are observed, without each late payment triggering a serious rift after the sale.]*

Permission for the sale transfer will be obtained from Spry Print Corporation (the franchisor) with the mutual cooperation of the buyer and seller. Consent to transfer the premises lease will also be obtained with the mutual cooperation of the buyer and the seller.

In the event that the location is resold, the full balance of the Promissory Note will be due and payable at that time.

*[Note: The seller can avoid inheriting a new note holder by demanding full payment at the time the business is resold.]*

Deposit to bind the sale will be $10,000.

The payables at date of closing will be the obligation of the seller. The receivables at date of closing will be either collected by the seller or collected by the buyer and remitted to the seller, with any uncollected receivables after 90 days following the closing being forwarded to the seller.

*[Note: The seller might pursue collections too aggressively without this clause.]*

It is understood that the buyer may elect to have a representative attend the SP training course, such training to be scheduled by SP Corporate.

*[Note: This clause is in the event the franchisor has a policy of providing training.]*

As the buyer deems necessary, the present owner, Michael Dance, shall remain with the buyer for a period up to one month for a fixed salary of $2,000.

*[Not'e: Paying the seller for his or her time causes the buyer to become independent more quickly.]*

_____          _____

David Money, Buyer                              Absolute Corporation, by its President,
                                                Michael Dance

_____

Della Money

# CHAPTER 15

# The Motivations Behind the Sale

### Starting or Buying a Business

"But I want to start taking an income from the first day." This is a statement heard in many classes on "how to go into business for yourself." Although it is a normal comment for the uninitiated, it certainly flies in the face of reality for those people who have already gone into business for themselves.

**The New Business**

The fuel that feeds the fire in all businesses is the customer base. Building that customer base takes time. You need to get the word out so that people know that your product or service is available. You've got to prove the quality and price of your product or service in relation to your competition. And then, you've got to inspire loyalty among your customers in order to maintain continuity and have your customers speak well of you to others. This is the beginning of establishing your foundation. And getting to the point where there are enough customers and enough sales to generate sufficient dollars for all your business expenses as well as your own compensation takes time. This time is equivalent to dollars. You will need to spend dollars to reach this point before the dollars grow enough to service you and the business.

## Is There an Alternative?

Buying a business is often a viable alternative to building one from scratch. Whatever trade or industry interests you, it is quite likely that there are already businesses of that kind in your neighborhood, and don't be surprised if one of them is for sale. If you buy a business, you don't have to worry about the start-up time and you can begin taking money from the business for your compensation immediately. In fact, that's the main reason for buying instead of building. If you buy a business correctly, you should be able to put a down payment toward the purchase price; then the balance of the purchase price and your income should come from the business itself. Sound like a good idea? Yes, it can be.

## Examining the Differences

Be sure to examine this possibility before you decide to start from scratch. Buying actually costs less than building, more often than not. And the existence of the customer base gives you every reason to believe that you can do as well as the seller—maybe, even better.

## Some Loyalties Are Not for Sale

The consultant represents a different picture, a real conundrum. Some consulting businesses—hair salons, personal chefs, therapists, business consultants, and the like—have usually developed personal relationships that are not so easily transferred to a buyer. These kinds of businesses must be examined very carefully before assuming that the seller's success can transfer or convert to the buyer. The customer base will likely be much more unstable than for the average product or service business. That's why the average consultant starting a practice today should have a customer base before deciding to depend on the consulting business to generate enough income. Experience suggests that a consultant attempting to build a customer base could be looking at a number of years to reach a profit position, rather than a number of months, which might be the case in the more conventional business venture. And, if you're acquiring such a practice, be sure to create alternative measures to adjust for this vulnerability. There are many ways to accommodate for this contingency and make the purchase a success. Be sure to consult with the appropriate professional for good advice on this issue.

## The Bottom Line

Owning a business is a dream that can turn into a delightful success or a disaster. Be careful that you do the appropriate, necessary research and analysis before making the decision. Remember: when you're on the diving board, be sure to check for water in the pool before doing your swan dive. Failure to do so might make it your swan song.

A successful business sale requires both buyer and seller to know the motivation and mind-set of the other as the negotiations proceed. The motivations of both parties have important implications long after the papers are signed. What most sellers do not realize is that the buyer's motivations often revolve around business style and concepts of entrepreneurship. How and whether your buyer delegates authority and how quickly your buyer learns the business may determine whether he or she pays your purchase money promissory note. Is your buyer prepared for the training involved in taking over business operations? Will he or she need your help during this period?

If the buyer doesn't succeed at the business and does not meet the payments on your promissory note, you have not succeeded at selling the business. Make sure that you contribute to the future success of the business by understanding the motivations behind the sale.

## Why Are You Selling?

Whether someone is interested in buying a car or a business, the potential buyer always wants to know why the seller is selling. The reason, obviously, shouldn't be that the car isn't performing well or the business is not gratifying or profitable. This reason will hardly motivate the buyer. Explain your reasons in such a way that the buyer can understand and feel comfortable with them. If someone is selling a car, it may be that he or she wants a better car, a faster car, or a four-door car. Why are you selling your business? Do you want to retire from business? Are you planning to move to Hawaii? Would you like to travel to Europe? Do you need to deal with health problems?

Whatever the reasons, think them through, make them solid, and make sure that your partners, professionals, and others involved in the negotiations are properly informed. You do not want to fabricate reasons in order to make the sale. Misrepresenting yourself or your business could cause the buyer to rescind the sale later on. It is a good idea to discuss this with your attorney.

You must also make your selling story believable. In most industries, no one would ever say that operating a business is easy. Business is exacting and requires constant attention to detail. If the potential for growth and profit is extraordinary, however, then the exercise is worthwhile. How you explain this fact of business life is important. Carefully prepare your presentation to respond to your buyer's thinking. If the business is too easy, everybody would be doing it. If the business is too tough, only the experts could handle it. Make sure the buyer understands that it is a good day's wage for a good day's labor and an equity potential in the bargain. Nobody really expects more—and nobody wants to pay for less.

Sometimes, sellers think irrationally about the value of their businesses. They have put much of their life, money, and energy into building and maintaining them. A seller's emotional ties to his or her business can cause a kind of paranoia during negotiations.

The value of a business is really based on the value it represents to its owner or a buyer. Value can be interpreted in many ways. A business that generates sufficient income to accommodate the needs of a family is valuable. When no one shows an interest in buying a business, it seems less valuable. When more than one person is interested in buying a business, its value rises. You may be willing to make concessions in price and other variables when few people are interested in buying it. It is quite a different story when you find a person who is qualified and motivated. Such a potential buyer may increase the value you perceive in your business. However, you can also blow the sale if your desire to get a high price prevents you from properly assessing the business's value.

---

### Illustration 15-1. A Seller's Paranoia

Al Morrow had a potential offer on his business that would have eliminated his creditor problems. In the face of this good fortune, he took a somewhat irrational emotional attitude.

"I'll be damned if I'm going to let someone steal this business from me after all I've done to build it up from nothing. I'd rather see it go down the drain than give it away."

Al was offered a fair price and probably could have consummated the deal if it were not for his attitude. Every minor point of the negotiations became a deal breaker. He became so paranoid as to believe that everyone was working against him—the buyer, the buyer's attorney, the broker, and, on occasion, even his own professional team. Everyone was suspect.

---

It is essential that you, as a seller, build a team of professionals in whom you have confidence. You must give them the responsibility for helping you make decisions that will be good for you and your family in both the short and the long terms. You must then accept their advice, with the understanding that it is still ultimately your decision. Remember: a fair price for both buyer and seller exists within very logical parameters. A little objectivity can go a long way in recognizing those parameters.

## The Buyer's Motivations

In the long run, however, your reasons for selling are secondary to the buyer's motivations to buy. Your buyer's motivations may be much more subtle. You must draw them out, however, because they affect the buyer's style and approach to operating the business,, the forces driving the payment of your promissory note.

You have every right to examine your potential buyers. The Sample Confidential Business Application below asks for your buyer's financial status, educational background, and business experience. However, this kind of information may not reveal whether the business will fulfill his or her goals or whether he or she likes the industry, the business, the marketplace, the geography, the people, or the hours—all of which are vital to bringing about a successful sale.

**Confidential Information**

Applicant's full name: _____ Social Security #: _____

Spouse's full name: _____ Social Security #: _____

Address: _____

City and state: _____

How long at this address: _____ Own ❑ Rent ❑

Business phone: _____ Home phone: _____

**Personal Data**

Single ❑ Separated ❑ Married ❑ Divorced ❑ Widowed ❑

Number of dependents _____ Ages of children _____ _____ _____

Monthly alimony/child support _____

**Record of Employment**

List most recent position first.

| Applicant | | | | |
|---|---|---|---|---|
| **Employer** | **City/State** | **Position/ Title** | **From/To** | **Annual Income** |
|  |  |  |  |  |
|  |  |  |  |  |
|  |  |  |  |  |

**Figure 15-1.** Sample Confidential Business Application (continued on pages 209–211)

| Spouse | | | | |
|---|---|---|---|---|
| Employer | City/State | Position/Title | From/To | Annual Income |
| | | | | |
| | | | | |
| | | | | |

## Gross Monthly Income and Monthly Living Expenses

| Applicant | | | |
|---|---|---|---|
| Gross Monthly Income | | Monthly Living Expenses | |
| Dividends/Interest | $ | Total Rent | $ |
| Net Rental Income | $ | Additional Financing | $ |
| Pension Income | $ | Other Expenses* | $ |
| Other Income* | $ | | |
| Total Income | $ | Total Expenses | $ |

| Spouse | | | |
|---|---|---|---|
| Gross Monthly Income | | Monthly Living Expenses | |
| Dividends/Interest | $ | Total Rent | $ |
| Net Rental Income | $ | Additional Financing | $ |
| Pension Income | $ | Other Expenses* | $ |
| Other Income* | $ | | |
| Total Income | $ | Total Expenses | $ |

* Please itemize. If necessary, attach a separate listing.

**Credit References**

| Creditor's Name | Address | Account Number | Present Balance | Date Paid |
|---|---|---|---|---|
| **Applicant** | | | | |
| | | | | |
| | | | | |
| **Spouse** | | | | |
| | | | | |
| | | | | |

**Financial Data**

As of _____, 20____

Individual Statement ❑  Joint Statement ❑  (If individual statement, a separate statement for spouse is required.)

 Applicant ❑

Spouse ❑

Assets* _____

Liabilities and Equity _____

**Checking Account**

Accounts Payable $_____

Bank Name _____

Bank Loans (Unsecured)*$_____

Address _____  Account No. _____

Balance $ _____

**Savings Account**

Bank Loans (Secured)* $_____

Bank Name _____  Address _____

Account No. _____

Balance $_____

Credit Card Balances* $_____

Stocks/Bonds (Negotiable) $_____

Money Market Funds $_____

Certificates of Deposit $_____

**Real Estate**

Taxes Due and Accrued $_____

Estimated Market Value $_____

Mortgages Payable $_____

Type of Property _____

**Other Loans or Notes Payable**

Personal Property $_____

Automobiles $_____

Loans Against Life Insurance $_____

How Many? Year(s) _____

Other Debts* $_____

Retirement Plans (Vested) $_____

Other Assets* $_____

**Total Assets (A) $_____**

**Total Liabilities (B) $_____**

**Equity (Net Worth) (A – B) $_____**

**Total Liabilities and Equity $_____**

*Please itemize. If necessary, attach a separate listing.

You will likely encounter many types of buyers. Be prepared to deal with their different qualifications and characteristics. Keep in mind that some potential buyers will be sales-oriented and others mechanically inclined. Make sure you don't accept the square peg for the round hole. Here are some possibilities:

- Marketing or salespeople
- Engineers
- Shopkeepers
- Professionals

- Military people
- Blue-collar workers
- White-collar workers

Some businesses perform both manufacturing and retail sales. Manufacturing can require technical skill or experience, which can intimidate a potential buyer who lacks that skill or experience. You may want to reassure a hesitant buyer by explaining that technical people are available at a price and that the ability to sell is probably more critical to successful business.

An ideal buying candidate is helpful, pleasant, conversational, smiling, knowledgeable, and caring. No one person has all the personality traits necessary to properly operate a successful business all the time. As long as you find someone interested in your business who has one or some of the talents necessary to operate it, can admit to the ones he or she lacks, and knows how to rely on others to fill the gaps in their experience, you have a potential buyer.

## Entrepreneurship and Business Style

Most people have read so much about owning a business that they have what is sometimes called the "entrepreneur bug." Even if they have been behind a desk in a big company for the past 20 years, they are sure that they have the qualifications to own a business. For the benefit of the potential buyer and as a reflection on your own entrepreneurial talents, examine the differences between a do-it-yourselfer and a good supervisor. How would your potential buyer handle these two roles?

The goal of the do-it-yourselfer and the supervisor is the same—to get a job done successfully. The difference is in their methods. In many businesses, like picture framing or button making, the owner is a retailer and a manufacturer. He or she is also the advertising department, bookkeeper, inventory manager, customer service representative, procurement manager, equipment buyer, personnel manager, and salesperson. The owner must take control to get these jobs done.

You know the old attitude, "If I don't do it, no one will." This can be a business owner's strength; it can also be his or her greatest weakness.

**Illustration 15-2. A Franchisor's Evaluation**

Franchisors deal with the question of a potential franchisee's business style every time they sell a new franchise. John Scott, former CEO of Fastframe USA, called the type of buyers he looked for "soft entrepreneurs":

> It is certainly true that we are always looking for aggressive, driving, creative, self-motivated people, but you have to be careful. The man or woman who recognizes that we've spent a lot of money over a long period to "get it right," who sees the real benefits, that's the soft entrepreneur. That is the man or woman we are looking for.

## Be a Leader and a Teacher

The very characteristic that makes a good entrepreneur—doing it yourself—is the one that can prevent you from delegating responsibility. Sometimes, your employees know better or less expensive ways to get things done. Sometimes a previous owner or your franchise company knows the industry and the market better than you do. Take time to examine how your business can grow and leave enough room for your employees, partners, or investors to use their creativity and ingenuity. In this way, you can depend on your people to help you adapt to changing times and a changing marketplace.

Being personally involved in every aspect of your business operations at the beginning is clearly appropriate. Total understanding of each working element is necessary for your ultimate success. However, you must eventually depend on other people in order for your business to succeed. At that point, you will have two more roles to add to your repertoire: teacher and leader.

The key to converting your business style is not only delegating responsibility, but also giving the commensurate authority that goes with it. If you give someone a job and then stand there while he or she does the job, then you are quite right: you might as well do it yourself. But if you have taught your people properly and shown them by example how you expect a job to be done and then you let them do it, you will be an effective supervisor, an important skill for any business owner. Yes, your people will make mistakes, and some may be costly, but a well-planned program of supervision will minimize the magnitude of these risks.

## Give the Buyer the Benefit of Your Experience

Some businesses work well when they're smaller or when the owner participates actively. Other businesses function more effectively when the owner leaves the basic operation to his or her staff. The buyer will be looking at these alternatives. It is your job to encourage this examination. While your business may have achieved its maximum productivity under your management, it may also benefit from a change in management technique. The success of your buyer might well depend on his or her ability to recognize a better way to do something you have been doing the same way for years.

If the buyer wants to change management style, it is in your best interest to give him or her the benefit of your best, objective judgment. You can operate a small business successfully in many ways. You may send some collateral functions outside, like bookkeeping to an accounting firm. Your buyer, however, may need to maintain control over such processes internally.

When you start a business, you need to find the time to do almost everything yourself, yet you lack knowledge of the different job functions. As the business grows and you become more knowledgeable and efficient, you develop time savers. Share with the buyer your experiences. Be careful, however, that the tale of your business education excites, rather than overwhelms your buyer.

## Learning the Business

If potential buyers are not knowledgeable about the industry, they will be concerned about a training or familiarization period that will enable them to successfully take over the business. You may ease their minds by telling them the philosophy of most franchise companies—they would rather sell a new franchise to someone who knows absolutely nothing about the business than to someone from inside the industry who may have bad habits that are difficult to change.

Learning the basics of properly operating a business is much more important than learning the specifics of any particular industry. Statistics show that the vast majority of franchise owners had never been involved in the particular industry before their purchase. This news should give potential buyers a much greater comfort zone if they are not especially expert in the industry they are entering.

In most situations, the franchise company makes some arrangements for a training period. Some companies charge for this and some don't. In any event, you should always be willing to devote whatever time is necessary to properly orient your buyer to take over the business in the most successful way. Make sure the buyer understands that you will not leave him or her to the whim of the fates after the sale.

Remember: the buyer's success is what pays your note and what secures your peace of mind until he or she pays it off completely. Buyers' attitudes change dramatically when the sellers remind them of this fact during the early discussions. Also keep in mind that the time you devote to initial training or post-franchise training or even to serving in a supervisory capacity need not be without compensation. In fact, if the buyer is paying you a salary for orientation and training, he or she will be eager to release you as quickly as possible.

## Key Points to Remember

- You must be able to present a logical and understandable reason for wanting to sell your business.
- Be careful not to let greed or principle prevent you from negotiating a good price.
- The buyer must satisfy you that his or her talents, experience, and goals are consistent with the size, profit, and growth potential of the business.
- Make sure the buyer understands the fundamental principles for operating a business successfully.
- Make sure that the buyer's personality and business style are consistent with the needs of the business's customer base.

# Before the Sale

## Bankruptcy: Not Yet

Yes, it is true. Economic times are pretty tight today, to say the least. For some people, some financial problems have become disastrous. The reasons are myriad. Some families have lost the basic income flow from the head of household's salary. As a result, they have been living on credit cards and savings. Other families have found themselves in a deep chasm, facing medical bills without health insurance to pick up the bulk of the costs. In some small businesses, for one reason or another, profits have turned into losses and maintaining continuity is no longer possible. The only alternative for some people and some businesses may be to declare bankruptcy.

## Another Business Alternative

There are those who suggest that bankruptcy is merely another business alternative and that "you've got to do what you've got to do." In other words, "Damn the torpedoes, full speed ahead." This lack of caution or, at least, failure to properly examine the problem can lead to unwanted consequences when other alternatives might be available. The short-term and long-term implications of a bankruptcy filing might not be the total taint they were a decade or so ago. However, they still have their tarnish, which, in many cases, takes time to erase before the business and its owner can return to normal. It is true, on the other hand, that in some cases it might be the only thing to do. Keep in mind that the bankruptcy legislation of 2005 makes it more difficult to file than previously was the case and that substantial time is required between filings. Make sure you understand the laws before you make the decision.

## The Business Alternative

In the business context, some people think that if you get behind six months, it will take another six months to catch up. Be careful of the simplicity of this concept. Falling behind six months in your business bills might mean taking 18 months or more to catch up. After all, the simplest part of this equation is that you have to pay taxes on your profit before you can use the money to pay off debts or loans. That means that only a portion of the profit is available. There are other reasons why this concept is too simple. Suffice to say that you need to examine all alternatives before making a judgment about bankruptcy. For example, a business that is using all its profit to pay back old debts may be a good business to buy because, if the old debt can be eliminated, the business could be very profitable. A good down payment can wipe out the old debt and the business can be successful for the new buyer. This has been a positive alternative for hundreds of owners facing financial difficulties. Be careful that you don't miss this possibility.

## More Than One Bankruptcy Alternative

Keep in mind that there are different kinds of bankruptcies. One is the "endgame." Everything you own and everything you owe go into a theoretical big box and, with some exceptions, they are both gone. As soon as you file your bankruptcy papers, you start all over again. Another type of bankruptcy allows you to keep your business, providing you can show that, aside from the debts that you've accumulated, the business can be profitable. And yet another kind of bankruptcy allows you, as a wage earner, to file for bankruptcy yourself and take advantage of the cleanup process by having certain dollars allocated to your debts over a limited period of time; thereafter, you start fresh. In other words, there are several ways that the bankruptcy laws can be helpful.

## Preparation for a Sale

Real estate brokers say a well-maintained, well-manicured, and recently cleaned house sells faster and for more money than a deserted, unkempt house. The same is certainly true for a business. Take the time to invest that extra energy or creativity—or money—to make your business more attractive.

This chapter focuses on how to prepare your business for sale—to cut costs and deal with outstanding debt before the sale. It also discusses how to prepare an ailing business for sale and when it may be necessary or appropriate to consider bankruptcy as an alternative.

The chapter begins with a successful and financially sound business and then examines various business problems of increasing severity—their symptoms, diagnosis, and treatment. By the end of the chapter, you will know how to deal with creditors and cut excess costs to improve your asking price. If you are concerned about needing bankruptcy protection, the chapter compares the bankruptcy alternatives to help you decide which best fits your situation.

## A Successful Business

Even the best-run business with an optimum operating profit has creditors. Buyers assume they will purchase the business free and clear of all encumbrances, including debt, unless it is built into the selling price. If you plan to sell your business, you should notify all your creditors at some point.

Normally, the buyer's counsel will file a bulk sales transfer notice in the appropriate newspaper or other periodical. This notice gives the buyer the protection of having notified any creditors that the business is being sold. The creditors can then seek protection for their obligations before the sale is consummated. If they fail to seek protection for their debts after the buyer publishes the bulk sales notice—even if they have not read the notice—they cannot then hold the buyer responsible for obligations incurred by the seller before the sale. However, municipal, state, and federal taxes are not necessarily wiped out by such a notice and might remain a problem for the buyer after the sale.

Consult your accountant or attorney for advice regarding tax obligations and the bulk sale transfer notice. In particular, ask your attorney if your state's bulk sale law has been repealed. Numerous states have recently repealed or are in the process of repealing these laws. If your state has repealed its bulk sales law, then you, as the seller, may be asked to guarantee all unpaid obligations.

Whether or not your state has a bulk sales law, notify your creditors of the pending sale in a businesslike fashion to ensure a smooth transition of the business from seller to buyer. Embarrassing situations can arise if the creditors find out through third parties or rumors.

You may be wise to put your sale through an escrow, a relatively inexpensive process that will ensure the creditors their payments in full before the business is actually turned over to the buyer and you receive the proceeds of the sale. If creditors are unsure whether you will pay what you owe them, they will probably put their claim into the escrow.

An escrow is a trust account held by a third party who is charged with the responsibility of holding all monies and papers until all conditions of the escrow are observed. A creditor submits his or her bill to the escrow agent and will normally take no other action, such as filing a lawsuit, that could cause the buyer to back out of the sale. As always, it is to your advantage to ensure that the buyer's relationship with all your vendors starts off positively.

If creditors are unaware of the escrow or the pending sale, they might bring a lawsuit against both buyer and seller after the fact. No matter what legal rights a creditor has, you and your buyer do not want to contend with a lawsuit after you consummate the sale.

As long as your creditors know you will bring their accounts current before the sale, they will normally not do anything to jeopardize your sale. As always, discuss this with your professional advisers when the time is right.

# A Good Business with Insufficient Operating Profit

If your business is suffering from insufficient operating profit, this will affect your asking price. Reevaluate the business to find the reasons for the insufficiency. You will need to look at many potential problem areas:

- High inventory
- Unnecessary personnel
- Employee benefits
- Inadequate collection efforts
- Owner compensation too much
- Personal bills too heavy for the business to carry
- Rent increase
- Too many locations for the business to handle
- Improper margins maintained for selling purposes
- Older equipment
- New competitors
- New price structure for retail customers
- Theft by personnel of goods or money
- Maintenance costs or service contracts too costly

You can work at resolving the problems in several ways, depending on the diagnosis. The following examples will give you a good start in identifying the causes. See also the worksheet for this chapter on the accompanying CD.

- Do an immediate analysis of the profit and loss statement to determine the causes of the problem. Compare the statement with statements from prior years and months to find out if the problem is connected to seasonality or to a permanent change.
- Evaluate the industry to determine if the problem is widespread or if it's specific to your business.
- Reexamine the margins for profit potential and look for extra costs of sale that have affected the profit. Very often, businesses neglect to pass cost increases on to their customers. For example, they may add pickup and delivery to their services without adding the costs of the extra services to their prices.

- Think about all of your employees in relation to their jobs, their incentives, and each other. Find out whether the team concept is working and what is required to make all employees more effective.
- Examine changes in customer preferences, styles, attitudes, and levels of sophistication. Sometimes, a product or service that was peripheral in the past becomes a customer priority.
- Think about training or retraining your employees. Because the marketplace is evolving so rapidly, your personnel need to keep up with sales and marketing techniques, computer innovations, and customer relations strategies.
- Consider updating your personnel manual, benefits packages, and salary scales to ensure your employees stay satisfied, challenged, and productive.
- Reevaluate your facility from the customer's perspective. Look at its size, appearance, convenience, parking, competition, and niche in the marketplace. You can too easily become complacent about your facility and fail to notice the cracks in the walls. New customers see these things as soon as they enter your business.
- Consider how to expand business through your current customers. How can you make better use of that valuable asset? How can you get your customers to buy more products or use more services? If you have been in business long enough, you know that it is easier and less expensive to build on your current customers than to find new customers.
- Look at the current advertising-marketing approach to new business. Advertising is not an expense of doing business; it is an investment. A good marketing analysis will often dictate the most cost-effective advertising approach.
- Get some research and development advice about the latest equipment technology, to maintain a competitive balance. Be careful to get an objective analysis and not just a sales pitch.
- Get a physical examination and perhaps a mental evaluation. Make sure the problems you are facing are not emotional. People may go through periods or phases in their lives, such as midlife crises, which may have

many implications for their businesses of which they may be completely unaware.

- Consider procedures for collecting outstanding debts, including compromise and litigation. More success in collecting could be at least a partial answer to dollar problems.
- Analyze your total asset portfolio to minimize the possibility of a business failure causing a personal disaster. An analysis of your assets will show any vulnerability of your personal and family holdings. You will sleep much better knowing that your life's savings are not at risk.
- Deal with your creditors to avoid legal action during sale negotiations. Even if your business is fairly strong, you probably have some creditors with whom your account is not current. If they find out about a sale, they may retain attorneys to protect their interests. You may want to reassure them in writing that you will take care of their accounts before closing the sale.

## A Good Business with Some Standing Debt

Some businesses continue operating successfully despite outstanding debts on which the owners have not made payments for some time. If you have some standing debt, you may be considering selling in order to pay those creditors from the purchase price. Again, a buyer normally expects to receive the business free of such obligations.

You can handle more serious creditor problems in several ways. Your first task is always to step back from the day-to-day business details and prioritize the problems you need to resolve. The earlier you get to a problem with creditors, the easier it is to negotiate with all the people involved and the more time you have to pursue alternatives. The numbers are lower, your creditors are less frustrated, and you have more money with which to negotiate.

## A Business with Serious Solvency Problems

Again, your solvency problems may result from a variety of causes. For example, you may have used your credit cards for business purposes or overextended your capacity to move your inventory and are facing a large debt to suppliers. Either of these situations can cause creditors to start lawsuits.

If your situation has become serious, your best course is to have your attorney contact the creditors directly and immediately to ensure that they don't do anything to interfere with the sale. You do not need to share these problems with your buyer because you will resolve them before transferring the business, free and clear of all debt. If the problems derive from situations other than the business itself, as is very often the case, it is really none of the buyer's business. A lawyer normally has credibility in the business community that can eliminate these potential problems before they get out of hand.

When the escrow closes and the buyer takes over the business, these debts will be paid out of the escrow by prearrangement and will not be a part of the buyer's ongoing obligations. In fact, if one of your solvency problems is excess inventory, you may choose to sell off some of the inventory before the sale, providing the amount to be retained in the sale is not affected, and you can pay off the account even before the escrow closes.

## Business Disaster Pending

If you are on the verge of a business disaster, you definitely need to retain a business advisor who understands your alternatives for dealing with your business problems. If you are facing some serious business problems and are not sure of your ground, get some good advice as soon as possible.

In analyzing your debt, keep these three basics in mind: communication, consistency, and credibility. More specifically, try to do the following:

- **Maintain communication.** However embarrassing or stressful it is to talk with someone to whom you owe money, that person is entitled to at least the courtesy of your recognition that the debt exists.
- **Create consistency.** It matters less how much you pay on an overdue debt than the fact that you pay something! Send something consistently and you show good faith and extend the patience of your creditor.
- **Don't lose credibility.** Promise to pay what you can and always fulfill your promise. "The check is in the mail" gets stale very quickly. If the

check doesn't arrive as promised, you may not get a second chance—probably when you need it most.

In addition to these generic means of staving off financial disaster, your accountant and attorney should be able to suggest specific steps you can take, depending on your situation.

### Illustration 16-1. Protect Your House and Your Business

Ted Foster bought a business in 2002 and operated it as a sole proprietorship. He paid $50,000 down and signed a purchase money promissory note for the balance of the purchase price. The note required him to pay $3,000 per month for five years and then pay off the balloon balance of $70,000 at that time. He made payments on time until 2003, when the recession got so bad that he fell behind. He still has 12 months of $3,000 payments and then the balloon payment of $70,000. The seller is threatening to take the business back if he continues to be late with his payments.

He has used all his cash, including the money from a second mortgage on his house. The house still has equity in it, but the bank won't lend him any more because the salary he gets from the business is not enough for a larger monthly payment and the business cannot afford to pay him more.

Ted's biggest problem is that he has waited a long time before dealing with the situation. He has fallen behind in the promissory note payments and lost the seller's faith in his ability to recover. He now needs to step back from the day-to-day business details and prioritize the issues he needs to resolve.

First, Ted needs to deal with the balloon balance of $70,000. He paid $50,000 down and has been paying $3,000 per month for four years. He obviously has a serious investment in the business and doesn't want to lose it. Further, the business has been successful during most of this time, so the viability of the business, the strength of the industry, and Ted's ability to operate the business are not in question. The balloon balance of $70,000 due in 12 months is a serious concern if the seller refuses to arrange for a new note and a less onerous payment schedule. The fact that Ted is now two months in arrears obviously makes his situation worse. Rescheduling the note to pay the balloon balance on a reasonable monthly schedule is his first priority toward saving his home and his business. He should contact a lawyer or an accountant immediately, preferably whoever worked on the sale.

Next, because Ted's house still has equity, he should protect it from the creditors who may bring lawsuits against him. It's probably the asset they would find most convenient to attack if they get a judgment from the court.

If, like the business owner in Illustration 16-1, you are concerned about protecting your home from creditors, you should know that you have some protection. Most states have a protective device called a *homestead act*. It allows you to protect a certain amount of the equity you have in the residential property in which you live. In one state, for example, you can protect only $7,500; in another, you can protect all the equity, regardless of amount. Some states have different protections for individuals and for married couples. In California, for example, the protection amounts to $250,000 for a single person and $500,000 for a married couple. Check with a competent lawyer in your state to find out just how much of your equity you can protect. Once you've taken action to protect your home, you can devote your attention to protecting your business.

## The Bankruptcy Alternative

Many sellers think that if their business has financial problems so severe that they need to declare bankruptcy, they have lost everything. Bankruptcy does not have to mean the end for all entrepreneurs. Some types of bankruptcies allow you to sell your business in pieces. Chapter 17 describes the circumstances under which a buyer may purchase a bankrupt business from the trustee in bankruptcy. A seller can continue to operate his or her business after the bankruptcy or resurrect parts of the business that still have value and start over.

For example, one entrepreneur in trouble found that he had no alternative but to file a Chapter 7 bankruptcy. In due course, a trustee in bankruptcy was appointed and took over all the assets to be sold for the benefit of the creditors. Among those assets was the customer list, which was technically the property of the trustee, but the trustee found it difficult to find a buyer who thought that it had any intrinsic value. However, the personal relationships of the business owner allowed him to start up his business immediately following the bankruptcy. All of the customers who had learned to trust him over the years didn't allow the bankruptcy to be a barrier; they started doing business with him again. It wasn't long before he opened another shop and started building the new business based on the start he got from his old customers.

No one is going to put you in jail or ask that your firstborn be sold just because you can't pay your bills. Declaring bankruptcy is embarrassing and can be a major setback to achieving your business goals, but if it is your reality, then you must reckon with it. You will do the best you can within the parameters of your financial strength, your available personnel, your creativity, and your energies. But it just might not be enough. Some people want to blame market conditions, unfair competition, or the franchisor. Some blame themselves. What difference does it make? All that really matters is that you need to face your problems and deal with them.

If there is a business solution to your business problems, certainly you will take it. If you can sell the business (even without a profit) and get out of trouble, you will sell it. If this type of solution is not possible, then you must consider the alternatives. In any case, consult a good bankruptcy lawyer for all the details.

Remember these two very important things if you are contemplating protection under the bankruptcy laws:

- Certain tax obligations as well as some personal debts don't get wiped out in any bankruptcy.
- If you are filing as a corporate entity, any personal guaranties or joint and several obligations leave you vulnerable to your corporate creditors. They do not get wiped out in the corporate bankruptcy proceeding. The only way to eliminate these is by filing a personal bankruptcy.

If you are thinking about bankruptcy, think of all the ramifications. Speak to your attorney, particularly in the wake of the Bankruptcy Abuse Prevention and Consumer Protection Act of 2005. Despite its "protective" title, the new bankruptcy act has more onerous filing requirements that make it harder for individuals to start again with a clean slate.

Finally, if you are contemplating the possibility of bankruptcy, be very careful about how you use the word in conversation with your creditors. Don't be arrogant. Bankruptcy is a delicate matter: even with the protection the bankruptcy acts provide, you want to handle your creditors carefully.

In your presentation to your creditors, you must be prepared to answer their questions candidly and accurately and understand exactly how the bankruptcy act works. You don't have to become a lawyer or an expert, but if you expect your creditors to pay attention to any entreaties you make regarding a bankruptcy solution, you must understand what it will do for you and for your creditors. You must be prepared mentally and emotionally to file bankruptcy, if it becomes appropriate. If your creditors are not convinced that you are ready to take whatever steps are necessary to secure your future, they will not change their positions. If you are not willing to do whatever it takes, this empty threat may well destroy your ability to use other options.

## A Chapter 7 Bankruptcy

The worst possible bankruptcy scenario is a Chapter 7 liquidation. Under a Chapter 7, all the money and property you own and all the obligations you owe are immediately transferred to a trustee in bankruptcy. The trustee's responsibility is to expeditiously convert your assets to cash and distribute the proceeds (after paying the costs and expenses of the bankruptcy) to the creditors in a pro rata manner, with some deference to the creditor status (secured or unsecured).

Once you have filed, the matter is taken out of your hands and you have no influence with respect to how creditors are paid. In fact, a bankruptcy precludes you from making any payments to old creditors, family, and friends in a preferential fashion. However, you have the prerogative of rehabilitating any debts that you choose to take on personally. You might want or need to do this if you intend to stay in business under a new name, since you may need to continue dealing with some of your creditors. Keep in mind, however, that you can file for bankruptcy only every seven years. If you take on too much debt, you may not only lose the advantage of the bankruptcy, but also create a similar financial disaster and not be able to file for bankruptcy again.

Certainly, the language of the bankruptcy act contains some intricacies, but that is basically all that is involved. You can protect certain things from the trustee, like a portion of the equity in your home. And certain obligations are not wiped out, such as certain taxes. Finally, any money that you earn after filing for bankruptcy is not subject to any of your old obligations, with certain exceptions, like the taxes.

You may find it difficult to see the benefit of this approach. Even though you eliminate your liabilities, you also lose all your assets, except for the equity in your home. But losing all your assets in bankruptcy does not have to be debilitating. If you have the kind of business that depends on customer relationships, you may be able to resurrect your business contacts in a matter of minutes after filing the bankruptcy petition and none of your future earnings or assets are in jeopardy from former creditors. The trustee in bankruptcy technically owns the names of your customers, but, as noted earlier, if the relationship is personal, then no one can take that selling advantage away from you. Having the ability to resurrect your business via customer contacts is not a good reason to file the Chapter 7 petition; it is merely a way to pick up some of the pieces if filing becomes inevitable. A good lawyer or business consultant can help you orchestrate this new beginning if you find yourself trapped in this position.

If you understand how bankruptcy works and can explain it to your more belligerent creditors, you may convince them that another alternative would be better for them. If the trustee is obliged to sell your assets quickly, he or she would get considerably less than market value for them. A forced sale always brings bargain prices. The proceeds that creditors would be sharing might be as little as 10 percent of the true value of your assets. Most creditors don't even want to go through the paperwork for so little. If, on the other hand, you can convince your creditors that the business is strong and viable and that, with a little more time, they will get much more than they would in a Chapter 7 liquidation, possibly even 100 percent of what you owe them, they may allow you some breathing space.

## A Chapter 11 Bankruptcy

Before you decide to file a Chapter 7 petition, you must examine the Chapter 11 reorganization. Some people consider the Chapter 11 a much better alternative than the Chapter 7. The positive aspects of the comparison are certainly encouraging.

The Chapter 11 allows you to remain the "debtor in possession." In other words, you may continue to operate the business exactly as you did before filing the Chapter 11 petition—with one difference! After filing the petition and during the entire bankruptcy period, you are entitled to many kinds of relief, as with any bankruptcy filing. For example, no one can bring a lawsuit against you for any reason, all lawsuits that have been brought against you must immediately stop, and no one is entitled to harass you for any obligation incurred prior to the filing of the petition.

To take advantage of the Chapter 11 reorganization, you must qualify. This qualification entails proving to the court that the business has sufficient revenue (cash flow) to pay all business maintenance costs and to pay at least part of the outstanding stale debt in a reasonable time. If you can't show this, the court and your creditors will see no reason for the business to continue. A Chapter 7 liquidation will be the more likely course.

If you can qualify, the court grants you some time (usually about 90 days) within which to formulate and present a plan to the court explaining how the business can continue to operate, pay all its current bills, and pay its old creditors. You may be able to pay your creditors 100 percent of what you owe or you may be able to offer only a percentage of what you owe.

You may ask at this point, "If I haven't been able to pay my old debts before filing the Chapter 11 petition, why should I expect to be able to pay them after filing?" Chapter 11 reorganization means just that—permission to reorganize and restructure your business.

Let's take as an example a business owner with a lease for premises that are too large and too expensive and with leased equipment that the business really doesn't need. These leases are called *executory contracts*—contracts with certain aspects yet to be performed. (Another example of an executory contract is a franchise.) A person filing any kind of bankruptcy has the right to reject an executory contract. If the owner was paying $5,000 a month on her old lease and could reject it and obtain a new lease for only $2,000 a month, she could free up $3,000 a month toward paying off her old obligations. If she was paying $5,000 per month on the two pieces of equipment that she didn't want or need, she could reject the lease and free up $5,000 toward paying off her old obligations. The business could continue, she would meet her current obligations, and she would now have an additional $8,000 per month for her old obligations.

If you can free up any money by rejecting executory contracts, you can present a plan to the bankruptcy court showing how you will use that money to pay old obligations. As long as the creditors would receive more money from a Chapter 11 reorganization than they would from a Chapter 7 liquidation, the court will likely approve your plan.

The people whose executory contracts you reject (in our example, the lease for the premises and the leases on the equipment) are not left without recourse. However, their recourse is only through the bankruptcy court, where the balance of their obligations is put in with the obligations of the other creditors. They may receive proportionately more than some of the other creditors, but the amount of money you pay on your plan each month will remain the same. Meanwhile, you can essentially get out of the leases, and when you follow the plan to completion in about five years, you will have eliminated all those obligations. The five-year period is somewhat arbitrary and will depend on the circumstances of the bankruptcy, including the nature and strength of the business and the attitude of the court and creditors. The courts are not eager to monitor these plans over an extended period. They usually allow only a reasonable payout period; nationwide, courts do not look favorably on periods longer than five years.

The bottom line is that you would be able to eliminate some debts and free up some cash monthly with which you could pay creditors on old bills. The court would reschedule your old obligations to fall within the plan presented by your counsel.

## A Chapter 13 Bankruptcy

The last possibility is a Chapter 13, originally referred to as a wage earner's plan. It has been expanded to include entrepreneurs, but business owners qualify only if they operate their business as a sole proprietorship, not a corporation.

Qualification for a Chapter 13 is different from qualification for a Chapter 11. You must owe no more than $307,675 in unsecured debt and no more than $922,975 in secured debt. The reason for the larger figure for secured debt is that the legislators recognized that many entrepreneurs own their homes. These homes are secured by mortgages (trust deeds) to banks. (Check with your local counsel to see if new legislation or case law has altered any of these figures.)

You must show that your business is viable and that it can support your family and pay old obligations. If you can show these things, then you may be able to take advantage of this approach.

Chapter 13 is the same as Chapter 11 in that you continue to operate the business after filing the petition just as you did before filing. You have available the relief against lawsuits and harassment, the homestead act protection, and the prerogative to accept or reject executory contracts. Chapter 13 is different from Chapter 11 in that you pay all your *excess* cash to a trustee, who deducts 10 percent for fees and costs and remits the balance to your creditors. Chapter 13 is a less expensive bankruptcy in terms of filing fees and attorney involvement. Also, the time allowed by the court to finalize your bankruptcy is somewhat shorter than under Chapter 11; courts are more inclined to allow about three years. At the end of that period, just as with the Chapter 11, you will be free from your old debts.

## Bankruptcy: The Bottom Line

Bankruptcy has a negative impact on your life: you must recognize this before you decide to go forward with it. A financial housecleaning is preferable to bankruptcy. However, if your creditors are not willing to give you that opportunity, you may have no alternative but to seek protection under the bankruptcy act.

A bankruptcy is embarrassing. Much of the feeling about bankruptcy depends on the national economy. In difficult times, all businesspeople recognize the need for a new beginning. In prosperous times, many businesspeople are much less apt to be sympathetic. Because you will consider filing a bankruptcy petition only when it is absolutely necessary, the embarrassment will normally not occupy a high priority in your thinking.

A bankruptcy affects your credit and it stays on your credit report for years. Even though you are not allowed to file a bankruptcy again for seven years, many people will not be eager to extend you credit immediately after a filing. Many of your business vendors may not be eager to extend you credit until you prove the stability of your business.

However, understanding the legal remedies can be a springboard to settlements that do not require legal recourse.

For example, assume that you have $500,000 in old debt. Assume further that you have assets, apart from the equity in your home, that have a market value of about $100,000. If you filed for Chapter 7 bankruptcy, a trustee would sell these assets for $50,000, optimistically. Your creditors would, therefore, get about $0.10 on the dollar. If you filed for Chapter 11 or Chapter 13 bankruptcy, you could reject executory contracts to free up $8,000 and you could present a plan to make payments over five years, less the bankruptcy expenses, to pay back approximately $375,000 of the $500,000 owed. If you settle with your creditors out of court, you can avoid the legal expenses and possibly pay the entire amount you owe them.

Thus, you can make the following presentation to your creditors, plugging in the figures you calculate:

- If you file a Chapter 7, the creditors will probably get $X.
- If you file a Chapter 11 or a Chapter 13, the creditors will probably get $Y.
- If you work out an informal plan outside the bankruptcy court, the creditors will get the entire amount you owe or at least a substantial portion of it.

You can work out a nonjudicial plan with the creditors that may not take

90-120 days to be accepted by the court, will not be subject to the expenses of lawyers and accountants, and will make the full amount available for distribution to creditors.

To prove to your creditors that you are completely serious about these alternatives, you will probably have to prepare financial paperwork for them to review. It will be very similar to the information you would have to prepare for the bankruptcy court. In other words, you will be naked before your creditors just as you would be before the court; therefore, you must be prepared to file the bankruptcy petition once you allow yourself to be this vulnerable to your creditors.

Creditors are much more willing to cooperate with a debtor who has been communicative and cooperative during the normal business relationship. It is always a good idea to stay friendly with the people to whom you owe money. Don't be guilty of trying to hide from them because the confrontation is distasteful or embarrassing. It will not help your situation later, when you may need their help the most. Creditors are always willing to give up a portion of the monies owed them when they know they could lose it all and they will always accept some cash as a good-faith introduction to a repayment plan, even if they will be losing part of their debt in the long run.

> The only caution here is that any payments made on old debt within 90 days of a bankruptcy filing can be "called back" by the bankruptcy court. In some cases, where family is involved, this time frame can be extended by the court.

## Key Points to Remember

- Different levels of business problems require different approaches to solve them. The least problematic may require simply good judgment. The most problematic may require a good bankruptcy lawyer.
- If you're considering serious measures, make sure your business problems are serious enough to require them.
- Examine your business problems carefully to see if they can be solved internally.

- Find out if your problems are specific to your business or general in the industry. They may require an entirely different solution if they are industry-wide.
- Know the differences among the types of bankruptcy protections—Chapter 7, Chapter 11, and Chapter 13. The outcomes for you and your family as well as the costs can differ dramatically.

# CHAPTER 17

# Negotiating the Sale of a Troubled Business

### Illustration 17-1. The Toy Shop

Allison and Marvin Beyer had operated a retail shop selling toys and games. The products included items for all ages, so the location needed to be in a high-traffic area. Unfortunately, instead of choosing to pay the higher rent on Main Street, they decided to save some dollars and picked a location on a side street. Even though the storefront was only 50 feet from Main Street, it was out of the pedestrian flow of the central part of town. Although the business got off the ground, the old debts that had accumulated in the early days kept swallowing up the profit. Allison and Marvin decided to close the shop.

During the five years they had been in business, they had accumulated a bunch of debts but also a pretty good and pretty loyal customer base. They didn't know what to do and were considering filing bankruptcy to get out from under the debt structure.

They went to a business consultant for advice and were very surprised at his suggestion.

It is interesting that many entrepreneurs think that their old debt is part of the selling package of their business. After all, if they can't make any profit because they were constantly paying off old debt, why should anyone else be interested in acquiring their business? This just isn't the case.

When a bankruptcy court is deciding the viability of a business, it doesn't consider "old debt." It is interested in whether the operating expenses against revenues will leave the business with a profit.

This is the way an owner should examine the salability of his or her business. Remember that when a buyer acquires a business, he or she is not going to take over old debt. Just as the cash earned belongs to the seller, it is also the seller's obligation to handle old debts. The buyer takes the business free from these debts; otherwise, the debts are a deduction against the purchase price.

Allison and Marvin put their business up for sale and got a good price. The down payment was used to take care of the old debts and they were no longer facing bankruptcy. In fact, after they paid their debts, Allison and Marvin had a nice nest egg to move to their next adventure.

## Preparing a Business for Sale

Part Three has discussed how to prepare a business for sale, what information the buyer will want, and how to determine an asking price and defend it during the sales presentation. However, rarely does a sales negotiation go smoothly. Many issues will arise for which you will feel unprepared.

This chapter will give you some more specifics about what to expect during the negotiations, what some of your legal responsibilities are during the negotiations, and how to negotiate the problem areas of your business without losing the sale. It will also explain how to posture the sale of a business that is in serious financial difficulty or has no profit at all.

## What a New Owner Offers a Troubled Business

Many businesses are offered for sale that show stability, vitality, and exciting prospects for the future. More often than not, however, a business is for sale because it's something less than successful. The problems may vary from lack of working capital to inexperienced personnel to obsolete equipment. Chapter 16 helped you to pinpoint potential problems, analyze them, and decide which alternative solutions might prove most effective. Depending on the severity of your business problems, you may want to have a professional adviser analyze your situation.

Selling a business is often one of the more practical solutions to a business problem. Many people don't seem able to understand why a business that is not performing adequately for the current owner would necessarily perform any better for another owner. This question has many answers, the simplest of which is that a business needs financial blood flowing through its veins and creative energy to constantly uplift and upgrade its levels of expectation. Someone who has owned a business for a long time may have lost much of this needed energy. A business owner can get tired of trying to match the competition with new and exciting advertising campaigns. An owner may not have the capital necessary for a new storefront, new equipment, or a whole new concept of inventory.

A new owner brings many things to the table—money, energy, initiative, creativity, and more. If you are considering selling your business, you should not take this personally. It may simply be your time to sell or even retire. Your business needs a new leader, a new manager, a new player.

If you are a seller in this situation, turn to Chapter 16 and read or reread the steps that will help put the best face on your ailing business. Because the basis for this book's valuation method is operating profit, you will have a hard time applying that method to a business with little or no operating profit.

For example, the profit and loss statement (Figure 17-1) shows a shop with annual gross revenue of approximately $220,000. Unfortunately, it has product costs of almost 34 percent and labor costs of 41 percent. Fixed expenses take an additional 22 percent. As a result, the operating profit shrinks to 3 percent—$7,173 per year! Based on a ten-year note at 10 percent (which gives the seller the maximum asking price), the owner of this shop would be hard-pressed to substantiate a price of $45,000.

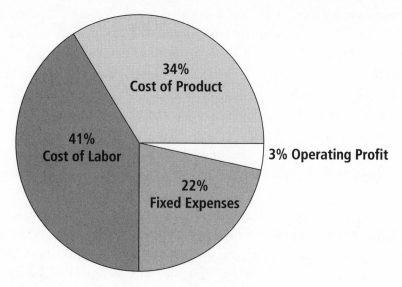

|  | Year to Date | % |
|---|---|---|
| **Sales** | | |
| Printing | $102,090 | 46.24% |
| Bindery | $13,056 | 5.91% |
| Copier | $7,389 | 3.35% |
| Other | $38,547 | 17.46% |
| Kodak | $59,709 | 27.04% |
| **Total Sales** | **$220,791** | **100.00%** |
| **Cost of Sales** | | |
| Paper | $14,544 | 6.59% |
| Subcontracts | $30,564 | 13.85% |

**Figure 17-1.** Sample income statement for a shop operated with poor percentages (continued on the next page)

|  | Year to Date | % |
|---|---|---|
| **Cost of Sales** | | |
| Supplies | $7,746 | 3.51% |
| Equipment Rental | $3,156 | 1.43% |
| Kodak Paper and Maintenance | $18,538 | 33.76% |
| **Total Cost of Sales** | **$74,538** | **33.76%** |

Product costs take 34% of total sales.

| **Gross Profit** | **$146,253** | **66.24%** |
|---|---|---|

| **Operating Expenses** | | |
|---|---|---|
| Salaries | $79,335 | 35.93% |
| Payroll Taxes | $7,386 | 3.35% |
| Employee Benefits | $3,000 | 1.36% |

Labor costs take 41% of total sales.

| Office Supplies | $426 | 0.19% |
|---|---|---|
| Postage/Freight | $1,386 | 0.63% |
| Advertising/Promotion | $4,107 | 1.86% |
| Auto Expense | $4,470 | 2.02% |
| Rent | $16,326 | 7.39% |
| Telephone/Utilities | $2,604 | 1.18% |

Fixed expenses take 22% of total sales.

| Outside Services | $1,164 | 0.47% |
|---|---|---|
| Insurance | $1,038 | 0.46% |
| Royalties | $16,824 | 7.62% |
| **Total Operating Expenses** | **$139,080** | **62.99%** |

| **Total Operating Profit** | **$7,173** | **3.25%** |
|---|---|---|

Only 3% remains as operating profit.

**Figure 17-1.** Sample income statement for a shop operated with poor percentages (continued)

If you are selling a business in similar straits, you have some work to do. Again, Chapters 13 and 16 have discussed how quickly a percentage point can drop to the bottom line, elevating your potential asking price. Examine your P&L closely and determine where you can make the most effective changes.

However, as you begin this process, you may also want to think about how you will explain in a sales presentation your business problems, the changes you have made, and the changes a new owner can make. The danger in this kind of explanation is that the buyer will probably ask, "Why haven't you made all these changes yourself before putting the business up for sale?" But the answer, of course, lies in the very reasons for the sale—not enough money, not enough energy, not enough personnel.

## Your Legal Obligation to Disclose
### Mandatory Material Disclosures

The first thing you need to consider in selling any business, particularly a business with serious financial problems, is what disclosures you will make.

If the matter under consideration is a material fact—a fact that is significant to the business—then disclosure is mandatory. Telling someone an untruth about a material fact is a disclosure problem—it is very simply a lie. Hiding a material fact is also a disclosure problem.

If the matter is a nonmaterial fact, you may need to decide if it is important enough to discuss at all. If some tiles in a bathroom are coming loose, it's probably not material. On the other hand, if you know that it's because the plumbing is bad, that would be a material fact requiring disclosure.

If you decide that a matter is significant, the next decision is how to make the disclosure. If you make the disclosure correctly, it becomes a basis for further discussion. If you reveal the information badly, you could end the negotiations.

In all cases, ask yourself the question, "If I don't tell the buyer about this, could the backlash cause the sale to fall through or cause the buyer to withhold payments or start a lawsuit after buying the business?" The answer to this question will lead you pretty quickly to the material disclosures.

## Mutual Trust Ensures Payment

If the buyer is going to pay you the purchase price of the business over time, you also want to ask yourself another question: "If I don't tell the buyer about this problem, will he or she wonder what other things I've failed to disclose?" If you fail to create a relationship of trust with the buyer, you will always wonder how secure the payments are on your purchase money promissory note.

For example, perhaps you purchased equipment on time at a bad price or on a bad payment schedule. If the equipment is not state-of-the-art or not appropriate to the purpose for which you bought it, your disclosure might cause the buyer to break off negotiations or, at the very least, insist on a serious adjustment in the price of the business. Failing to make this kind of disclosure before the sale could lead to a lawsuit later. On the other hand, if the equipment is serviceable and state-of-the-art, a bad price or a bad payment schedule will likely lead to a minor dollar adjustment in the figures at the negotiating table.

Another disclosure you may have to consider making is about any large delinquencies that cause payments to exceed income. However, while this may be material with regard to your operating profit, it should not affect the buyer. If you pay these delinquencies out of the purchase price, they will not affect the buyer in any way. This is not a disclosure problem because the delinquencies are is not material to the buyer.

However, an excessive equipment rental or a rent increase on the premises could be disastrous: it definitely constitutes a material fact. You must disclose such things to the buyer because they could go to the very essence of the business, its ability to survive and meet its obligations.

In some cases, the law says, "Buyer beware"—buyers are responsible for finding out certain matters for themselves. It is always the buyer's obligation to diligently examine the business and make his or her own judgment as to its viability in all respects. The buyer should consult with his or her professional advisors early in the buying process for this reason.

On the other hand, there has been much legislation—franchise legislation, for example—that requires the seller to completely disclose all material facts before selling a business to an individual. A seller's failure to disclose can allow the buyer to later rescind or call back the contract.

When specific legislation is not involved, common law dictates that the average buyer should be protected at least from fraud and misrepresentation. What happens in situations that are just short of fraud and misrepresentation is anybody's guess. It will depend in each case on the particular facts, the sophistication of the buyer, the intent of the seller, and the attitude of the court.

## At the Negotiating Table

Successful negotiation requires timing, posturing, and expectation adjustment. When you negotiate the sale of a troubled business, the timing of certain disclosures and your overall negotiating posture take on even greater importance.

## Posturing

For your first meeting with a potential buyer, you need to decide, for posturing purposes, whether you want to have your partner, spouse, attorney, or accountant present. You may find the first meeting easier if you meet with the buyer alone. Meeting alone allows you to do the following:

- Ask questions and offer responses that might not be appropriate if someone else were with you—perhaps items of a more personal nature.
- Assess what approach might work best with the prospect. This might be much more difficult if others are at the same meeting and the prospect is on guard.
- Tell the prospect, "I can't really make any decisions without consulting my _____ (spouse/partner/lawyer/accountant/banker)." This is a good way out of many embarrassing situations.

On the other hand, a spouse or partner will be able to complement the perspective you bring to the table. He or she can share the responsibility of asking the right questions and will surely be able to give you a slightly different reading of the person or people on the other side of the table.

Having a professional at the table with you has obvious advantages. A professional advisor will likely have negotiated business deals before and can help you elicit the basic information you need to make your decision. Your professional can recognize certain peculiarities or anomalies in the prospect's presentation that a less experienced listener might miss. The question of which posture to adopt will depend on the kind of negotiating in which you expect to engage, the strength or weakness of your presentation, the length of time you expect to devote to the project, and the gravity of the timing involved.

Using a glass-top table analogy is a good way to illustrate how negotiations between a legitimate potential buyer and a seller should proceed. Everything from both sides ought to be on top of the table; if something is under the table, all parties should be able to see it anyway. In other words, no one should have a secret agenda.

## Timing

Neither a buyer nor a seller wants to disclose information without knowing what kind of response he or she may get.

You would be unwise to tell a prospective buyer, for example, that you have already bought a house in another community. This timing secret would give the buyer some additional bargaining power.

A prospective buyer doesn't want to disclose how much money he or she has available for the purchase until a price is discussed. If you have not yet discussed price, you may end up basing price exclusively on the buyer's financial position rather than on the value of the business. Pricing the business exclusively on the buyer's ability to pay is in his or her favor if the business would otherwise be priced too high. However, it is a serious disadvantage to the buyer if his or her finances can support a price well above the value and the price is therefore inflated.

A prospective buyer is wise to begin negotiations by explaining how much money he or she needs from the business to take care of his or her family. You must then consider the buyer's income needs along with the business's value if you want to sell to that buyer candidate. On the other hand, you could start the discussion with the kind of dollars you need from the business for your plans for retirement, travel, or purchasing a business in the future. Both you and the buyer are forced to examine each other's needs as the negotiations continue and you get to know each other, your professionals, and your families.

If an all-cash deal is possible, this kind of approach has less appeal. After all, it's like buying a used car from a stranger: it is unlikely you will have any concern with what he or she intends to do with the money or the long-term benefit it may have for his or her family.

You need to assess each negotiation as it proceeds to decide what kind of personal involvement may or may not be effective. Your professional, who has experience with negotiations, can help you adopt the most appropriate negotiating posture.

## Have Your Professionals Present

Always be wary of a buyer or a seller who is not represented by an attorney. Having an attorney on your side when negotiating may add the necessary degree of authority and strength to your negotiating posture. While you may sometimes want to begin negotiations without your professionals, most of the time your professional advisors are the most important part of your negotiating team.

Discussing the possible purchase or sale of a business with the appropriate professional will allow you to determine your posture, your timing, and ultimately the success of your negotiations. Professional advisors will help you make an effective sales presentation, interpret the offer you are given, and determine the questions to ask to make a knowledgeable decision. Working out a deal without an attorney can be a very risky endeavor. Take, for example, the story in Illustration 17-2.

---

### Illustration 17-2. Larceny in His Heart

In the recent sale of a hardware store, the buyer and the seller chose not to work with attorneys. Later, the buyer, Jake Thompson, felt the seller had misled him during sale negotiations. He began to threaten the seller during the repayment period and wrote him the following letter.

"I can't believe how you led me down the garden path and right into the cemetery. I am shocked at the debts people are trying to collect from me. You told me you would take care of all the debts from the down payment I made. Why did you lie to me? You told me your manager would be delighted to stay with me until I could learn the business for myself. He tells me that he has a job in Michigan and that you

---

knew this all the time. If you think I'm going to pay you any more money, think again. I'm going to use the money I owe you to sue you, and I'm not going to stop until everyone knows just what kind of person you are."

Both Jake and the seller thought that because the business was relatively small, they didn't need to spend the money on lawyers. It just shows how badly these situations can become when both parties are left to their own devices. In this case, the seller had a little larceny in his heart and Jake didn't know how to protect his investment.

## Bankruptcy as a Selling Posture

One of the last items you should reflect on is the possibility of using the Bankruptcy Act to posture the business for sale. If you are getting ready to sell a business that has serious financial problems and your creditors will not work with you out of court, declaring bankruptcy may be your best alternative. If the business, apart from the current financial problems, is good, you can find buyers who would be happy to buy it from a trustee in bankruptcy as part of a Chapter 7 liquidation. The trustee, whose charge is to convert the assets to cash as quickly as possible, would obviously be delighted to have a buyer waiting for it. And you, as the debtor in bankruptcy, may be retained as a consultant to the buyer.

Remember: any money you earn after filing the Chapter 7 bankruptcy petition is not subject to the debts involved in the bankruptcy. Chapter 11 and Chapter 13 provide similar protection. You can sell the business under the auspices of the bankruptcy court and the buyer takes over the business without the old obligations. The normal bankruptcy scenario would merely close the door on any dollar benefit direct to the bankrupt owner from the bankruptcy itself. However, once again, a consulting contract is not out of the question. It's one way a seller can enjoy a piece of the business's future after a bankruptcy.

## Selling Your Customer Volume

When selling a business that shows little or no operating profit, you can still promote a positive aspect of your business to potential buyers. As long as your business has customers coming through the door, it has a value. To start a business from scratch usually takes time and working capital. The cost of this time can be very high, depending on the style in which the entrepreneur is used to living. You can, therefore, argue that selling a business even showing no profit means selling customer volume. The value of your customers should be the basis of your thinking and negotiating. If the business is showing no profit, the buyer is still purchasing customer volume, which has a monetary value.

In the face of great frustrations, closing the door and walking away may seem like the easiest path to take, but leaving a valuable asset on the table is not fair to your family or to yourself for the investment of time and money that you have made, however unsuccessful the venture may have been. Don't lose sight of the fact that you are involved in an important decision for yourself and your family. This kind of decision deserves your best judgment and the most professional advice you can bring to your side of the negotiating table.

## Key Points to Remember

- Sometimes the difference between a successful business and an unsuccessful business is the energy and optimism the owner brings to the front door every day.
- If you sell a debt-ridden business, you will pay old debts from the purchase price and present the business to the new owner free of its most onerous financial obligations. The new owner will have a head start toward success.
- Make all disclosures to your buyer that are material to the stability and success of the business. Anything less than full material disclosure can lead to a lawsuit after the sale and the buyer may be unable or unwilling to pay your promissory note.
- Professional business consultants and advisors have experience with all levels of business problems. Take advantage of their experience.
- You can posture a troubled business for sale in many ways, including putting it into bankruptcy. A trustee in bankruptcy is always eager to sell a business expeditiously.

# CHAPTER 18

# How to Value and Sell a Professional Practice

## Professional Practice Is Unique

The professional practice is unique because the relationship between the entrepreneur and his or her clients or patients (customers) is predicated primarily on loyalty. This loyalty has been created and fostered through time as each develops trust and confidence in the other. Transferring this loyalty from the seller to the buyer is the problem that needs to be accommodated in each case.

But don't be thinking that professional practices are limited to doctors and lawyers. Consider the following list of examples of the broad spectrum of people that this definition of "professional"

> encompasses: massage therapists, personal chefs, business consultants, personal trainers, veterinarians, insurance brokers, investment counselors, teachers, and accountants, to name only a few.

While this chapter specifically discusses the sale of a professional practice, any seller can benefit from reading how to develop a price structure for a business that has some unique concerns—like a professional practice. The pricing chart used in this chapter to develop the price of a law practice will give you some idea of the effect of a down payment and a transition period as discount factors on an ultimate selling price. The more difficult problem of a practice dependent in great part on referrals from other professionals is examined in the story of the orthodontist, later in this chapter. The formula designed to handle this problem can obviously be used for other businesses, such as physical therapy, neurosurgical, or periodontal practices, where referrals are a primary source of business.

The answer must involve the resolution of two basic issues:

- Degradation of the practice because of the difficulty in transferring loyalty
- A transition period intended to minimize the negative impact of the transfer

Certainly, the loss of clients cannot be prevented. Some clients will already have a second choice lined up, whether it is a relative, a friend, or merely another professional. It is clear from experience that the longer the transition period—the period of time that the seller stays with the practice during or after the sale—the more successful the transition is likely to be.

One suggestion that has proven fruitful, although somewhat deceptive to the clients, is the development of a partnership arrangement where both buyer and seller acknowledge at the outset that the arrangement will be consummated at a certain time, a target date, and based on a particular dollar amount, a valuation given to the practice. The parties either agree to the dollar value at the beginning of the partnership or predicate it on a formula that might relate to that portion of the practice surviving the transition period. In some cases, the parties use a more complex combination of these aspects.

Most business buyers look for a business that suits their temperament, their experience, and their innate abilities. Professionals make the decision to buy a business by virtue of their education. With a law degree, one does not practice medicine; with a medical degree, one does not become a certified public accountant. In turn, the seller of a professional practice has a limited pool of buyers from which to draw. A lawyer cannot sell to a medical doctor. An accountant cannot sell to a juris doctor.

Preference and capability still play a part in a professional's decision to buy a practice. An accountant who handles primarily tax work for small businesses is not going to be interested in buying an accounting practice that deals primarily with securities work. A research scientist will not, in all probability, be interested in buying the practice of a plastic surgeon. It is equally unlikely that a trial lawyer would be interested in taking over a law practice that prepares wills and files probates.

Geography also influences the pool of buyers. Since all practices are essentially local, the buyer must consider the climate and community in which a practice is located. Even when state boards, licenses, and other requirements preclude the movement of professionals from state to state, climate will still be a consideration (except for the smaller states like Rhode Island). Choosing between a big city and a small suburban community is also a significant consideration. To some, the ethnicity of a particular area may be important.

## Special Concerns for Transfer of Ownership

The kind of relationship that is established between a psychiatrist and his or her patient is not one that can easily be transferred. Similarly, a client who has disclosed all his or her personal information to an accountant or lawyer may not want to make the same revelations to a stranger.

If you are selling a professional practice, you need to be prepared, to a greater extent than in the average business transfer, to introduce the buyer to your clients or patients. You need to overcome the unfamiliarity of the new owner and infuse an element of confidence into the new relationship. You cannot rush this process.

The client or patient also has the prerogative to take his or her business to another professional. Clients often take their business elsewhere when their long-time professional sells or retires. On the other hand, in the professional world, patients or clients also have some fear about looking for a new doctor, lawyer, or accountant. As a result, most people are willing to try the new owner if he or she receives a satisfactory endorsement from the former owner on whose advice, presumably, the client or patient has learned to depend.

Still, it is in the nature of this professional relationship that clients make many personal disclosures that have nothing at all to do with the specialty of the practice. Patients, for example, will often speak of their personal or business problems with their doctor, their medical problems with their accountant, and their tax problems with their lawyer. A connection develops that is very difficult to transfer to a stranger.

The best you can hope to do is present the buyer to your clients or patients as a consummate professional who has the appropriate education and experience. The process of introducing the buyer should, indeed, be a marketing program of the highest standards. As with any type of business sale, this advertising-marketing strategy is as important to the seller as it is to the buyer.

The continuity of the client base may not be as sustainable as it might be in a more conventional type of small business. The ability of the buyer of a professional practice to retain its clients depends in great part on the seller's willingness to devote the time and energy necessary for proper introductions.

## The Partnership Period

Most sales of conventional businesses contain an arrangement for the seller to stay with the business for some period after the buyer takes over. This transition period is sometimes referred to as the *partnership period*. During this somewhat delicate transition period, your buyer learns the idiosyncrasies of customers and employees with your help. You may want to do the following:

- Train the new owner on equipment or computer programs.
- Introduce the new owner to certain customers or accounts of particular size or merit.
- Create a continuity or comfort zone for employees.

The seller may stay on for days or months. In some cases, the seller includes this accommodation in the purchase price. In others, the seller receives compensation during this period.

In the sale of a conventional business, the partnership arrangement is a financing option. The sale of a professional practice is somewhat different. Buyers are frequently taken on as partners with the opportunity to buy out the seller after a certain length of time. The buyout could be based either on a predetermined price or on a formula to which both parties agree in the contract of partnership.

A transition partnership has an obvious advantage to the buyer. It allows the buyer to become familiar with clients or patients under the seller's actual sponsorship. The buyer can build a rapport with each client or patient.

Some might say that a partnership period is deceptive to the clients or patients, because the seller is not going to be a partner for an extended period: the partnership is intended exclusively to consummate the sale. Whether this is a deception depends in great part on exactly how it is handled. The best approach is for you, the seller, to disclose your imminent departure to your patients or clients during the transition period.

## Degradation of the Practice

No matter how successful the marketing strategy, your practice will likely experience a loss of clients or patients, a degradation of the practice, during the change in ownership. Many clients or patients will, at the very least, give the new professional a try. If the buyer proves himself or herself at that first meeting, the clients or patients are more likely to remain.

Some clients, however, will leave immediately—some because the changeover gives them an excuse to make a move they were considering, some because there are other professionals in the community with whom they are more familiar. In any case, the practice that the buyer takes over will normally not be as hardy as the one you sell. The likelihood of some kind of degradation of the practice creates a problem determining the purchase price. It is difficult, if not impossible, to assess this degradation before it actually happens.

You may be able to partially assess, during the price negotiations, which clients will stay with the new owner. In some cases, an accountant can retain clients because taxes are due shortly and because the seller has already done much of the work. A lawyer may be in the middle of a trial or final preparation of a business reconstruction. A doctor may have followed a medical problem for a long time to maintain a delicate balance of medication and treatment, not all of which the new professional can absorb merely by going over the former practitioner's notes.

## Structuring the Price

At this point, instead of reading how to prepare a price structure for a professional practice, study and compare the two letters relative to the law practice, located at the end of this chapter, and the story of the orthodontist, appearing within this chapter, to get two entirely different views on the attitudes of two professionals selling for different reasons. The remainder of this section discusses in detail the letters regarding the law practice.

---

January 15, 2008

Harrison Aldrich, Esq.

1200 Manomet Avenue, Suite B

Elmar, CA 92764

PRIVATE AND CONFIDENTIAL

Dear Harry:

Our current order of business is to set a value on your professional practice to posture the business for sale. As I indicated to you at our first meeting, we are going to participate in this project as a team. In order for us to do this, there are certain basics on which we need to agree. One of these is the concept of valuation.

---

**Figure 18-1.** Sample client letter establishing an asking price (continued on next page)

**Owner Compensation and Reconstituting the Profit and Loss Statement**

One of the prerogatives of entrepreneurship is to use the business's profit as owner income. It is very difficult to put a value on a business because this arbitrary salary (owner's compensation) does not allow us to formalize the labor base of the business. The first thing we have to do is decide how much we would have to pay someone who has the necessary qualifications to replace the owner. In our case, because it is a professional position, it is difficult to make a clear assessment. However, considering the nature of the practice, the costs and expenses of living in the general area of Elmar, California, and the number of professionals available in the marketplace, I am prepared to use the figure of $35,000 as an annual income. This size salary is appropriate for someone who would be operating the business. And this salary would be augmented by the "profit" of the business.

Another issue that we must address with some care is the profit and loss statement. We all understand that a P&L prepared for Uncle Sam is not necessarily the P&L we want to prepare for the buying candidate. After all, the IRS allows you to take certain business deductions that are personal choices and that the buyer may or may not include as expenses. In your case, you maintain a small plane that you consider essential to your practice but that another owner might not. In order to have a P&L that properly reflects the costs and expenses of the business, leading us to a realistic profit picture, we must reconstitute the P&L to eliminate those things of a more personal nature, leaving what is necessary and appropriate to the proper operation of the business. In this way, we find that your business with gross revenues of $150,000 and net revenues of $45,000 can legitimately show a net profit of $65,000 without a change in the gross business.

**How to Find the Proper Value**

Because the professional practice may degrade somewhat with a change in ownership, it is reasonable for the buyer to want a return of his or her investment in one to three years, as opposed to five to ten years. The conventional business can support a return of investment over a longer period because the continuity of the business and its customers is more secure.

If we then consider the actual figures of the business, plug in a manager's salary, and reconstitute the P&L, we find a profit of $30,000 per year. If we agree that, due to the

**Figure 18-1.** Sample client letter establishing an asking price (continued on next page)

degradation problem, the business should provide a return on investment in one to three years, we should be looking at a selling price of somewhere between $30,000 and $90,000. The transition period is going to be a key factor, as it would be in any professional practice. How close we come to the higher figure depends on how substantial an argument we can make for the stability of the clientele, the continuity of the business activity, and the length of time you decide to devote to the practice during the transition after the sale. The following will give you an idea as to the differentials depending on both the transition period and the down payment.

***Note:*** *The seller wants as much cash upfront as possible and is willing to make the corresponding adjustments in price to get it.*

| Down Payment | Selling Price Purchase | Money Promissory Note |
|---|---|---|
| No down payment | $120,000 | $120,000 |
| $10,000 | 100,000 | 90,000 |
| 20,000 | 80,000 | 60,000 |
| 30,000 | 60,000 | 30,000 |
| All cash | 40,000 | 0 |

If you include a transition period in the deal, you could increase the selling price by 10 to 30 percent, depending on the length of the period.

Keep in mind, Harry, that there is no magic to these figures. They are figures similar to those I have used in other sales, which I found to be understandable to buyers.

One last issue—the potential buyer I mentioned to you in my earlier correspondence decided against examining your practice any further due to the climate in Elmar. We need to prepare some marketing materials that present the community and climate in the best possible light.

Cordially,

Ira N. Nottonson

**Figure 18-1.** Sample client letter establishing an asking price (concluded)

> ### Amount of Information
> The amount of information in this type of communication depends on the nature of the relationship between client and advisor, the level of sophistication of the client, and the purpose to be served. Too much information to the wrong person can be just as problematic as too little.

You may notice that the concept and details of a purchase money promissory note are absent from the sample client letter establishing an asking price. The seller had already considered a promissory note and a partnership arrangement and had decided against both options.

Harry Aldrich was not interested in a long transition period or a partnership arrangement because he intended to embark on an entirely new career as soon as possible. He was aware that a shorter transition period meant a lower price for the practice. He was also not interested in a payout situation—he wanted an all-cash deal so that he could invest in his next business enterprise—but he recognized that he might have to compromise on this point in exchange for some negotiated payment plan. As you read the letter, you will find many of the elements discussed in this book. Note in particular the possible reduction in selling price in exchange for a larger down payment.

Harry responded to this letter with a pretty good recognition of reality. He had received various figures for the value of his business from various sources. This was the first time he had been given a rationale for any asking price.

His only comment was whether he could ask for more at the outset, even though he recognized the ultimate validity of the valuation concept. The answer is really twofold.

Once you establish an asking price, it is difficult to raise it during the course of negotiations. You should, therefore, ask the highest defensible price. On the other hand, you must be careful not to ask a price that suggests to the potential buyer that you have severely overestimated the value of your business. The buyer may decide that your thinking is so unrealistic that a reasonable negotiation is impossible. Remember that this is not the sale of a house, where substantial negotiating for a better price is often the standard.

## Getting the Project Moving: Selling

Having established the parameters within which the price should be structured, the next order of business was to get the project moving. After some discussion, Harry agreed to prepare a list of potential buyers from the general area whose names and reputations he knew firsthand. These people then received a telephone call from Harry's representative, which allowed Harry to maintain anonymity and avoid injuring his practice during these early discussions. Harry and his attorney established the following as a working scenario.

### Illustration 18-1. A Cold Call Scenario

"Hello, my name is Ira Nottonson. I am a California attorney and part of my practice is dealing with the purchase and sale of businesses.

"I represent an attorney who has an estate planning practice for sale within the general geographical area of Quansot, Elmar, and Haystack. I am not at liberty to disclose the name of my principal or any details about the specific location of the practice. Since we both would like to keep any such communication private, this is a very preliminary inquiry. The only question I would like to ask is whether you would be interested in discussing this matter further with me on a completely confidential basis?"

If the recipient is interested: "I would like to discuss this further, but I would rather discuss it with you when you are home. I'm sure you can understand the delicacy of the matter; I wouldn't want to feel that anyone could intrude on our conversation in any way. I'm sure you feel the same way."

If the recipient is not interested: "Why don't I give you my telephone number in case you have any further thoughts?"

If the recipient presses for some additional information: "The practice has been in place for 17 years and has a stable client base. The excellent reputation of the practitioner will precede you; all you have to do is to enjoy the benefits of another location in your practice, sit down at the desk, and go to work."

If the recipient asks about price: "Price is based on a mutual understanding of value. I believe very logical parameters exist within which the price of a business makes sense to both buyer and seller. If you decide to acquire the practice, you and my client will find a logical price structure that works for both of you."

## Advertising the Practice

After making contact with a half-dozen candidates and finding one who might be interested, albeit not immediately, Harry decided to go forward with the next logical step. He chose the most appropriate print medium and structured an advertisement that would generate interest without risking his anonymity. He decided to use the magazine of the California Bar Association, which would reach all the most obvious and qualified candidates. The buyer would have to be a member of the California Bar Association to buy the practice and maintain it. Harry considered the possibility of reciprocity between states that might allow an out-of-state lawyer to buy the practice, but this kind of candidate would be the exception, not the rule.

The sample client letter to begin advertising the practice discusses the advertisement and is a good example of the step-by-step process Harry and his attorney started to advertise and sell the practice. They also advertised the practice with the placement officers at all the California law schools. They also discussed the possibility that brokers might respond to the ad. They maintained confidentiality by referring any respondents to Harry's advisor. Because Harry was so eager to sell the practice and move on to his new venture, he and his advisor agreed that the commission to a broker would be a good investment should a broker produce a qualified candidate.

March 17, 2008

Harrison Aldrich, Esq.
1200 Manomet Avenue, Suite B
Elmar, CA 92764
PRIVATE AND CONFIDENTIAL

Dear Harry:
There is always an excitement about the prospect of hitting the target with the first shot. However, even though we have a candidate who might turn out to be a buyer, we both agree that it is time to move expeditiously to the next stage of our program.

**Figure 18-2.** Sample client letter to begin advertising the practice (continuedon next page)

Most magazines have a closing date for submitting advertisements that usually precedes publication by many weeks; if we don't make arrangements now for inserting our ad, we may miss the deadline. If the pending candidate decides to buy, we can still consider the advertising dollars as an appropriate investment. The following includes the information necessary to generate responses from serious candidates:

| | |
|---|---|
| ESTATE PLANNING PRACTICE | 24 spaces per line |
| SO. CAL. DESERT COMMUNITY | 25 spaces per line |
| 17 YRS. EXCELLENT REPUTATION. | 29 spaces per line |
| TURNKEY OPERATION: 150K/YR/W/ | 28 spaces per line |
| GROWTH POTENTIAL. SELLER WILL | 29 spaces per line |
| REMAIN FOR TRANSITION. INQUIRIES | 32 spaces per line |
| HANDLED WITH DISCRETION AND | 27 spaces per line |
| CONFIDENTIALITY: 858-555-1212 | 28 spaces per line |

The number of spaces per line will be critical, but they can be worked out only when you get the parameters of the particular print format you will use. Advertising is predicated on size and frequency. Some magazines give you the opportunity to use boxes surrounding the ad or gray or white backgrounds to make the ad stand out. We need the ad to appear over a six-month period to be sure we have properly tapped the readership. Not everyone reads the whole magazine every issue. The last item to consider is the ad itself. Most ads use abbreviations, though using an extra line or longer word can sometimes be very effective. Let me know your thinking.

Cordially,

Ira N. Nottonson

**Figure 18-2.** Sample client letter to begin advertising the practice (continued)

## Closing the Deal

The advertisement worked: it attracted candidates. Harry interviewed them and discussed the price. Professionals representing both parties became involved. Harry sold the business. The buyer is excited at having acquired a jump-start in a new community where he and his family are happy to live. Harry is on his way to his next professional adventure.

The approach taken in this section does not guarantee a successful sale. You need to work out a marketing and advertising scheme with your professionals that will work best for you. You may not be as concerned about anonymity or as opposed to a transition period as the seller in this example. Nevertheless, you can probably find the secret to a successful sale in a line from the first letter included in this chapter: "As I indicated to you at our first meeting, we are going to participate in this project as a team." In this situation, consultant and client combined their efforts for maximum effectiveness.

## Valuation of a Specialty Practice

The next and more complex aspect of a professional practice is where the seller must deliver to the buyer the referrals from other professionals as part of the business. Although many businesses, professional and otherwise, depend on the ability of the buyer to build a relationship with the customers after the seller leaves, the dynamics of the problem are always a question of degree.

Usually, a retail business will maintain the continuity of its customer base so long as the quality, timeliness, and pricing of the service or product are maintained. On the other hand, the neurosurgeon depends, for the great percentage of his or her business, on referrals from primary physicians. It would be quite unusual for a patient to ask to see a neurosurgeon without having been examined by a primary physician first. The appointment would likely be set up by the general practitioner, who would recognize the symptoms requiring the need for a more expert opinion and who would have the experience to recommend a particular surgeon. One the other hand, a plastic surgeon, because of the general acceptance and growing numbers of people seeking cosmetic surgery, may get the great percentage of his or her practice from a good marketing program. The orthodontics practice in the illustration below is between these two extremes, with equal numbers of patient and physician referrals.

**Illustration 18-2. The Referral Problem**

When Don Grimsdale decided to help his son buy an orthodontics practice, he ran across a problem that was more than he was prepared for. It wasn't the first business deal that Don had negotiated. In fact, over the years he had been both a buyer and a seller at different times. So, putting himself in the seller's shoes was not difficult. The problem he faced, however, was one that had not surfaced in his other business deals, which hadn't involved businesses that depended so dramatically on referrals.

Don's son, Alex, was finishing his orthodontics program at the university. Alex had already met Dr. Bronson, the seller. They liked each other and both felt that the sale would be mutually beneficial. When Alex returned to school, he left the negotiating to his dad. Don, fortunately, sought the advice of professionals in order to establish a value for the practice. What was the practice worth, how much should he pay as a down payment, and how should the balance be paid?

With about 50 percent of the business coming through referrals by patients and the other 50 percent coming through referrals by primary physicians, the general practitioner dentists, these are the questions to answer:

- How many of these referrals will the buyer realistically be able to enjoy once the seller leaves the practice and perhaps the city?
- To what extent will the loyalty of referring physicians to the seller transfer to the buyer?
- What will be the deciding factors?
- Can the seller promise to deliver these referrals and to what extent can the buyer expect the seller to fulfill that promise?
- How can this problem be handled in terms of valuing the practice?

The problem with referrals from dentists is that they are usually based on the acknowledged experience of the orthodontist or, more often, the personal relationships between the orthodontist and the referring dentists or both. The new graduate will have neither the reputation nor the relationships.

If the practice is valued at its full potential based on the previous activity of the seller and then the referral expectations go unfulfilled, the buyer may be buying a practice of less value than expected for the price. On the other hand, if the risk of not delivering the level of referrals expected is so great as to dramatically lower the price of the business, the seller may be selling a practice of much greater value than the price would indicate.

Another significant element that must be factored into this complicated equation is the transition period, the period after the sale during which the seller maintains a relationship with the practice to help ensure and stabilize the continuity. In most businesses, this involves introducing the customers and the vendors to the buyer to establish a comfortable relationship. In some instances, it involves establishing a working environment and a familiarity with personnel. In other cases, it involves training the buyer to handle any and all aspects of the business.

In the illustration, Dr. Bronson, as the seller, is also aware of this problem, especially since his former associate and very good friend is the source for a substantial number of referrals. Dr. Bronson knows that, after the sale, many of these referrals will go to other orthodontists in the community instead of to his buyer.

But the seller's problem is equally as serious as the buyer's, especially if the seller is going to carry back a purchase money promissory note for the balance of the purchase price after the down payment. The seller doesn't want the practice to be valued based on such a risk and then find that he or she is expected to deliver more referrals than might have been anticipated.

This dilemma is a good reason to establish a method by which the buyer pays for the referrals he or she gets and the seller receives payment for the referrals he or she delivers.

The seller and the buyer can agree to certain aspects of a sale, aside from the referral problem. In this case, it was agreed that if the practice remained stable—that is, the number of patients coming to the office for their initial conference remained the same, approximately 30 per month, 15 from patient referrals and 15 from dentist referrals—then the value of the business would be $500,000. It was further agreed that the seller had no control over the patient referrals. This part of the practice would likely remain the same or, certainly, would depend on the ability of the buyer—not the seller—to maintain it. Therefore, neither disputed setting a price of at least half the value of the business, or $250,000. This amount was scheduled for payment over a ten-year period at an interest rate of 10 percent. The promissory note representing this $250,000 was payable at $39,646 per year or $3,304 per month.

The question arose as to how to handle the balance of the purchase price, $250,000. If the pattern of 15 referrals per month from dentists represented about $3,000 per month in payments—assuming the second $250,000 was scheduled for payment in the same manner as the first $250,000 of the purchase price—then how much would the buyer owe for a single month when only ten dentist referrals came into the office for their initial conference? They decided that the buyer would pay 10/15 of $3,000 or $2,000 for that month.

## Referrals and the All-Cash Deal

The problem becomes somewhat different if the buyer borrows the money from a third party to buy the business, allowing the seller to receive all cash. This makes any payout extending over a period of time and subject to a formula impractical. In such a case, a good approach would be similar to almost any business sale where there are likely to be payments for which the buyer is responsible but that are attributable to the seller.

To handle this situation, an escrow is set up, so a third party is holding the money. The money is in escrow until a certain time period has elapsed, during which the buyer is able to find out if there are any such liabilities for which he or she may be responsible that the seller incurred before selling the business and did not disclose or for which payment arrangements had not been made, either inadvertently or intentionally.

In the sale of the orthodontist's practice, for example, it may be appropriate, if the seller is receiving all cash for the practice, to set up such an escrow for a period of six months. The escrow agreement can reflect that a portion of the money will be released to the seller, depending on the percentage of referrals that occur during the escrow period. There are many variations on this theme and the parties can presumably agree to some sort of an arrangement that will be fair. After all, if the referrals promised are not delivered, the buyer has no recourse against a seller who has received 100 percent of the purchase price in cash. And the bank will not be interested in the equity or lack of equity involved.

The next section looks at specifics for valuating professional practices and handling the referral problem.

## Patient-Physician Referral Valuation Model

The best way to grasp the valuation process of a professional practice is to start looking at actual numbers. Take a look at the patient-physician referral valuation model (Figure 18-3). This model, which is from the sale of an actual professional practice, shows how the numbers look for different scenarios of referrals delivered. The model is divided into three sections. The first section lists the assumptions. A change in any of these assumptions will, of course, change the entire spectrum of results on the chart.

Here are the assumptions you will need to make for your own model:

- Monthly new patient exams. This will be the method of determining just how many of the anticipated referrals are actually delivered.
- Value of the business. This figure represents the full value without considering the risk factor.
- Patient referral percentage. The critical factor is the remaining percentage from 100 percent, which represents the physician referrals.
- Interest on the note.
- Number of years over which the note will be payable.

The second section of the model contains the scenarios for differing rates of physician referrals delivered. This shows the dollars to which the seller is entitled, based on the number of referrals delivered out of the number that the buyer is entitled to expect: that is, the number that is based on the history of the practice.

The total of new patient exams is approximately 30 per month, 360 per year. The number attributable to physician referrals is 180 per year, 15 per month, 45 per quarter. If the seller delivers 100 percent of the historically expected referrals (HERs), then the seller will be entitled to 100 percent of the dollars that are represented by the physician referral half of the business's value. If the seller delivers only 75 percent of these HERs, then the seller, for that period, will be entitled to only 75 percent of the total revenues attributable to the physician referral half.

**Assumptions**
Current business generates 30 new patient exams (NPE) per month.
Total business value is based on 30 NPE per month.
Portion of price based on patient referrals is a percentage of the total business value.
The down payment represents the portion of the business supported by patient referrals.

Business value: $500,000
Patient referral: 50%
Interest on note: 10%
Years on note: 10

| Scenario | | Qtr 1 | Qtr 2 | Qtr 3 | Qtr 4 | Qtr 5 | Qtr 6 | Qtr 7 | Qtr 8 | Remaining Payments | Grand Total |
|---|---|---|---|---|---|---|---|---|---|---|---|
| 1. Physician Referrals | (100%) 180/yr Payment | 45 $9,959 | 45 $9,959 | 45 $9,959 | 45 $9,959 | 45 $9,959 | 45 $9,959 | 45 $9,959 | 45 $9,959 | $318,690 | $398,362 |
| 2. Physician Referrals | (75%) 34/yr Payment | 34 $7,469 | 34 $7,469 | 34 $7,469 | 34 $7,469 | 34 $7,469 | 34 $7,469 | 34 $7,469 | 34 $7,469 | $238,017 | $298,772 |
| 3. Physician Referrals | (50%) 23/yr Payment | 23 $4,980 | 23 $4,980 | 23 $4,980 | 23 $4,980 | 23 $4,980 | 23 $4,980 | 23 $4,980 | 23 $4,980 | $159,345 | $199,181 |
| 4. Physician Referrals | Declining 5% Payment | 45 $9,959 | 43 $9,461 | 41 $8,988 | 23 $4,980 | 23 $4,980 | 23 $4,980 | 23 $4,980 | 23 $4,980 | $159,345 | $199,181 |
| 5. Physician Referrals | Cliff/12% Ramp Payment | 45 $9,959 | 20 $4,426 | 20 $4,426 | 22 $4,957 | 25 $5,552 | 28 $6,219 | 31 $6,965 | 35 $7,801 | $236,246 | $286,551 |
| 6. Physician Referrals | Bathtub (15%) Payment | 45 $9,959 | 38 $8,465 | 33 $7,195 | 28 $6,116 | 32 $7,034 | 37 $8,089 | 42 $9,302 | 48 $10,697 | $319,983 | $386,840 |
| **Patient Referral Note** | $250,000 | $9,959 | $9,959 | $9,959 | $9,959 | $9,959 | $9,959 | $9,959 | $9,959 | $318,690 | $398,362 |

| Payment Summary | $250,000 | | | | | | | | | | |
|---|---|---|---|---|---|---|---|---|---|---|---|
| Scenario 1 | Total Paid | $19,918 | $19,918 | $19,918 | $19,918 | $19,918 | $19,918 | $19,918 | $19,918 | $637,380 | $796,725 |
| Scenario 2 | Total Paid | $17,428 | $17,428 | $17,428 | $17,428 | $17,428 | $17,428 | $17,428 | $17,428 | $557,707 | $697,134 |
| Scenario 3 | Total Paid | $14,939 | $14,939 | $14,939 | $14,939 | $14,939 | $14,939 | $14,939 | $14,939 | $478,380 | $597,543 |
| Scenario 4 | Total Paid | $19,918 | $19,420 | $18,947 | $18,498 | $18,071 | $17,665 | $17,280 | $16,914 | $547,100 | $693,812 |
| Scenario 5 | Total Paid | $19,918 | $14,385 | $14,385 | $14,916 | $15,511 | $16,178 | $16,924 | $17,760 | $554,935 | $684,913 |
| Scenario 6 | Total Paid | $19,918 | $18,424 | $17,154 | $16,075 | $16,993 | $18,048 | $19,621 | $20,656 | $638,673 | $785,202 |

First Section

Second Section

Third Section

**Figure 18-3.** Sample patient-physician referral valuation model

Next in the model, you will find some alternative scenarios that might indicate the results of a shorter transition period, leading to a permanent degradation of the numbers and variations on that theme. The Grand Total column is the amount of the payments for the entire period based on the particular numbered scenario. Keep in mind that you are looking at only one-half the total number of referrals in this model, since the other half is represented by patient referrals and is not dependent on the activity of the seller during transition.

The third section of the model shows the total payments for referrals from both patients and physicians for each of the scenarios. The Remaining Payments column represents the amount for the balance of the quarters remaining in the ten-year note, based on an average of the last two quarters on the chart. This figure can be calculated in any number of ways. This model demonstrates only one way—a method that allows for a final computation at some appropriate point after the initial period during which the referrals are most vulnerable. The degradation will, presumably, have reached a maximum level at that point, after which it is up to the buyer to maintain the balance. The seller then gets a definitive price based on his or her good-faith transition effort.

The Grand Total numbers in the bottom section represent the entire amount that would have been paid, based on the physician referral dollars to be received and the full complement of patient referral dollars to be received.

Your accounting professional can help you create your own models. An accountant can also show you different views of these figures, presented as a revenue model, for example, showing the actual revenue stream that the buyer would receive based on patient and actual physician referrals for each of the scenarios.

## The Referral Problem—The Real Secret Formula

In many professional practices, particularly those where the practitioner is a specialist, he or she receives referrals from the general practitioners in the community. Good examples in dentistry would be periodontics and orthodontics. As previously stated, in orthodontics, the percentage of referrals in relation to the entire practice on a nationwide basis is about 50 percent. In periodontics, the percentage can be 80 percent or more. It is clearly a problem that cannot be left out of any valuation concept.

If you follow the philosophy that the price must be adjusted in relationship to the risk of not maintaining continuity, then the value of these businesses would suffer dramatically. The transition period becomes even more critical than it normally appears, since it will be the obligation of the seller to deliver these referrals in order for the buyer to enjoy the full revenue stream of the business. But how can this problem be accommodated in real-dollar terms?

In other words, the seller will agree to stay with the business long enough after the sale to maintain the continuity of the referrals and the buyer will pay a price based on this promise. What if the seller fails, either intentionally or otherwise, to deliver the referrals as promised? This means that the buyer is paying for a revenue stream that he or she will never enjoy.

The alternative to this is to predicate the value of the business on the risk of nondelivery, in which case the seller is likely to receive less than the value that is ultimately delivered. Another alternative eliminates the loss to either buyer or seller. It is a formula by which the buyer pays for the referrals actually delivered. This plan creates an incentive for the seller to remain for a long enough transition period to ensure the continuity of the referral base. However, if the seller fails to deliver as promised, then the buyer is obligated to pay for only that percentage of referrals he or she is actually able to enjoy.

## Key Points to Remember

- The highest priority in maintaining the integrity of a professional practice after its sale is to transfer client loyalty.
- A partnership period allows clients to meet the new owner while still having the comfort of the former owner's presence.
- Potential degradation of the practice is the most serious issue in structuring the selling price of a professional practice.
- A seller is entitled to be paid for the business being sold, but the buyer should be obligated to pay only for the business that can be delivered.

# PART FOUR

# Legal and Financial Considerations

Three of the four following chapters are addressed directly to accountants, lawyers, and brokers who may not have extensive experience with buying or selling a business. The fourth chapter relates the lender's expectations and perspective to the borrower. Part Four is designed to give buyers and sellers some insight into what to expect from their professionals, on whose shoulders much of their success rests.

You should expect your professional advisors to help you with certain aspects of the transaction. In each case, the help should be within their scope and capabilities. Chapters 19, 20, and 21 will help you distinguish the boundaries of expertise and professional responsibility within which your accountant, lawyer, and broker should operate. Then, Chapter 22 and Chapter 25 will provide insight into the demands of your lender so you can get the loan you need.

Part Four discusses difficult-to-quantify issues, such as the client-advisor relationship and what types of personal traits in the advisor will make that relationship a success. Your professionals need to stand behind you as a team throughout the process of buying or selling. These chapters, therefore, will also devote some time to how accountants, lawyers, and brokers can work together for the most successful business transfer for their clients.

The professionals to whom these remarks are directed should note that the information contained here is not designed to be a treatise. It is rather information taken from experience in the field. Hopefully, it will remind professionals of the tools that are so important and effective to the proper representation of the client.

# CHAPTER 19

# The Accountant's Job

**Illustration 19-1. Buying a Manufacturing Business**

John and Evelyn Stover decided to buy a manufacturing business. They did a lot of studying of the marketplace and did a careful analysis of the income statement given to them by the seller. Since both John and Evelyn were fairly sophisticated, they took a careful look at the line items on the income statement. Although there was only one line item on advertising, they did a statistical analysis of the advertising account together with the different products manufactured by the company. What they found was that 80 percent of the advertising budget (the Yellow Pages) appeared to generate activity for only one product, a product that represented only 20 percent of the company income. They immediately recog-

> nized that they could revise their advertising schedule and make at least two important changes to their profit position after acquiring the business. They could reallocate their advertising dollars to save substantial money on their advertising commitment and, at the same time, spend more of their advertising dollars to increase the sales of their biggest product, which represented 80 percent of their business. A much smaller amount would be allocated to the product responsible for only 20 percent of the business. Increasing sales and decreasing costs would make this business a very positive acquisition.
>
> Do you think you would invest the time to search for this kind of post acquisition profit potential? Would you know how to do it? If you didn't know how to do it, would you seek advice from a professional? Do you think it would be worthwhile?

Chapter 19 is devoted to the accountant who may not have handled many business sales. The chapter will help lead him or her through some of the elements that are of particular concern to both buyer and seller. Obviously, an accountant cannot anticipate all the business situations in which his or her advice could be helpful. Hopefully, this will be a good beginning.

As an accountant involved in a business purchase or sale, you must think ahead, place yourself in the path of business judgment, and, presumably, be there when the time comes to make the big decision. You are the only professional who is involved with the client periodically, if only to file his or her income taxes. Your advice or recommendation could make the difference between success and failure of the sale. Educate your client to seek advice before the fact and avoid the pitfalls of judgments based on inadequate knowledge or bad advice from well-meaning but inexperienced advisors.

## Representing the Seller
### Creating the Client Relationship

Some businesspeople say that accountants should keep the figures in their proper columns and avoid being creative. Yet sometimes, putting the numbers in a particular column or creating a particular chart of accounts that helps a business owner with day-to-day operations requires creative thinking. Some accountants prefer not to participate in the business itself, but rather limit all activity to their area of expertise. Others want to be involved in the business and management decision making.

A good accountant can do a lot to help the business owner achieve his or her goals. The owner must decide, however, to what extent he or she wants an accountant to contribute to the future of the business. The relationship, trust, and confidence that exist between a business owner and his or her accountant take time to establish.

You want to begin by making sure your client understands the need to have a good bookkeeping system, to prepare a consistent and accurate periodic profit and loss statement, and to compare balance sheets on a periodic basis—in other words, the essence of good financial housekeeping.

## Working Out the Purchase Price for the Seller

No one knows better than an accountant the need for defensible numbers. When all the philosophical aspects of the business have been laid out, all the sales puffing has faded away, and all the emotional involvements have been exhausted, the buyer and his or her professionals will look at the numbers. If the numbers don't stand up, the sale will inevitably fall down.

If you have prepared a reconstituted financial statement for the sale, then you are presenting a stronger case for the business with figures that are defensible during negotiations. If you have removed from the P&L all advantages personal to your client, it will show only those items that are basic to proper business operations. The numbers must be precise to prove that the business depends on those figures and nothing more. After all, in the final analysis, you will be explaining these numbers to the buyer's accountant. Never anticipate that your counterpart is less sophisticated than you are. If the buyer's accountant gets the idea that you are trying to hide something, he or she will notify the buyer that there is a problem and that every issue must be examined with care and caution. You do not want the negotiations to turn on you because the buyer gets suspicious of your numbers.

## The Tax Ramifications of the Sale

You need to look at the tax aspects of the sale long before your client commits to the sale. The tax issues can often, as you know, make the difference between a good sale and a bad sale.

Your client must understand, for example, that an all-cash sale may not help achieve his or her long-term goals. The taxes are immediate in the year of the sale and seriously deplete the potential investment dollars your client expects to have available after the sale. Carrying back a promissory note is a constant problem, because scheduled payments to your client will depend on the stability and success of the business. On the other hand, the interest rate reflected in the note is normally higher than those dollars would earn if invested in the financial marketplace. The seller must carefully weigh these equations. As the seller's accountant, your job is to point out the various alternatives and refer the more complex options to a professional investment counselor.

You need to show your client the many more sophisticated tax implications of taking depreciation, possible recapture problems, different methods of inventory accounting, and depreciating long-term equipment purchases. Don't scare your client with a bombardment of the myriad details involved in complex tax ramifications. On the other hand, don't try to retain your client's confidence by being disingenuous about how difficult the preparation process is. Neither approach will secure your reputation as a professional. Your job is to analyze the financial situation of your client and explain the alternatives available and what each alternative represents in terms of dollars. Then, help your client make a knowledgeable decision based on the short-term and long-term effects on his or her financial portfolio.

## Presenting a Clean Set of Books

A real problem arises when the client has not maintained adequate financial records. You may not be the accountant of record, yet your task is to prepare financial documentation to present to the buyer candidate. The financial records may have been kept professionally; if so, then the job is easy. However, they may also have been kept incorrectly, even inadvertently weakened, and then your job is enormous. Your experience should enable you to make an early assessment of the problem. Part of your job will be to explain the time required to properly prepare for the presentation and give the client a good idea of the anticipated costs and the reasons for them.

## The Buyer's Financial Statement

Your client will want you to assess the qualifications of potential buyers. If the sale is going to be in cash, financial qualifications are less important. If, on the other hand, your client is going to carry any part of the purchase price with a purchase money promissory note, then the question of financial stability is very important. Your client might ask for a form containing information similar to what a bank would require during the application for a mortgage loan. See the Sample Confidential Business Application in Chapter 15. The form asks about assets, liabilities, length of job and residence, and family size and obligations. Most buyer candidates are reluctant to submit these details; most sellers are not interested in serious discussions without them. At some time during initial discussions, the seller is entitled to see this information and the buyer must recognize the need to disclose it.

Although the confidential business application forms are not really difficult to read, they often require an analysis and an explanation for anyone who is unfamiliar with this presentation of financial information. As the seller's accountant, you have an obligation to ensure that your client understands the meaning of the elements involved and that nothing appears misleading or inconsistent. He or she can then make a more educated judgment about the buyer.

The financial statement is sometimes done with great care and in great detail and other times quite casually and with minimum definition. In the latter case, you should request additional information from the buyer. In either case, verify the more important disclosures. During initial disclosures, you may also want to run credit checks on any potential buyers. This can tell you if they are already "over their heads" on credit card debt, for example. If your client wants additional security on a promissory note, you will need to find out the amount the buyer has still outstanding on mortgages and second trust deeds. Any available equity can serve as a support system for your client.

Finally, you may want to review Worksheet 19, the Accountant's Checklist on the CD that accompanies this book to help you better represent your client.

# Representing the Buyer

If you are representing someone interested in buying a business, you have several jobs to perform. You need to present your client's financial data in a light that makes your client look financially able to operate the business successfully. However, if your client's resources are not sufficient to meet the capital requirements of a particular business, you also have to advise against the purchase. You must analyze the business and interpret the information the seller provides—the profit and loss statement, balance sheets, and cash flow analyses. You need to work with the other professionals involved on both sides of the table to work out a payment plan that provides your client with an adequate annual income.

## Preparing the Buyer's Financial Statement

Your first step is to go over your client's financial resources in detail and prepare a financial statement to present to the seller. Any buyer who thinks he or she can buy a business exclusively on charm ought to be given a very large dose of reality. P.T. Barnum may have been correct when he said there is a sucker born every minute; however, there are not that many suckers around these days. If a seller is going to take a down payment and carry back the remainder of the selling price, the seller wants a buyer with sufficient capital resources to weather occasional storms and make note payments on time.

You will have to discuss the financial statement with your client in some detail. It cannot be deceptive, misleading, or simplistic. It must contain a real picture of the client's entire asset portfolio of your client. If there are things your client would prefer not to disclose, you need to give your professional advice about the implications of any failure to disclose.

## Explaining the Purchase Price to the Buyer

A buyer is basically interested in two things:

- The ability of the business to generate an immediate income
- Cash flow sufficient to pay the balance of the purchase price if he or she makes a down payment or, if the sale is in cash, a reasonable return on investment over a reasonable period of time

The income must be consistent with your client's needs and he or she must be able to get the purchase price out of the cash flow within a reasonable time, about five to ten years maximum. The actual dollar amount is negotiable, but you should never lose sight of your client's goals. Don't argue over price just for the sake of winning.

The appropriateness of the price must be based on your client's resources and needs and on the business's operating profit, not on any emotional involvement. Always keep in mind, however, that two businesses similar in all other respects can bring much different prices if they have been operated differently. The owner of one may have reconstituted the P&L to present a much more accurate picture of the business than the owner of the other. Don't let your buyer be deceived by the numbers alone until you have evaluated their accuracy and validity. You know how deceiving they can be.

## The Profit and Loss Statement

A seller needs to present the buyer with a map showing how the business has developed from its inception or at least over the past few years. The buyer will want to examine this history in light of the particular industry. The buyer will be able to analyze comparative months, seasonality problems, differentials due to competitors opening or closing, the utility of new equipment, and the ability of the business to service debt. Without this financial tracking, the buyer would have no idea as to the validity of the business. This financial history is one of the best looks into the future.

A road map can have too much detail, including every little town and village along the highway, or too little. The same is true for the P&L. As the buyer's accountant, you must know enough about the business your client is purchasing to decide what level of definition its P&L should have. If the seller presents a reconstituted P&L during the sale negotiations, your client may ask you, "How can a profit and loss statement for the buyer be different from the one prepared for the IRS?" As Chapter 2 points out, the P&L leaves room for some flexible record keeping with regard to expenses personal to the owner among other things.

This flexibility may also allow a creative accountant for the seller to represent different aspects of business operations. A good accountant will design a P&L to serve whatever purpose he or she chooses, consistent with industry and professional standards and the needs of the client.

In representing the buyer, you must be careful to recognize the difference between those expenses personal to the owner and those basic to the operation of the business. For example, the choice of a particular car may be personal to the owner, but the use of some vehicle, with its associated costs and expenses, may be mandatory for the business's pickup and delivery service.

## The Balance Sheet

Your client may need for you to explain the difference between a balance sheet—a business standing still—and a P&L—a business in motion. He or she must know how to read and interpret each financial record, as each makes a particular statement. If it sounds like your job as an accountant involves teaching your client, you are right. Because of the tax implications—particularly the personal liability of the individual, regardless of corporate protection—your client must understand at least the basics of the financial map. Without such an understanding, he or she may end up as one of P.T. Barnum's suckers. These buyers do not make good clients.

Impress upon your client that a single balance sheet does not provide enough information for judging the progress of a business. It's the changes in the numbers from balance sheet to balance sheet that show the progress or lack of it over time. By explaining to your client the basics of the balance sheet, you will enable him or her to quickly monitor some of the long-term business decisions that are so often lost in the details of day-to-day business activity. For example, the P&L will show the monthly interest being paid on a long-term obligation, but not the total obligation over the years of the particular lease, note, or purchase contract. This information is found only by examining two or more balance sheets.

## The General Ledger

The balance sheet and the P&L represent the financial map of the business. You must make it clear to your client that these two reports cannot be prepared without a general ledger. The general ledger is the engineer's tool to initiate and design that road map. This ultimate record allows the accountant to find all the information necessary to prepare a clear financial picture of the business. As the buyer's accountant, you should prepare a chart of accounts that will allow you to designate and access each element of the business and put it in its proper category to analyze the business. Your client must keep the chart of accounts clearly and accurately. As noted earlier, a Chart of Accounts that reflects "advertising" may be too simplistic to recognize the dollars that are "good earners" and the dollars that are not.

## The Need for Detail

Every business functions within certain parameters to be most effective. Some must maintain a particular ratio between labor and revenue to realize a profit. Others require a particular ratio between cost of product and revenues. Still others require a particular inventory level. The ratios you analyze depend on the type of business your client is purchasing. Many of the appropriate ratios can be found in the financial road map, providing it has sufficient detail. Without a detailed financial history, your client cannot properly analyze the business.

For example, if you are looking at a service business that has experienced an increase in labor costs without a commensurate increase in the price for services, you should recognize this as a danger sign to the profit of the business. An increase in cost of product without an increase in retail pricing structure is another signpost of danger.

## Taxes

A buyer faces even more precarious tax obligations than a seller. Your client must realize the personal liability of federal, state, and municipal tax obligations, such as sales taxes, payroll taxes, excise taxes, personal property taxes, and real property taxes. You must ensure that, whatever the financial situation of the business, the buyer never, never, never falls behind on any of these obligations.

## Costs and Fees

Closing costs, whether in the sale of a house or a business, are invariably a surprise to the parties involved. After paying the escrow costs, rent, deposits for gas and electricity and telephone, accountant's and attorney's fees, and other incidentals that arise, the buyer may have depleted the cash reservoir he or she thought might be available for working capital.

Make sure your client is prepared. In the end, your client will be grateful that you discussed costs and fees early in the process.

## Employee Requirements

Learning the employees' salary and bonus structure is only the beginning of your client's investigation into the business's employee requirements. For example, some sales may come from outside commission salespeople, who are not only a labor factor but a control factor as well. They may have more control over some big customers than the buyer would prefer. Bring this issue to your client's attention as a concern you should both examine.

Each business has its employee benefits, from a health program to vacation plans and accrued vacations for older employees. The buyer may even be obliged to honor some strange bonuses that the seller initiated at some point for some reason. You have an obligation as a financial investigator to find as many of these problem areas as possible. Unfortunately, being an accountant involves not only examining what you see, but also searching and finding the things that are not so obvious.

Although it is not your job as the buyer's accountant to restructure the business, your advice in this context can be tremendously helpful. Your experience will have put you in touch with various outside services and state-of-the-art equipment for maintaining good financial bookkeeping. Examine with the buyer which of these might eliminate excess personnel expenses. You may help the buyer make the difference between a brilliant first year and a mediocre one.

Many business owners decide to sell because the financial maintenance, among other things, has just become too onerous in terms of costs and/or time. If you can bring these alternatives to the attention of your client, you may help him or her recoup your entire fee for the year. This grateful buyer could become a long-term client.

The buyer can create a positive atmosphere in the business and solidify the relationship between the business and its employees in many ways. If the business is big enough and profitable enough, then creating plans to ensure employee longevity is appropriate, in some cases even necessary, to the continued success of the business. In other cases, this may be an opportunity for the owner of the business to begin developing a retirement plan and conditions may be just right to take advantage of some of the tax benefits available. A business owner could make big mistakes without good advice from a competent accountant, a pension administrator, or other investment advisor.

## The S Corporation

Most businesspeople without much legal or accounting background think that the corporate entity is the answer to all personal liability situations involved in business. They are not aware that many taxes are normally excluded from this protective device and that most people in the business community require personal signatures or guarantees to corporate contracts of any substance. You must ensure that your client understands the rationale behind both of these exceptions to limited liability.

In the event, however, that the corporate entity can still serve a good purpose, you must explain to your client that a C corporation could represent a double tax on the business profits. The corporation pays a tax on the profit of the business and the shareholder pays a tax on the dividend if the profit is distributed.

When you explain that the S corporation is taxed only once, on the profit of the business only, you will have a very grateful client. Be careful to point out, however, that profits are assessed to the partners and each must pay a tax on those profits whether he or she actually receives the money or not. Carefully discuss the alternatives with all the appropriate professionals to avoid this situation. One approach might be better than another based on the kind of business, the kinds of investments that have been made, or the financial position of the investors.

## Borrowing Money for the Business

You also need to explain to your client the potential dangers of borrowing money on behalf of the corporation. If your client submits a credit application on behalf of the corporation to a vendor, your client is not completely protected by his or her corporate position. If the application contains information that is incomplete or untrue, the officers and directors of the corporation may be personally liable. Unfortunately, many clients fill out these applications, thinking nothing of it. By the time their accountant gets to the problem, it is too late.

If the business has cash-flow problems, your job is not so much to find money as it is to know when it is a good or bad idea to borrow it. Your client has options for obtaining money and needs your advice as to which is the best. A buyer has the following options:

- Discount retail prices to generate additional cash flow.
- Discount receivables to a bank or other institution.
- Get a long-term commitment by applying for a loan secured by hard assets or accounts receivable.
- Sell stock or other participation in the business.

In fact, you can find many ways to service a money problem without borrowing. Make sure your client understands the alternatives.

## Investing Retained Earnings

Finally, your client may want help deciding what to do with excess profits. He or she should obey three important rules of investing: the investment must have security, return, and flexibility. If an investment meets the first two criteria but not the third and then business immediacies necessitate taking back the investment early, the penalties may eliminate whatever profit your client anticipated. In the worst-case scenario, the officers and directors who made the decision might be liable to the shareholders for bad judgment.

## Negotiating the Purchase

You want to have an eye on all your client's needs as you assist with purchase negotiations. You must look at the business in relationship to all the other financial aspects of your client's personal and business life. If you don't, you could misdiagnose the problems and give bad advice.

If you can develop a relationship of mutual trust with your client, you will probably save him or her money in the long term. You will be able to catch mistakes before they happen. Most clients are beginning to realize that asking the professional for advice before the fact saves money most of the time.

Finally, you may want to review the accountant's checklist worksheet on the accompanying CD to help you better represent your client.

## Key Points to Remember

- Never underrate the value of a strong relationship with your client.
- If you're the accountant for the seller, your first priorities are to work out the selling price and its tax ramifications, prepare the financial disclosure documents, and examine the financial capabilities of the buyer.
- If you're the accountant for the buyer, your first priorities are to prepare his or her financial statement, explain the seller's financial disclosure documents, and ensure that your client will have an adequate working capital reservoir.
- The buyer must be able to understand and discuss the financial history of the business, including the balance sheet, the profit and loss statement, the cash flow analysis, and the general ledger. If you're representing the buyer and your client cannot do this, you need to educate him or her.

# CHAPTER 20

# The Lawyer's Job

### Illustration 20-1. A Hug and a Handshake—The Problem with a General Partnership

Alex and Kelly had been together for a few years when Kelly decided to go into business. She wanted to open a yoga and tai chi studio. Kelly was capable of teaching and coaching both types of activities as well as supervising some collateral exercise programs. Because of their ongoing relationship, Alex agreed to help Kelly get started. He essentially put his bank account at her disposal. Since Kelly did not have a substantial financial portfolio, Alex was necessarily involved in the business to the extent that his signature was required on the five-year lease for the premises, at $5,000 per month. In addition, Kelly hired contractors to build out the studio, leased equipment for collateral exercise programs, and contracted with an advertising agency to develop the marketing program, the website, and the advertising materials. After a year in business, Kelly met John and fell in love with him. It wasn't long before they decided to get married and, because of John's business interests, move to Europe, leaving Alex holding the proverbial bag.

When Kelly left Alex, he was left with more than just a lingering memory of a lost love. The simplest part of this scenario is that Alex is responsible for the lease on the premises because he signed it. Since this is a five-year lease at $5,000 per month, the obligation is $300,000. But this was only the first surprise for Alex. Although it was Kelly who retained the ad agency, hired the contractors, and leased the equipment, as Kelly's partner, Alex was responsible for all these bills.

A partnership, without adequate protection, can create vulnerability for all the partners. In a general partnership, there is joint and several liability among all partners. Moreover, the law imputes a partnership when two or more people are involved in a business together, whether anything is in writing or not. The fact that Alex had little to win and a lot to lose does not change this liability. It doesn't make any difference if the partnership is created by a verbal affirmation, a hug, or a handshake. In fact, even if the two or more people do not agree to be partners, a partnership is actually created by action of the parties. Because Kelly was using Alex's money and his name with his permission and acting as if they were partners, Alex had become a general partner. And, in a general partnership, each partner is 100 percent liable for all the debts and obligations of the partnership, regardless of who contracts for the services or signs the documents.

## Limited Liability

The question of limited liability looms large in the small-business community. It's always a good idea to prepare clearly for any contingency. Although Alex could hardly have anticipated Kelly's change of heart, he should have taken a more professional approach to their business relationship. It's not a question of trust to formalize a business relationship with contracts and other legal documents. If somebody wants to do you wrong, they can usually do it however carefully drafted a contract might be. It is merely a matter of good sense. Remember: a contract is not to protect against bad intentions. It is basically to avoid ambiguity and bad memory.

Limited liability is available in all legal entities aside from the general partnership. Take advantage of this protection early on.

## Attorneys in General

A lawyer must be a good listener, a clear thinker, and a skillful tactician. Lawyers obviously need good communication skills, not only to argue cases, but also to explain issues to their clients and to advise their clients on which alternative is the shortest, least expensive, and most productive. Finally, a lawyer must be a good presenter to convince the other party—another lawyer, a judge, a jury, or a board of directors—with logic, emotion, and substance, in order to achieve the result desired by the client.

A lawyer cannot afford to make a mistake. To a client, it could mean as little as a bump in the road or as much as life itself. To the lawyer, it could mean censure, disbarment, or, in the case of criminal involvement, incarceration. Lawyers sell a strange product: time and expertise. Neither is something you can see, hear, or feel.

While selling or buying a business, your client may not be able to point to any one thing you did to help the transfer succeed. However, a buyer or a seller will benefit from good representation by a skilled lawyer and sleep well at night.

The checklist at the end of this chapter will help you identify those areas in which your client needs the most legal help. Be sure to review Worksheet 20 on the accompanying CD with your client.

## Creating the Client Relationship

Every lawyer knows that you don't instill confidence in a client by telling him or her which school you attended, whether you were on the law review, or how much money you made last year. Each of these things means something a little different to each client and becomes part of the picture.

The substance of the relationship, however, is based on a much more personal level. The relationship is often based on things over which you exercise little control—your voice, your demeanor, your clothes, your desk, the pictures on your wall, or the location of your office.

You build the most satisfactory relationship by listening to the problem and responding to the issues objectively and dispassionately. By listening and responding appropriately, you give your client a comfort zone—confidence in a professional who appears to understand the problem and to have a clear picture of how to most expeditiously help.

To ensure that you can best serve your client's needs, you need the most accurate and reliable information from him or her. If your client is concerned about disclosure, it may be because he or she doesn't know who may ultimately have access to the information disclosed. By explaining the attorney-client privilege and stressing that it can be waived only by the client, you may be able to eliminate that concern.

Some lawyers look at every problem from a negative perspective and think of reasons why the client won't be able to buy or sell a business on advantageous terms. Other lawyers address the sale in a positive way to maximize the benefits to the client. Your best approach is to remember that the client is looking for a lawyer who can get the job done. If you fulfill your purpose in an appropriate time frame and for a reasonable fee, you have indeed gotten the job done.

## Representing the Seller
### Defending the Selling Price

Whether the price is set by the client or by a professional appraiser whom the client has retained, it is incumbent on you, as the client's representative, to understand the price structure and be prepared to defend it. Understanding and defending does not mean you interfere with the valuation of the business; however, a price that is clearly out of line will eventually lead the buyer or his or her professional advisors to cancel the deal. You will have charged a fee with little concern about the ultimate result sought by your client—to sell the business.

Many clients fail to make appropriate adjustments in their price expectations because they're emotionally involved with the business. At that point, it is necessary for you to put logic before emotion by explaining what price your client can realistically expect. A lawyer cannot do any better under the circumstances.

## Preparing the Initial Memorandum

You are well advised, as counsel for the seller, to prepare an initial memorandum to memorialize the basic elements of the sale early on. This memorandum can reference the fact that more formal documents are being prepared, but the memorandum will also call for a down payment. When the buyer candidate puts down hard cash to bind the deal, even though he or she may be able to retrieve these dollars if the deal falls through, it brings the parties much closer to a real discussion. This memorandum is often referred to as a Letter of Intent.

With buyer's remorse a chronic problem, you must act to tie the deal down in whatever way you can, pending the preparation of final documents. The memorandum must be simple to read and understand and contain no ambiguities. Put in as many of the basics as you can without complicating the document. The objective is to get it signed and a down payment in the bank or into an escrow of some kind. (See the Sample Memorandum of Sale in Chapter 14.)

## Preparing the Final Documents

Because documents very often survive the relationship between attorney and client, it is always a good idea to go over the final document with your client to ensure that he or she understands the language, including those elements in which legal language has no simple equivalent. Have your client take notes and add those notes to his or her copy after the sale is consummated to be sure he or she can reconstruct the proper interpretation of the language whenever necessary. Like everything else you do as an attorney, this kind of extra service will earn you the reputation of making your client's best interests your highest priority.

## Protecting the Seller Until the Balance Is Paid

If the buyer's expertise is essential to the survival and success of the business, what would happen if he or she died before paying off the purchase money promissory note? The seller may have difficulty getting the dollars he or she anticipated from the sale. One solution is to have the buyer take out an insurance policy for the balance of the note and name the seller as beneficiary.

What if the buyer fails at the business? If the original down payment was large enough and if the seller has the right to take the business back, he or she may be able to sell the business again, even if for less than the original purchase price.

What if the buyer has not only failed at the business but also run it into the ground? The seller will take back a mere skeleton of the business. You should seek to protect your client against this misfortune. (See Chapter 14 for more on seller protections.)

After the sale, the seller should be able to monitor the business as long as any part of the purchase price is still outstanding. Some sellers merely want assurances that the taxes are paid; other outstanding debts are usually easier to negotiate in the event that the seller is forced to take the business back. The seller also wants to ensure that salaries and other labor costs are held to a certain percentage of income to be sure that the business is not being systematically destroyed. Some sellers even go as far as to seek assurance that the cost of product stays within certain parameters. The more sophisticated will even monitor the advertising. You need to arrange for your client to monitor the business during the repayment period.

Much depends on the type of business involved and the size of the down payment. In fact, much also depends on the amount of supervision to which the buyer is willing to submit. You, as seller's counsel, will have to make the judgment once you and the seller have developed a good working relationship.

## Representing the Buyer
### Explaining the Selling Price

You will not make the ultimate decision as to whether or not your client should buy a business. Your job is to examine pricing alternatives and explain the ramifications of each potential price structure. It is not your prerogative to accept or reject the price of a business. As long as the price is sensible, you have certain obligations to your client. You must examine with the buyer various issues regarding money. Does your client have the following?

- Enough income to pay the bills, including the purchase money obligation, if any?
- Enough money as working capital for the business to survive and prosper?
- Enough money for his or her needs while paying the promissory note and building the business?

Make sure your client is aware of these financial necessities. Then he or she should use good judgment and, hopefully, the advice of a good accountant.

### Protections for the Buyer

A buyer is invariably emotionally involved in the project of buying a business. After all, not only is he or she investing very substantial time, money, and effort, but probably also risking the future of his or her family and retirement. It is incumbent upon you as buyer's counsel to offer whatever objective, dispassionate advice you can to temper this emotional involvement. You are not expected to know everything about every business; however, very much like a bar examination, it is not as necessary to know the specific answers to the questions as to recognize the questions themselves. The buyer must get the answers. These questions could include the following:

- The history of the industry
- The adequacy of the equipment included in the purchase
- Competitors and what they mean to the future of the business
- The personnel as an asset or a potential problem

- The ratios of labor and cost of product to the income stream
- Any seasonality in the business

You should be able to recognize that answers to these questions could dramatically change the buyer's perspective. You would be doing your client a disservice if you did not enter into this area to at least some degree.

## Examine the Lease

The longevity of a business in a particular location could substantially affect its success. If your client needs to move the business or face a dramatic increase in rent or lease-related expenses, such as taxes or common-area maintenance, it could devastate profitability. You should look at the lease and lease options carefully to avoid these potential problems.

Many options to renew leases state that rent will be discussed at the time the lessee chooses to exercise the option to renew. This is hardly an option. It is merely an opportunity to negotiate. Explain this to the buyer, along with any of the other ambiguities that so many leases contain.

## Broker Agreements

Discuss also any agreements with brokers for sales commissions. These commissions can lead to very tricky situations; you should scrutinize any relationship that the seller had with a broker at any time. If a seller has had relationships with other brokers before the current one, an earlier contract may create problems. If a broker once under contract with the seller brings a lawsuit against him or her, the buyer might become embroiled in the problem, like it or not. Be careful to look out for this hidden danger for your client.

## Examine Any Franchise Agreement

Some lawyers think that because they have eaten at a McDonald's they understand franchising. This kind of thinking can be a dangerous mistake. There is really no reason for it. State and federal legislation has made the lawyer's job much easier in this regard. Buying a franchise is not much different from buying any business, if you find out just what's involved in the business.

Your first step is to request the franchise disclosure document from the franchise company. It will, by law, contain the nature and history of the business, name the people who are responsible for the operation of the franchise company, and state any obligations the buyer is about to assume. This information will lead you to any other questions about the local marketplace and competition. See also Chapter 9 of this book or *Franchise Bible* by Erwin J. Keup (Entrepreneur Press, $6^{th}$ edition, 2007) for more information on buying or selling a franchise.

## Long-Term Leases and Contracts

While you cannot save your client from every lurking disaster, long-term leases or contracts your client purchases with the business are places where potential disasters can hide. Long-term obligations, whether for equipment or for buying or selling products, can have unforeseen long-term consequences for the business.

Take a quantity discount purchase, for example. If a new component is designed that makes the product obsolete before the entire quantity is sold, your client will be buying a deteriorating inventory. If a seller wants to get out of the business because he or she has a long-term lease on equipment that is about to become obsolete, raise the issue with your client as a possible deal-breaker.

## Legal Business Entities

There are several forms of holding title to a business. An owner may be a sole proprietor, a general partner with one or more partners, the general partner in a limited partnership, the president of a corporation, or the managing member in a limited liability company. On a more subtle level, an individual can control a business in many ways without appearing to be the driving force on a day-to-day basis, such as by controlling the money or corporate stock.

As the buyer's lawyer, you need to assess just what your client is trying to accomplish and then recommend the form of ownership most appropriate under the circumstances. Explain also that your client may have a reason to change the form of ownership as the long-term goals of the business change. For example, the company may grow to a stature that warrants a public offering. If the company goes public, a different corporate package may be necessary to facilitate large investments while allowing present management to stay in control of the day-to-day activities.

## The Personal Signature

The average businessperson understands that the corporate form of ownership affords the owner a certain amount of protection. Unfortunately, many business agreements for which the owner would like protection, like leases and long-term purchase arrangements, require either a personal signature to the contract or a personal guarantee. The corporation cannot protect against the liability of this personal involvement.

Many people do not understand the ramifications of their signature on a legal document. They are even unaware that "The Corporation, by Jack Terry, President" is an entirely different signature from "Jack Terry." You need to ensure that your client clearly understands the dangerous difference between the two. The first signature will bind the corporation to a contract but will not create an obligation on Jack Terry the individual. The second signature, on the other hand, will bind Jack Terry to the obligation regardless of whom or what he may purport to represent.

Since a corporation can be costly and problematic to use as a business entity, the decision to incorporate depends on the kind of business and business obligations for which the owner expects to be responsible. Your client needs to understand the potential holes in corporate protection.

## Joint and Several Liability

Some less sophisticated businesspeople think that if they sign a document along with other people, they are responsible for only a portion of the obligation. They are devastated when they find out their signature obligates them to the entire debt. Certainly they may have the right to seek contributions from the other signatories; however, if they have the most money, their money will invariably pay the bill long before contributions come from the others. Make sure your client understands joint and several liability.

## The Partnership Relationship

The best relationships will have disagreements. That's only natural and logical. The best framework for a partnership agreement is to have, from the beginning, a method by which either or any partner can get out or buy out the other(s). It is a good idea to explain to your client that one partner can legally bind the other(s) to long-term business obligations. A decision that might appear to be brilliant at one moment may turn out to be terrible in hindsight. The partnership agreement must be drafted carefully to keep either or any partner from binding the partnership to a long-term obligation detrimental to the future of the business.

## Collections and Contracts

Someone who has acted as a sales representative for a large company may never have dealt with the problem of collecting from the accounts he or she sold. That sales rep merely picked up a commission check at the end of the week, verified that the commission was properly calculated, and made the deposit. Operating a business, particularly collecting for the goods or services sold, is a new world for many of these new entrepreneurs.

Entering into contractual relationships with customers may also be new territory for a person who formerly just took orders. Any long-term, contractual arrangement that is important to the success or survival of the business should always be reduced to writing, partly to avoid ambiguities and partly to help secure payment.

You must decide how much education your client needs about collections and contracts to survive and prosper in the business after buying it.

## Employee Relations and Contracts

The employees of a business can either be incidental to the core elements of the activity or essential. Losing key employees can devastate a successful business. You need to examine any contractual relationship between management and employees. If no documented contracts exist, you still need to get into the substance of the relationship. Suggest to your client that he or she examine the employees' loyalty and what promises, if any, have been made to the employees that the new management will be obliged or expected to keep. If the business is large enough to involve a union, you may need to consult an attorney who specializes in labor law.

## How to Handle a Bulk Transfer

The purchase of a business can involve the acquisition of stocks or assets. In the case of stocks, the buyer is knowingly taking on the full responsibility of the corporate business. In the case of assets—the buyer's intention is normally to take on only what he or she knows—what is disclosed.

But what about the things that are not disclosed? The question of the buyer's responsibility to the seller's creditors can be problematic. In most jurisdictions, technically, creditors can be notified officially by publishing notice of the pending sale. They are then obliged to put their claims in the escrow and are precluded from seeking payment from the new buyer. Some jurisdictions have legislation under the title of "bulk transfer of assets"; others reference the sale in different ways. It is appropriate to check your particular jurisdiction to ensure that the law has not been repealed.

## Buying Assets Free and Clear

Because your client expects that whichever assets he or she purchases are free and clear of any outstanding debt, you need to verify that no one else has an interest in the property. Check all the appropriate agencies for the filing of legal documents that indicate an interest in the property by someone other than the owner who is selling them. Check any filings made under the Uniform Commercial Code to ensure that no others hold title to the property that your client is buying.

By examining any outstanding contracts or debts on the business's assets, you will also examine any contractual relationships between the seller and vendors and manufacturers with whom the seller does business. If you cannot find a filing on record, the chances are greater that your client is getting the assets he or she expects.

## Issues Beyond Your Expertise

Many lawyers like to think of themselves as a one-stop shop, a place where clients can address all legal problems. With the constant passage of legislation in every area of the law, it is practically impossible for the average lawyer to keep up with the changes in every field. Smart lawyers keep current in their own specialty and seek advice from others when their practice takes them into an area away from their expertise.

In dealing with a business purchase or sale, you may need help in these areas:

- Labor law—to deal with unions or other employee concerns, including, for example, preparation of an employee manual, where appropriate or necessary
- Securities law—to deal with stock participations in public companies (and sometimes private companies)
- Litigation—to deal with lawsuits involving a wide range of matters, including collection on delinquent accounts, contract issues, and protection of proprietary interests and intellectual property

You may be able to handle a given matter without being affiliated with another office; sometimes, a little advice in the right direction can save you time and save your client a lot of money. Your own good judgment should prevail.

In other areas of the law, the experience of dealing with the people involved is just as important as the law itself. In negotiating the specific elements of a lease, for example, your experience and negotiating skills are as valuable as your knowledge of the law. In many of these situations, you must depend on your judgment. After all, the highest priority is always to serve your client professionally and expeditiously.

Be sure to review the worksheet on the accompanying CD to be better prepared to cover these important issues with your client.

## Key Points to Remember

- Your first priorities are to create a relationship with your client that instills confidence and to explain the attorney-client privilege.
- If you're representing the seller, make sure you and your client understand your responsibilities regarding preparing the sales presentation, negotiating the purchase price, and protecting the sale.
- If you're representing the buyer, make sure your client understands the premises lease, any franchise agreement, and any contracts with vendors, customers, manufacturers, or employees.
- If you're representing the buyer, you may need to educate your client regarding the rationale behind the purchase price, available cash flow, personal liability, and relationships with partners, investors, and key employees.

For additional information on partnership relationships of all kinds, see *Forming a Partnership and Making It Work* (Entrepreneur Press, 2007) by Ira Nottonson.

# CHAPTER 21

# The Broker's Job

**Illustration 21-1.**
**The Story of Multiple Brokers**

When Alan and Barbara decided to sell their business, they were told that they would probably get more money if they let a business broker handle the sale. They were not very familiar with the business community, even though they had run a retail business for a number of years, but they did know a couple of brokers. They decided to work with ABC Business Brokers. Jay Federer was handling their account. They signed all the forms without reading through them, because Jay told them that the forms were standard among brokers. Jay did not discuss the forms or offer any cautions about them. Six months went by, the business had not sold, and the contract with ABC expired.

During this period, they met another broker, Sally Quinn, who they felt would be a little more personal. They signed a contract with Sally for six months. In about three months, Sally resurrected a person who had expressed an interest in acquiring the business five months earlier but who then left the country on business. Negotiations took place and a sale was consummated. Sally was delighted about being able to help Alan and Barbara as well as earn a 10 percent commission on the sale. Shortly after the sale was completed, Alan and Barbara received a bill from Jay Federer of ABC Business Brokers for an additional commission of 10 percent.

It seems that the contract that Alan and Barbara had signed with ABC Business Brokers contained a clause stating that the broker would be entitled to a full commission if, during six months following expiration of the contract, any person whom Jay had contacted bought their business. This is exactly what happened and Alan and Barbara had to pay an additional 10 percent commission. This kind of language is usually included in the "standard" contract that Alan and Barbara had signed. In some cases, the follow-up period can be years.

No one can be an expert in all businesses. Nonetheless, the broker's obligation is to understand the nature of the business that he or she is negotiating on behalf of a client. After all, if a broker is only going to obtain signatures on the listing agreement, what real value does he or she have to any buyer or seller? A broker must never forget that his or her client is dealing with tremendous emotional pressure.

Every business has its nuances. No one would expect a broker to be as experienced with the business that he or she represents as the seller. It is, however, incumbent on the broker to have a fair understanding of the basic elements. Whether you represent the seller or the buyer, you should discuss the business with your client carefully. You need to appreciate just what the seller is putting on the market and the kind of involvement for which the buyer anticipates paying. You should read whichever section of this chapter is appropriate—"Representing the Seller" or "Representing the Buyer"—or both sections and then, to review your responsibilities to your clients, refer to Worksheet 21 at the end of the chapter.

# Representing the Seller
## Creating the Seller-Broker Relationship

The relationship between seller and broker is different in different jurisdictions. The most restrictive is the *exclusive authorization to sell*. Under this kind of agreement, the broker is entitled to collect a commission on the business sale whether or not he or she brings the buyer to the table. As long as a sale is consummated with a buyer who was introduced to the business during the term of the agreement, whether by the broker or not, the broker is deemed to have earned the commission.

This may seem unfair. Clients should recognize, however, that in some cases a broker spends an inordinate amount of time and even substantial money to advertise the business—time and money for which the broker cannot be compensated unless and until the business sells.

This type of agreement can also call for an earned commission if the sale takes place after the agreement has expired, as long as the broker prepares a list of buyer candidates and gives it to the client within a certain time frame. Indeed, if the seller withdraws the business from the market or interferes with negotiations that might otherwise have led to a sale during the term of the broker agreement, the broker might still be entitled to the commission. You can, of course, develop other less stringent arrangements with your clients.

The commission is another element you and your client need to consider. Most brokers earn a 10 percent commission when a business is sold, but the percentage could be less or more. A broker may even work without a commission. Some brokers charge for their time and then receive a bonus if the business is sold.

The type of agreement and the amount of the commission are, in a sense, secondary considerations. The key issues are disclosure and mutual trust. The client must feel that the broker is experienced, competent, and trustworthy. The broker must feel that the client is realistic, honest, and trustworthy. Full disclosure will always eliminate the ambiguous and uncertain elements between you and your client.

## Preparing the Asking Price

If an asking price for a business is substantially below its market value, the business may sell quickly, but the seller may lose a good portion of his or her earned equity. If the business is priced too high, it may remain unsold, much to the chagrin of both the seller and the broker. As a result, your obligation as a broker is to find a selling price that maximizes the equity position of the seller while attracting the largest number of qualified buyers.

To find the asking price, always examine the marketplace from the perspective of the potential buyer. After all, the deal must serve the buyer's goals or there's no sale. You know from experience that there is no magic to price. The buyer is looking for two things: an immediate income consistent with his or her needs and a cash flow that can essentially pay back the purchase price. The real question is what income is consistent with the buyer's needs. If the buyer needs more income than the business can produce and the only way to make the sale work would be by lowering the price far below the seller's expectations, then the buyer is the wrong candidate.

On the other hand, the seller must be given the appropriate dose of reality based on the number of other businesses available in the same profit range. It is the seller's prerogative to set the minimum selling price—and it is the broker's job to analyze the situation and to advise and counsel the seller.

Remember always, as the broker, that price is based on much more than just the dollar amount put forward at the beginning of the negotiating session. Price can be adjusted by many items with which the seller is normally not very conversant. Here are some of these variables:

- All-cash vs. down payment and carryback loan
- Amount of the down payment
- Rate of interest on the note
- Length of time for the promissory note
- Possibility of a consulting contract for the seller as part of the purchase price

Any one of these could turn out to be the key to the sale, the point that allows the buyer and the seller to succeed in their negotiations. Explain these pricing variables to your client at the beginning of your involvement. By discussing price structuring with your client, you will show that you have a handle on the nuances of selling and that you are the best-qualified person in the field to handle the sale for the seller.

## Preparing the Business for Sale

The key to an attractive business is good housekeeping—cosmetic, hygienic, and financial. You can play an important part here.

A business owner frequently does not see his or her business as others see it—the cobwebs in the corners, the torn carpet, or the plastic panel coming off the counter. It is your job to point these things out. In some cases, a small cosmetic change can make a difference in the price; in other cases, it can determine whether or not you make the sale. Don't ever hesitate about bringing these things to your client's attention.

A new bookkeeping system can help put a better face on the business and get it ready for sale. The bookkeeping system should be easy to access, read, and understand. If the buyer can understand it, you will spend less time with the buyer's accountant. In addition, the books must tell the financial story of the business. Remember: whatever it is that you are representing for sale, the information must be honest, accurate, and easy to access. Anything less will suggest that someone is trying to hide something from the buyer, which will make a sale more difficult, if not impossible. Trying to resurrect credibility is always an uphill battle. It's very much like the expression, "You don't get a second chance to make a first impression."

Whatever the reality of the business, it has a value. The business might not be valued as high as the seller would like, but it has a value. A good broker is interested in maximizing that value without distorting the facts or the reality of the business. Your reputation for honesty, candor, and concision is your stock in trade. If it becomes tainted, you may become less effective in the business community. You will be of little value to your prospective clients.

If the business has a substantial price, you may even want to structure a business plan. A business plan can take many shapes, from a few pages to something as complex as a franchise disclosure document. Because writing a business plan is time-consuming and expensive, discuss it with your client. This may be worth a separate retainer agreement for a substantial business presentation.

## Preparing the Seller's Negotiating Position

For every negotiating session, there are three basic categories of things to consider:

- Things your client must have
- Things your client would like to have
- Things your client is willing to concede

Before every session, you should confer with your client to ensure that you both understand which items fall into which of those three categories.

Other essential elements to consider may be collateral to the asking price:

- How long is the seller willing to remain with the business after the sale for training, supervisory, or introduction purposes (the *transition period*)?
- Should the receivables be part of the sale or not? If so, should they be calculated at 100 percent of value or something less?
- Is any real property included or not? If so, what should its value be? Real property gives the seller greater flexibility in negotiating the total price structure.

The broker must constantly stress that negotiating is searching, not demanding. Buying and selling are based on compromise, not mandate.

## Discussing the Buyer's Financial Statement

Unless a business owner looks at financial statements regularly, discrepancies will probably not be obvious. You must examine the statement with your client for three purposes.

- To find out if there seems to be anything missing or misleading about the statement

- To make a preliminary judgment as to whether the statement qualifies the buyer financially
- To determine whether there are any assets that can serve as additional security if the sale is not all-cash

If any information is missing, you may want to order a credit report, check on the bank accounts listed to confirm balances, and even call business and personal references. After all, the broker's job, among others, is to ensure that the seller has enough credible information to make a satisfactory sale.

## Marketing the Business

Marketing the business can involve various things, from preparing a business plan to examining the basic categories of potential buyers. You, as the broker, will normally go to your largest source of candidates. Yet, this is not necessarily the best approach and, in some cases, this source can be exactly the wrong reservoir from which to draw.

If, for example, you are dealing with a business that may be vulnerable to employees or creditors if its pending sale becomes known, you are then bound to maintain confidentiality. The need to maintain confidentiality might severely limit your ability to expose the business to a broad spectrum of buyer candidates. If you make a mistake in such a situation, it can prove devastating to the client. It can even lead to litigation, which is the last thing a broker wants to face.

If the business is a professional practice—law, accounting, medicine, or even one of the less dominant professions such as massage therapy or business consulting—disclosure to the wrong people can cause the professional you represent to lose confidence in you, which could cause you to lose clients. In the case of a manufacturing business, inappropriate disclosure can mean the loss of customers significant enough to destroy the future of the business.

You must carry this responsibility with great care and exercise discretion. Discuss confidentiality with your client and put the details of the disclosure problem in writing. You will then have the necessary guidelines to reduce the possibility that you'll err inadvertently.

On the other hand, you may find in some situations that the best and most logical candidate is either a customer or a competitor. In either of these cases, your job is different. With a customer, you are dealing with someone who at least knows the nature of the product or service being offered. You must then find out what qualifications this customer has as a potential buyer. With a competitor, you don't have to sell the concept of the business. You merely have to convince him or her that acquiring the business will not negatively affect his or her business operation, but rather increase revenues and profits.

A customer or competitor will have a head start understanding the particular business and the industry. A stranger to the industry requires a different approach and a more detailed education about the business and the industry.

## Advertising the Business

Each broker has his or her personal preferences for advertising media. Much, of course, depends on the business and its industry. For every industry, you will invariably find a trade magazine. Advertising in this medium will get to people who already understand much about the business you represent. On the other hand, advertising in a newspaper that advertises employment opportunities might be a very good way to reach people who recognize that owning a business means never needing to look for a job again. The internet, of course, presents a greater reservoir of candidates than any other medium. You must, however, be prepared to discuss this with someone knowledgeable.

Because size and frequency are the keys to advertising, particularly in the print media, you must decide just how much of an investment is appropriate. After all, if you spend enough money, you may find a buyer and make the sale—but you may also be spending all of the commission you would make on the sale. And, what if, after such an extensive expenditure, you don't find a buyer? It is easy enough for the seller to say, "But that's your job!" You are not brokering sales as a hobby; you expect to earn an income. If the seller wants an extensive advertising campaign, it is completely appropriate for you to also discuss how the seller could invest in that campaign. If the seller is obliged to put his or her money into advertising the business, it may make him or her more reasonable about decisions on advertising.

## Working with the Accountant and the Lawyer

As you handle more business sales, you will become so familiar with some of the paperwork and protective devices that they will become almost second nature. However, the experienced broker must distinguish between the elements within his or her domain and those in the domain of other professionals, particularly the accountant and lawyer. Giving accounting or legal advice to your client may cause those professionals to become less cooperative and may even put your own professional practice in serious jeopardy if your advice is off target. You should understand the roles of other professionals so that you can explain and interpret their advice to your client and occasionally offer interesting comments to the other advisors on your client's team.

Make sure your client has a good lawyer and a good accountant. Each of these professionals has a specific role to play in preparation for the sale and the period following the sale. The protective devices and tax implications of a sale that is not all-cash are important to the seller. Leaving your client unprotected after a sale is a big mistake. It is sometimes difficult to know exactly when your representation of your client ends. Working with good professionals eliminates this danger and brings high endorsements from a satisfied client.

# Representing the Buyer
## Understanding the Business

In some cases, you may be representing a buyer who is a competitor with the seller. The buyer understands the nature of the industry and all the positive reasons for the potential acquisition. Your job then is to ensure confidentiality, confirm the revenues the seller is presenting, and make sure there are no substantial negatives for the buyer.

If you represent a potential buyer who is familiar with the business as a customer, you may need to point out the negatives. A customer or other type of buyer who is not familiar with the day-to-day frustrations of operating a business may be too excited or emotional about the purchase to see potential dangers. If you think your commentary on the negative aspects of the business might prevent the sale from happening, you are right. But what is your role as the buyer's representative? Is it to ensure that he or she buys something—or that he or she buys something that is likely to survive and succeed?

Your job is not to decide whether or not to buy, but to ensure that your client makes a knowledgeable decision based on all available information. Some information may be difficult to find and some may not be positive; however, you should certainly give the search for it your best effort. The business may not be the best for a particular buyer because of his or her personality, inclinations, aversions, or lack of basic knowledge. You can point these things out to your client; the ultimate decision is not in your hands. In all these cases, you should monitor the progress of the sale in writing. In part, this will show where you are at every substantial stage of the buying process. It will also ensure that your client cannot later accuse you of bad advice you never gave.

## Rationalizing the Purchase Price

Although purchase price is based on various factors, the acquisition must serve two basic purposes for the average buyer: it must generate the income the buyer requires and provide sufficient cash flow to service the purchase money promissory note or to pay back the money borrowed from a third party. Other, secondary reasons for buying may be as diverse as building equity for retirement or fulfilling the requirements for an alien to obtain a green card for permanent resident status.

A business that provides owner income and that services debt is the only kind of business a broker is normally hired to find. Buyers often view owner's compensation in a sole proprietorship as the money available to the buyer after the sale. You must point out to your client that the cash flow to service the purchase money promissory note must also come from this source. If the seller is handling more administrative activity than the buyer can handle until he or she learns the business, additional personnel or contracted help may be needed, which must be paid from that same income source. The buyer may not be able to meet his or her salary expectations as early as hoped.

## The Buyer's Financial Statement

The seller will be interested in the financial and, to some extent, the personal background of the buyer. If the sale is not all-cash, the information provides reassurance that he or she will be able to continue the business. If the sale is all cash, the seller may still want to feel confident that his or her vendors, customers, employees, and associates are going to be getting a fair deal from a competent businessperson. The seller may request the buyer's financial information before serious negotiations get under way, when neither the seller nor the buyer are sure what purchase arrangement they will structure. The seller asks for this information, in part, to ensure that the buyer is a serious candidate. Only serious candidates normally disclose this type of personal information.

On the other hand, although the information submitted must be complete, truthful, and not misleading, the buyer need not disclose many things that would be mandatory in a bankruptcy petition or a mortgage loan application. The degree of disclosure depends on the buyer. As the buyer's broker, you can help protect some more personal elements.

For example, potential inheritances, interests in capital assets (real estate) with others, and minority interests in unlisted stocks are not necessary disclosures to consummate the sale and could unnecessarily put these assets at risk. Keep in mind that the buyer must exercise a certain caution at this point. Although your advice is appropriate, you are wise to have an accountant examine these disclosures to be sure your client is adequately protected.

## How to Package a Loan

Putting together a package for a loan involves three basic elements:

- A picture of the business, including its history, current financial status, current management, and competitive position in the marketplace
- The growth potential of the business, including the state and condition of the equipment and the ability of management to maintain success in a competitive marketplace
- The reason for the loan, including a defense of the purchase price, plans to use the investment capital apart from the purchase, and the business's stability for repaying the loan and growing in the future

All these elements can be stated in different terms and with somewhat different priorities, but your client needs to know how he or she will be using the money and when he or she is going to be paying it back. Then the lender will ask how stable the business is and how secure the investment.

Where to apply for the loan is the broker's biggest problem. You probably have personal contacts in the banking and investment community. Keeping these sources viable is one of the keys to making investment capital available as and when your client meets the necessary criteria and the business opportunity is a good one.

## Working with the Accountant and the Lawyer

Some brokers feel that their job is to orchestrate the basic elements of a purchase and then suggest to the client that he or she bring an attorney and an accountant to the table. Many clients agree with this procedure, because they think bringing other professionals into the game later means lower fees. The smart broker knows that neither of these propositions is true.

Because your most significant contribution to the buy-sell process is to bring a willing buyer together with a willing seller, it is your obligation to harness the strongest team to do the job. That means working with a good accountant and a good attorney. Bring them in before mistakes happen in the preliminary negotiations. Once your client makes statements to the seller, it is difficult to go back and change them. Once your client has agreed to certain conditions of sale, even though they may not yet be in writing, it is difficult to retrench without causing a serious rift in the buyer-seller relationship. The cost of correcting an error can be significantly greater than the cost of using an accountant and an attorney from the beginning. By getting the right advice from the professionals before mistakes happen, you can make the negotiations smoother and the purchase more fulfilling for the buyer.

## Your Role in Pre-Purchase Research

The question of the extent of the broker's obligation to the buyer is always open. If your client purchases a house with a big hill behind it, you might suggest a geological survey be performed. If your client buys rural land with the intention of building a house, you might suggest a percolation test before signing the papers. These suggestions ensure that the property purchased serves the basic purpose for which the buyer is purchasing it. To what extent does this obligation apply to the purchase of a business?

Your obligation to recommend market surveys or other analyses does not extend beyond your knowledge or experience. The representation does not oblige you to become an expert in the field or industry of which the business is a part. You can become very involved in prepurchase research and analysis. Your level of involvement depends on the size of the business, the purchase price, and your relationship with the buyer, both personally and professionally.

If you want to really get involved in finding out about the nature of the business and its prospects, you take on a serious task. Just like the preparation of a business plan on a seller's behalf, an analysis can take many shapes. It can be as simple as a rough look at the marketplace or as complex as a presentation submitted to generate corporate investment or to take a company public. You would be involved in price comparison and analyzing the competition and the competition's quantity purchase advantages or disadvantages. You would do an analysis of population growth, traffic and shopping habits of the neighborhood, location of the business and comparative rents, potential for future growth, and availability of personnel, including public transportation or parking availability.

Regardless of the level of market analysis you decide to undertake, as the buyer's broker you should research the competition at least superficially. For example, many fast-food merchants don't consider a neighboring merchant a competitor if it is not selling the exact same food product. A newcomer to the industry may think that ten fast-food neighbors are a competition problem. You may want to point out the phenomenon of shopping mall food courts. All the food concessions are congregated in one place to draw lunch traffic to the area. Customers go to them not really knowing what they will be in the mood to eat. This concept has proven quite successful. Although it is not your prerogative to intrude on the buyer's decision-making process, you do want your client to have enough information to make an educated decision.

No one can foretell the future, yet business is based on outguessing the need for a product or a service. The ability to anticipate the needs of the customers is the key to success for many entrepreneurs. It is hardly your job as the buyer's broker to look into the future and advise your client as to whether he or she is making the right decision by acquiring the business in question. However, you know how blinded your client can be by the emotional involvement of the decision.

Whatever business your client is considering, have him or her analyze whether it is dependent on a strong or a weak economy. Make sure your client asks at least the simplest of all questions—whether the population size and the traffic pattern surrounding the location will mean enough customers. If you look at these questions with your client, your client will have the advantage of a somewhat more objective perspective from which to consider the important decision.

## Key Points to Remember

- Always document your broker-client relationship in writing.
- Although you do not need to be an expert in every business, you should learn enough about the business and the industry to properly represent the buyer or the seller.
- If you're representing the seller, you need to understand and help present and defend the price of the business.
- If you're representing the buyer, you need to negotiate the price based on the business's profits and its position in the marketplace.
- A delicate balance exists between a price that is too low, allowing the business to sell quickly but losing some of the seller's equity, and too high, which prevents a sale from taking place.
- You must work with the accountant and lawyer as an effective professional team to maximize success for your client.

# CHAPTER 22

# The Lender's Job

### Writing a Business Plan

Whether you want to borrow money to take your business to the next growth plateau,  to survive a current crisis, or to buy a business, your approach to a potential lender is going to require a similar presentation. This chapter will help you find the money for your business.

Be careful of conventional wisdom. You will be told that creating a business plan represents a terribly complicated problem. It isn't. You will be told to look at a business plan format and follow it to the letter. Don't. You will be told that every part is as important as every other part. It isn't. You will be told that "substance" is the important stuff and that "form" is not important. Wrong!

## Remember the Purpose

Most business plans are designed to be a tool by which management can monitor the growth of a business. A business plan will enable you to periodically do a comparative analysis to see which ideas have worked and which have not. You will be able to increase your efforts and maximize your results by examining and reexamining the most cost-effective ways to grow. There are, of course, other purposes. You might intend the business plan to be used for enticing a company to enter into a joint venture with you. You might want to convince a bank that your company would be a good lending risk. You might want to excite a venture capital group to invest in your company because it has an exciting future.

If you consider these different purposes, you should recognize that one generic business plan is not likely to satisfy the expectations of all of the above. In order to serve each purpose, you will need to adjust each business plan to meet the likely expectations of the reader. And you've got to make it interesting enough for the reader to get excited about reading it.

## What the Package Should Look Like

Make your business plan colorful, clear, and concise. Form is every bit as important as substance. If the reader can't read it easily, your entire effort is wasted. Don't try to put 100 words in a space that is only big enough for 50. Use bullets for emphasis and enough space between lines to allow for easy reading. For type, don't use anything less than 12 point and don't use some exotic type style that makes it difficult to read. Don't use words that only you or your peers will understand. Remember that the reader is not likely to know as much about your business as you do. Use pictures, color logos, and the like … without going overboard. Don't get wordy and expect the reader to enjoy your prose. That's not the purpose of the business plan. And these are only a few of the standard practices.

## Don't Ask Someone Else to Build the Plan

Aside from the fact that you must understand the business plan for your own purposes, you will likely have to face questions from the reader at some point. It would be foolish to have someone else prepare the plan and then fall on your face because you don't understand what it says. You need to understand the most significant features of your business and present them in the appropriate priority for the benefit of the reader and the purpose you intend the plan to serve. Only you can create these building blocks. Then, after getting some feedback on the readability from people who understand your business—and from people who don't—you might ask someone with proofreading skills to ensure that the grammar, spelling, punctuation, and the like are correct.

## The Most Significant Parts

Aside from the fact that every business has its peculiarities, the two most important features in most business plans are the marketing and the financials. Every reader wants to be sure that you understand your competitive position in the marketplace and that you have built your business in a way that will allow you to survive and succeed in that context. Because presentation of your business plan is usually for the purpose of getting something from the reader, it is important for you to understand the financial paperwork that will show the current or future financial success of the company.

Always keep in mind that you don't have to be an accountant, a lawyer, or a marketing guru to write a good business plan. If that were the case, then the American small business landscape would be naked. And you know that this is not the case. Learn what you need to learn in order to understand the nature of the competitive marketplace and your financial needs. And, don't forget, no one is likely to know about the nuances of your business better than you do.

# Approaching the Lender

Remember that there are basically two types of lenders. One lender will loan you money and expect you to return it with interest for the period during which you are using it. The other lender—sometimes called an investor, an angel, or a venture capitalist—will advance money on the basis of participating in the business: this lender comes along for the ride. There are, of course, combinations of lending and equity participation for investors, although banks do not normally engage in combinations of lending and ownership.

You should understand that both lenders have the same goal: they want a return of their investment and something more within what they consider an appropriate time frame. Your job is to create a comfort zone so they can feel secure in your ability to enable them to achieve their goal. This is often called the *exit strategy*, which will be better defined in further discussion. Since the approach to getting the money is more often borrowing from the bank, this will be the basic reference here.

## Know the Bank and the Banker

Banks, just like any other businesses, are not all things to all people. Each bank and each banker will tend to have a positive attitude toward those businesses about which they are most knowledgeable. After all, the lending decision must be based, in great part, on the banker's understanding of the particular business's competitive position in the marketplace, among other things. This is good reason to examine two aspects of the lending relationship early on:

- Know which industries the bank is most likely to receive positively.
- Be prepared to present information about the industry of which your business or prospective business is a part, the size of your business in relation to its competitors, and the particular niche market your business occupies.

Also make sure that you're in the correct department at the bank. Different bankers may well cater to different industries and, certainly, different bankers will have different levels of dollar responsibility. There is no point in talking with a banker about a loan for $250,000 when his or her dollar authority maxes out at $50,000. Also keep in mind that you can do some preliminary work and often save a lot of time by knowing what the bank's parameters are relative to their requirements of assets/income to loan amount. When you bring this up with the banker for clarification, it suggests that you have enough financial knowledge to be credible.

# The Business Plan

Bankers are not interested in participating in your business. Their product is money. Their expertise lies in the value of money—what a certain amount can generate during what period of time with what degree of security. Notice the word "security," rather than "certainty." You must understand that they are not so much interested in whether you can achieve your goals as in whether they can expect to get their money. You should expect them to be looking for additional security for their money, as we will discuss.

However often you have examined and reexamined the basic concept, the necessary elements, and the sequential aspects of preparing a business plan, you must recognize which of those elements are going to be of the highest priority to the bank.

## Focus on the Numbers

Bankers will go immediately to the numbers to see if a discussion is worthwhile. There are many significant elements, each of which may ultimately play a part in a bank's decision. First, the banker wants to find out if the dollar request is within the bank's lending parameters. Second, the banker wants to examine the nature of the business's activity to get a sense of the business's ability to repay a loan. These are both aspects of the numbers.

Venture capitalists and bankers have different points of view. Venture capitalists are primarily interested in the future of the business and what kind of a dollar multiple they might anticipate. Bankers are more interested in the historical financial picture, which might give them some assurance of stability and, in turn, the ability of the company to generate a payment schedule on the loan. As a result, bankers will be looking for the income statement, the rate of growth, the balance sheet, and three to five years of historical information documenting what growth plateaus were reached within what time frames and the money it took to achieve those goals.

Although tax returns will ultimately be required, primarily for confirmation purposes, that is not likely to be until after the application is actually in place. Similarly, a personal financial statement will also be required. This, of course, allows the bank to see just what other assets might be available as additional security for the loan. (Remember the reference earlier to additional security.)

## Make Your Case

How are you going to make your case for a loan? You should know what you are going to say. Bankers are not interested in your ability as an extemporaneous speaker. They are interested in the content of your remarks and the excitement that represents the energy, creativity, and initiative so necessary to the success of any entrepreneurial effort. In other words, bankers want to know that you're just as excited about and interested in the future of the business as you want them to be.

You should, of course, be prepared for questions. But, to begin, you should prepare what you want to convey. Practice it on others, perhaps people who might be friendlier and not involved, seeing if you can get a positive reaction to the approach you intend to take. Trial attorneys often set up mock juries to see what reaction they are likely to get to the presentation they're planning. Why shouldn't you?

Remember that the banker who sees your application likely knows nothing about your business or even the industry of which your business is a part. It is incumbent upon you to create a picture of both that is easy to recognize. Keep in mind that a banker could be handling from 50 to 150 business applications. He or she must have enough information about your business to be comfortable, especially if the banker is going to make a subsequent presentation to an underwriter.

For example, if your business deals in bauxite ore, make sure that your explanation includes the fact that bauxite is used in toothpaste. Without that information, the banker may never recognize the practical value of your product or service. Without that recognition, the banker may not be able to make any assessment of your position in the marketplace—the real world. Don't assume that a lender already understands this reality. This assumption could be your first and last mistake.

## Who's Managing the Business?

However exciting an industry or a business within a given industry may be, every business success is attributable to intelligent business management. Every bank is going to look at a loan application with particular interest in the people on whom the business will depend for its continuity and success. The experience of management personnel and key operational people is going to impact the decision on any application. The banker is going to want to know the people in charge of every aspect of your business's operation.

If, for example, your business plan indicates that a substantial portion of the capital you require is going to be used for marketing, you can be sure that the banker will be interested in the background and experience of your marketing executive. If a big portion of your loan is allocated to manufacturing, the banker will look to the background of your executive in charge. If your intention is to replicate your operation by franchising the concept, the banker will certainly want to examine the experience and prior successes of the individual in charge of creating the franchise program. Don't lose sight of this all-important aspect of your business plan and your presentation.

## Where Is the Money Going?

Even though a given banker might not be familiar with your business or your industry, they are all practiced in the concept of how much money it takes to achieve certain levels of activity and, in turn, generate certain levels of sales and revenues. It is your obligation, as part of your business plan, to explain how you will use the money, what levels of activity you intend to achieve, what business plateaus you hope to attain, and the relationship between this growth and the ultimate goal—profit.

Do your best to think like a banker. If you create a scenario in which you use every dollar to achieve your basic goals, it may be too tight a fit for the average banker. Bankers need to know that there will be enough money available to handle the inevitable contingencies, those things that invariably happen regardless of the most careful planning based on the most extensive investigation and the aggregate thinking of the best minds. If you build a fair margin for error into your business plan, the banker will be more inclined to assess the investment as a minimal risk. Be careful to address this question at every stage of your thinking.

## The Risk

Although there are many specific negatives that will crop up and that you will need to address, there is one that ought to be obvious but that many loan applicants fail to recognize. It was mentioned earlier that bankers want to know that you're just as excited about and interested in the future of the business as you want them to be. They also want to know that you have a risk in the future of the business, just like the one you expect them to take by lending you money.

Many entrepreneurs see the bank loan as an opportunity to get reimbursed for the dollars that they have invested to get the business started. Any lender, whether a lending institution or an investor taking an equity position, will be quite disturbed at the thought that you will not be risking your own money as you ask them to risk their money. They want to know that their investment is going to contribute to the growth of the business and not to reward you for your original investment of time, money, or both.

## Don't Forget the Sizzle

Banks are notoriously and historically known as dry institutions, but don't let that throw you off. As noted earlier, the banker is interested in both the content of your story and the excitement in your presentation. In other words, he or she is interested in the sizzle of your story as well as the meat and potatoes of your presentation. If there is any excitement in your industry, the reputation of your management team, or the particular niche you occupy in the competitive marketplace—anything that makes your business more interesting or explosive than the business next door—make sure to present it as a significant part of your business picture. The banker will never get a feeling for this excitement if you don't convey it!

Keep in mind that very often the banker will need to sell the loan to an underwriter. The banker will need all the tools to build a credible picture. Make sure you fill his or her toolbox with anything and everything that might help. You may get another bite at this apple, but, except under certain circumstances, the first bite may be the most important. Don't expect the bank to do the job without your help. Your loan application should be a joint effort.

## Special Circumstances

Some experienced financial people have a slightly different approach that would be defined as "special circumstances." They suggest that you apply first at a lending institution that you feel will likely reject your loan. The purpose would be to use the application as a test, to get an impression as to which items prove effective and which items are not so well received. This will allow you to restructure your application for maximum effectiveness without prejudicing your loan with an institution that would be likely to approve it.

There are two schools of thought in this regard, so you should discuss this tactic with your financial advisor before making any such decision. Since the banking community in any given city might be very close-knit, with bankers sharing stories with each other, such an approach could cause a dangerous backlash. Be careful before making this decision.

## Get Out of the Bank

Although your first meeting is likely to be at the bank, keep in mind that bankers like to see the collateral available. Invite the banker to visit your business—and do so clearly and early. A good banker is going to have a good idea what to look for. Be as honest with what you show as you should be with what you tell.

There is a story of a banker who was processing a loan to an oil company and specifically examined the oil reservoir owned by the borrower. It wasn't until much later that the banker made a terribly unpleasant discovery: the oil tank was three-quarters full of water and then just topped off with oil.

Most loan situations, of course, are not so fraudulent. However, keep in mind that the slightest variance from total truth and candor can lead any banker to quickly deny a loan application—no matter how good it looks!

## Exit Strategy

In any plan, the exit strategy must always be an integral part. Whether a lender is lending money or an investor is taking an equity position, the questions of return of capital and return on capital are high on the list of priorities. You must build into your presentation the method by which the company expects to repay the loan or the method by which the investor can anticipate the growth of his or her investment and the method by which he or she may ultimately expect to convert the equity position to cash—to cash out. The sophisticated investor usually recognizes that there are basically three ways for this conversion to take place:

- The company may grow so dramatically as to be in a position to pay a dividend to its shareholders. Most small companies will prefer, however, to use these extra dollars to either invest in new equipment or personnel or retire any debt that the company may be carrying.
- The company may present such a positive picture of growth as to attract a bigger company that would acquire it.
- Management may recognize the potential of taking the company public, which could make every investor's share worth a multiple of the investment.

There are, of course, other ways to convert, some of which are less optimistic than others. In the event of a bankruptcy, for example, the investor may get part of the original investment returned, but only after all creditors are paid. The likelihood of a return of any kind to the investor is quite conjectural, as you might well imagine.

Remember that the bank will not be actively participating in your business and your profit, although it may build into the loan a power to veto larger expenditures that it might not consider totally prudent. Be careful that you don't end up with a partner in decision making as part of your loan package. The bank's inclination to protect its investment in the short term might turn out to be inimical to the long-term goals of the company.

Keep in mind that, however you may excite the banker about the potential of your business, you must nonetheless convince him or her that you can repay the loan over a specific period of time within the structure of the business as you've presented it.

## The Essentials of Your Application

In considering your loan application, the bank is looking at many factors. Make sure that you have addressed all of them. These are the primary questions:

- Profitability of the business
- Liquidity of the business
- Solvency of the business

The answers to these questions drive the bank's analysis of your application and its decision:

- What is the ability of the company to repay the debt?
- How much equity do you have in the business?
- How do the industry, the competition, the economy, and the interest rates look for the foreseeable future?
- What is your personal credit history?
- What is available for increasing their security, in terms of your personal guarantee, the availability of any second trust deeds, liens on equipment, or liens on receivables?
- What kind of profits, depending on the outcome of the business plan, will be available to repay the loan?
- How fast are sales growing? Is profit commensurate with sales growth? If not, why not? And how long will this period last?
- What assets can be turned into cash, if necessary?

Last, but not least, keep in mind that, although banks will not take an equity position in your company, they may be able to advise you about alternative sources of investment capital—depending on the size and scope of the risk involved.

## Follow Up

Finally, don't forget that simple, basic courtesies still matter. Send a thank-you note whenever you consider it appropriate because someone has helped you in the loan application process. You never know the extent to which such a courtesy may find its way to the right desk.

Stay on top of the process. There is certainly a difference between bothering someone and following up. Make sure you understand the difference. Being a pain in the neck will not help your cause, but being an interested applicant can make a big difference.

## The Big Decision
### Rejection

You understand by now that there are many reasons for which a bank might reject your application for a loan. You also understand that rejection by one bank does not necessarily portend rejection by others. Banks have different philosophies, different levels of participation, and different criteria, depending on industry, size of loan, purpose of loan, and competitive position in the marketplace.

So, if you get rejected, don't fold up your tent! Go to the banker, in the correct frame of mind, and ask for his or her reasons for rejecting your application. You might, under the right circumstances, even ask him or her for advice as to which institution might be a good bet for you to try next. You might find that an adjustment in your business plan or your application might make a big difference in your next attempt. And from this follow-up interview you might find out that by making some changes in your method of operation, you might be a much more suitable candidate for a loan six to eight months down the road ... at the same bank!

### Acceptance

If the bank accepts your application, you might think that it's the end of the process. Actually, it might still be quite near the beginning. The bank may have approved your loan based on the general health and stability of the business, but at this stage, you might not yet have addressed some of the more mundane aspects of the loan. Consider the following issues:

- What is the method of funding? Is it a line of credit to be used as activity demands, is it based on periodic approval by the bank based on certain criteria, or is it a complete funding at one time?
- What is the interest rate? Is it different from what you've anticipated, because of a change in the federal rate since the time of your original inquiry or your application? Does the risk that the bank is taking demand a higher interest rate?
- Is the repayment schedule more difficult than you anticipated in your repayment plan? Was the subject of your collateral security specifically addressed?
- Are you willing to offer your personal guarantee as part of the collateral security for the loan?
- After all, if you're not willing to take the risk, why should they? Keep in mind that both collateral security and a personal signature can be reduced as you pay off your loan. Although it's unlikely, the bank may release any security that is in excess of the current balance.

## The Bankruptcy Loan

At this point we should consider another type of loan application, by a company that has declared a Chapter 11 bankruptcy, to enable reconstruction.

It is fairly obvious that, given the choice, the average banker would prefer to exclude from his or her portfolio any business that has declared bankruptcy. However, for those who understand the implications of a Chapter 11 bankruptcy, investment in such a project can often represent a lesser risk than normal and an opportunity to recapture the loan with greater security in hand and over a shorter period of time. It also means that there will be considerably greater supervision over business operations. In some cases, an earlier loan by the bank may be at risk; an additional loan could help restructure the business and, conceivably, rehabilitate the original lending position. An accomplished Chapter 11 might be well received by a knowledgeable banker.

You should not expect, however, to get any advice from the bank with regard to such position. There are potential liability problems with respect to any such advice and this is not within the purview of normal banking activity.

## Key Points to Remember

- Make sure your business plan shows your knowledge of the marketplace, your financial goals, and your competitive position.
- What the lender knows about your business will likely be limited to the information you present.
- Although lenders will assess risk primarily on your financial history, their examination of your management team will always be a high priority.
- Every investor will be particularly interested in how you handle your exit strategy—how the lender gets paid.
- A rejection can, in many ways, be converted into a learning process for the next presentation.

# PART FIVE

# Contract Elements

# The Noncompete, Nondisclosure Issue

### Illustration 23-1. Signing a Noncompete

Allison and Jimmy Lee were working for the Markham Collection Agency. As time went on, they became very close friends. As they climbed the management ladder, they became completely immersed in the concepts and methodologies that Ed Markham had developed over the ten years before Allison and Jimmy Lee joined his company. As the economy grew more problematic, the business started growing dramatically. Ed realized that any of his senior employees might leave the company and become competitors. Instead of developing some bonus or equity programs to retain them, Ed decided to have his lawyer prepare an employee manual that would include a nondisclosure, noncompete section. He insisted that all of his employees sign it.

About eight months later, Allison and Jimmy Lee decided to leave Markham Collection Agency and started their own agency. Ed brought legal action against the two of them, alleging that they were precluded from becoming a competing business because they had signed the employee manual.

- What do you think a court would do under such circumstances?
- Do you think it makes a difference that Allison and Jimmy Lee were employees instead of owners?
- Do you think it makes a difference that they were asked to sign the employee manual after they had been employed for some time?
- Do you wonder if Ed Markham had protected his "proprietary information"?

There are two aspects of the noncompete question that the owner of a business or the buyer of a business must understand. The first is the problem when an employee leaves his or her employer in order to join a competitor in the same marketplace. The second is the problem when a business owner sells the business and then starts a competing business.

This chapter addresses the issues and dynamics of both aspects of the noncompete question. They need to be examined in detail, because both have become the core elements of substantial litigation and deserve additional attention.

## When a Business Is Transferred

Someone who buys a business should certainly be entitled to the comfort of knowing that the person selling it is not going to set up a competing business across the street immediately after the sale and then lure old customers away to that new business. Such a move could jeopardize and maybe even destroy the business acquired by the buyer. This is why the buyer may require as part of the terms of the sale that the seller sign an agreement not to compete—a very usual request.

In general, a noncompete clause must be "reasonable." This means that it must be justified by some reasonable circumstances and involve reasonable consideration: the sale of a business would qualify on both counts. It must also be reasonable in geographic scope and in duration. Determining what is reasonable in terms of scope and time can be problematic. In fact, that's usually the only question a court has with noncompete clauses—whether geographic scope and duration are reasonable.

## When an Employee Leaves

The situation in which an employee leaves to go to work for a competitor is perhaps the more prevalent noncompete problem. It may come as a surprise that, in many states, a noncompete agreement between employees and an employer is not enforceable. The reason for this is that the broad interpretation of such an agreement would suggest that it is in restraint of trade. Technically, yes, it is a restraint of trade. After all, a noncompete agreement is intended to legally keep an individual from engaging in a lawful occupation in the venue of his or her choice. The key to a noncompete agreement that courts would enforce is in the language that would make a specific case an exception to the general rule.

The critical element is that, in the sale of a business, the departure of an employee can be detrimental to the buyer, the seller, or both, because both buyer and seller are likely to be vulnerable.

Most small businesses are not sold for cash, but rather with a down payment and the balance of the price paid over time. If a key employee unexpectedly leaves the business shortly after the sale, the buyer may believe that the seller misrepresented the business, even though the seller may have known nothing of the employee's intention to leave. The buyer may feel justified in not making payments on the balance of the purchase price.

The departure of the employee, then, could jeopardize the seller's ability to collect payment in full. The question, unfortunately, may have to be resolved in court.

Is there a way to protect against this possibility? To the extent that contract language can prevent an employee from leaving, the answer is no! To the extent that contract language can protect the seller against losing the balance of the purchase price, the answer is yes! The key is in the drafting of the purchase and sale agreement. The buyer must acknowledge that the employee structure of the company will be a responsibility of the buyer and not the seller. The seller may be protected if both parties reach this agreement with a complete and mature understanding of its implications.

## Trade Secrets and Nondisclosure

An agreement to keep former employees from making disclosures about trade secrets to a competitor or any third party is usually enforceable. The nature of the information, however, must be carefully defined. The information must be specific to the extent that it is either a development or an accumulation of data that has taken a substantial investment to acquire or that others could acquire only through a substantial investment.

The information must also be considered valuable, not only when it is protected from disclosure to outside sources but also when it is protected within close confines, even within the company itself. If the company does not consider it important enough to protect it, why should the court?

Ultimately, this is the question: does such disclosure give an unfair commercial advantage to a competitor that has not invested in its development?

## Special Access

The relationship of the employee to the company can have significant bearing on the enforceability of noncompete or nondisclosure language in a contract. An employee who is at the management level and who has management discretion or prerogatives is likely to be held to a higher standard than those who are not at that level. The special nature of management or executive personnel suggests that they have special access to the private, proprietary, and protectable information so necessary for the maintenance, continuity, and success of the business.

However, keep in mind that the nondisclosure or noncompete language is contractual. It is not inherent in the employer-employee relationship.

Follow these guidelines:

- Noncompete and nondisclosure language must be carefully designed and delineated.
- Noncompete and nondisclosure language must have consideration, as in any other contract. That is, the employee must accept the language as part of his or her employment arrangement; it cannot merely be added at some point after the fact.
- Although clearly a question of fact, the relationship must be one of trust and confidence that prevails on the management level.

## What Will the Courts Say?

The language used in drafting noncompete and nondisclosure agreements is obviously important. No matter how artfully you draft the document, however, keep in mind that if the employer chooses to enforce the contract or the employee chooses not to abide by it, the court must accept the language. It is important that the document carefully define the essential elements: the relationship, the information to be protected, the length of time involved, and the area within which the person is not to compete.

Here is an interesting point. Some courts will examine the language to see if it is reasonable and then decide, on that basis, to enforce it or not. In other words, some courts will take the language as they find it. It is both reasonable and appropriate or it is not. If not, it is simply not enforceable. Other courts take the position that the parties intended for the protection to exist even though the agreement was actually drafted by an attorney representing the employer. These courts tend to rewrite the language in order to make it acceptable and enforceable. In other words, if the language prohibits competition within the Commonwealth of Massachusetts and the court deems the geographic scope to be too extensive, the court may rewrite the language to include only the cities east of Worcester.

Remember that litigation is expensive, in terms of money, time, energy, and sometimes image and morale. An employer must make a careful judgment, before the fact, as to whether the cost of legally enforcing the noncompete or nondisclosure agreement is worth the protection it is intended to provide.

## Temporary Restraining Order

When an employer seeks to enforce a nondisclosure agreement, the first order of legal business is for his or her lawyer to seek a temporary restraining order to prevent any dissemination of the protected information until the entire problem can be examined and resolved by the court. Otherwise, if it took weeks or months for the case to come to court and for the judge to rule, the judgment would obviously come after the fact. Such a protracted decision would not afford any comfort to the employer. In order to prevent unauthorized disclosures, the lawyer will ask the court to make a preliminary judgment even before hearing both sides and determining all the facts. This must be done in order to maintain the current status and prevent any such disclosure before the court has an opportunity to fully examine the facts.

This may seem like a prudent solution, but there's a problem—cost. The lawyer must examine the entire case in order to make this plea to the court for a temporary injunction. This means that the cost of the temporary restraining order could conceivably be the most substantial of the legal costs of the entire action. It shouldn't come as a surprise to the commercially sophisticated employer that this figure could be $50,000. This should certainly suggest that an employer give a lot of thought to the question of enforcement before deciding to go forward with a legal action.

## The Intimidation Factor

From the employee's perspective, a nondisclosure agreement certainly deserves an equal amount of attention. Before choosing to violate the language of the contract, the employee must consider the following questions:

- Is the employer likely to go to court to enforce it?
- Is the court likely to find in favor of the employer?
- Do I have the money necessary to mount a defense?
- Are the dollars involved in the activity in question worth the risk?

As you can see, even if the contract language is never enforced in court, it certainly serves as a deterrent that would cause the employee to think before deciding to disregard that language.

Also, consider that any company that is contemplating hiring the former employee—even if part of the reason is to access privileged information—must understand that it could then easily become part of any legal action brought by the former employer. In other words, the new employer might be accused of having been involved in a conspiracy to obtain the privileged information. The former employer could also take legal action against the new employer for interfering with a contractual relationship or interfering with an advantageous business relationship. Either of these actions could result in substantial damages against the new employer. As you can see, there are good reasons why each of the parties involved should give serious thought to the consequences before entering this very conjectural arena.

## The Exit Interview

This is one of the reasons why an employer should always conduct an exit interview when an employee is leaving because of termination or expiration of a contract relationship. It lays the groundwork for a clear understanding of what is expected of the parties after the relationship ends. It is an opportunity to review any such language that might have been inserted in a contract at the outset of the relationship.

## The Danger with Salespeople

One of the biggest problems in the highly competitive marketplace is the aggressive nature of outside selling. Although some businesses have always depended on outside sales in the form of distributors or an internal sales department, there are many businesses that used to rely on advertising in various media. Today, the one-on-one relationship appears to be the most successful method of selling products and services. In this context, many businesses are not satisfied with the somewhat passive media. They are interested in a much more aggressive approach to sales.

When you hire a salesperson, you are putting him or her in direct contact with your customers. In many cases, the customers don't care or maybe even don't know that you are the owner of the business. They are concerned only with the person on whom they depend for the timely delivery, quality, and fair pricing of the service or product they are buying. So, your client or customer's business relationship is not really with the company at all; it is with your sales representative. If the salesperson decides to move to a competitor, your customers may very well follow to the competitor. It is a clear and present danger.

## Not Everything Is Protectable

Many things, even those that appear relatively mundane, can be protected if the company affords the information sufficient dignity to warrant its protection as valuable and secret. These items can include customer lists, business plans, financial information, research data, and methods of instruction.

However, you can't keep an ex-employee from using his or her knowledge of the trade and his or her general skills as a salesperson, an engineer, a paralegal, and so on. Generally, those things that are public knowledge or that can be learned by participating in a particular industry would be difficult to protect unless the company can show that its methodology is different enough to warrant a special or peculiar presentation. The question of proof becomes the key—and don't forget the costs involved in proving it.

## So What Is the Answer?

The answer doesn't lie so much in the language of the contract. It is easy enough to recognize that even the most carefully drawn language in a contract is not only subject to the ultimate discretion of a court but is also dramatically expensive. The real answer lies outside the contract relationship of the parties.

One of the reasons for companies to create profit-sharing and pension plans, such as the 401(k), is that the investment by both employer and employee gives the employee a reason to remain with the company. Years ago, loyalty was the primary adhesive element. Today, with corporations showing as much downsizing as loyalty, the vested dollar becomes the higher priority.

Even without the substantial investment in the more sophisticated plans, the small-business owner can create this vested-dollar incentive. When you hire a salesperson or a key employee without whom the business would not be as strong or whose absence could even mean a significant sales loss, you can set up a plan.

In many sales situations, a contractual arrangement is made that provides for a salesperson who leaves the business to continue to receive a percentage of the normal commission for any accounts that he or she sold while with the employer. This percentage usually declines over time until the dollar amount reaches zero. At the same time, the new salesperson receives the other part of the commission, a percentage that rises as the percentage paid to the former salesperson declines.

For example, when a salesperson leaves, he or she might get 80 percent of personal sales for the first year, 60 percent in the second, 40 percent in the third, and so on down to zero, while the new salesperson might get 20 percent in the first year, 40 percent in the second, 60 percent in the third, and so on up to 100 percent. This arrangement can be orchestrated in various ways. It is usually predicated on the salesperson leaving under pleasant circumstances; there are usually no payments at all if the salesperson leaves to work for a competitor.

In addition to this, part of the salary or compensation arrangement for a new employee could be for a certain percentage or dollar amount to be deposited in an escrow account, a holding account, which would continue to build up during the employee's tenure. When the employee would decide to leave the business, he or she would receive the money in this escrow account—but only under certain terms and conditions. For example, the money held in escrow could be paid out over a period of five years. This arrangement creates an incentive for the employee to think carefully before leaving to work for a competitor.

## One Last Caution

Be sure that you examine these alternatives with your attorney in order to be sure that you are not violating any laws mandating parity among employees for anything that falls within the area of profit-sharing and pension plans.

# Key Points to Remember

- In the purchase of any business, the seller's agreement to a noncompete clause is mandatory.

- Trade secrets and other proprietary information subject to nondisclosure must be afforded the appropriate dignity to ensure their protection.
- Noncompete language must be reasonable in terms of both time and geography in order to be likely enforceable.
- The more practical approach of the dollar incentive is becoming more prevalent in the business marketplace than the threat of legal enforceability.
- Whatever the problem of disclosure, never lose sight of the legal costs involved in enforcement.

# CHAPTER 24

# The End of the Franchise Contract

## Illustration 24-1. Franchise Goes South

Charlene and Justin had been owners of a women's clothing franchise for ten years. At this point, the franchise contract expired. The franchise company tried to get them to renew their contract for another ten years. Charlene and Justin decided not to. The language in their contract prevented them from staying in the business as independents. Worse yet, they had been buying their goods through the franchisor at a discount, which the manufacturer did not offer to independents. That was the deal that the franchisor had made with the manufacturer and the reason why all the franchisees had to buy through the franchise company, not from the manufacturer. If Charlene and Justin bought clothes from other manufacturers, their profit margin would not be sufficient enough for the business to survive.

Although the problem was difficult, Charlene and Justin realized that they had developed a very substantial and loyal customer base. They decided to change the business from women's clothes to children's clothes. The franchisor brought a legal action against them to prevent them from selling children's clothes as independents at their former franchise location.

- What do you think the court would do?
- Do you think it was a good idea to convert their customer base from women's clothes to children's clothes?
- Do you think that Charlene and Justin had any other alternatives?

What happens when the dance is over? When you own an independent business, it can go on forever. When you own a franchise business, the relationship eventually comes to an end. Then what do you do?

It is certainly true that buying any business is quite traumatic, since the decision will obviously involve a lot of time and money. To do a reasonably good job in the due diligence phase of examining the business and the industry takes a lot of work. Making judgments about working capital, personnel, training, equipment, and the myriad other things that constitute the basic structure of the business is mind-boggling. And it all must be done.

Then, in the case of a franchise, the buyer must examine the relationship under which he or she will be operating the business: this is critically important.

All the factors involved in making the decision whether to go into business as an independent or as a franchise affiliate can be overwhelming. Is this any time to consider what the alternatives will be when the franchise contract ultimately comes to an end? Unfortunately, yes.

## All Franchise Contracts Are Not the Same

Although time and legislation have created a basic format that most franchise companies follow, franchise contracts are not all alike. The amount of the royalty payable, most often calculated on the gross sales of the business, may vary from 1 percent to 10 percent or more. Some royalties are payable weekly; some are paid monthly. And some mandate that the royalties be automatically deducted from the franchisee's bank account. There is often an advertising commitment in addition to the royalties. The percentage for advertising also varies from company to company. Some of the advertising dollars are allocated for national advertising, some are allocated for local advertising, and sometimes the franchisor has complete discretion in placing the advertising dollars.

Although you will certainly want to compare any franchise contract with others in the same industry in terms of the above points, most franchise companies have adjusted their royalty and advertising policies to conform to industry standards. They usually correlate in some way with the amount of the profit that the franchise is expected to generate. After all, it would be silly for the franchisor to expect to collect revenues that would leave the franchisee without any income. It is unlikely that you will find a dramatic difference between one franchise company and another in the same industry. On the other hand, you should always make this initial comparison to be sure that you are not looking at an exception.

## Long-Term Plans

All the dollars-and-cents elements of the franchise relationship should certainly be factored into your business plan. The issue that is difficult to consider in the early stages of your entrepreneurial adventure is the purpose of your long-term plans. If you are in your early 20s, your perspective of the future may be considerably different from what it might be if you were in your 50s. Some people buy a business with the intention that it will be the family business for more than just a single generation, that ownership will pass to the children. Other people buy a business with the intention of building it into a dynasty that will consume all of their intellect, energy, and emotion for a lifetime. Still others have shorter-term goals for taking the business to a particular plateau and then converting their earned equity to a retirement income by selling the business. There are yet others, depending in part on the industry chosen, who recognize that they are essentially buying a job from which they can't be discharged and that they can abandon when they choose to do so.

## Why Did They Become Franchisees?

This, of course, brings us to the very nature of the franchise relationship. Without belaboring the concept of the franchise, suffice it to say that most entrepreneurs choose the franchise route because they lack the experience, education, or confidence to go into business alone. They want to take advantage of the experience of the franchisor, which, in most cases, has been considerable over an extended time. This enables the neophyte entrepreneur to enjoy many benefits, including training, supervision, and quantity discounts with vendors. The neophyte also benefits from research and development that most entrepreneurs have neither the time nor the ability to do themselves. The beginner can also reap the marketing and advertising savvy, which is difficult if not impossible to obtain on an independent's budget. He or she also has the opportunity to meet with franchisees from all over the country and compare notes with peers who may share private and proprietary aspects of their business with other franchisees with whom they are not in direct competition. Yes, these are reasons why buyers look to the franchise rather than scale the mountain by themselves.

## The Norm in the Seller's Marketplace

Most entrepreneurs, whether by design or by default, seem to end up converting their earned equity into a retirement income. Still others find, after giving the business their best efforts, that the profit is not sufficient to warrant maintaining the franchise relationship: the royalties are dollars that the owner would prefer to keep.

In the first instance, it is appropriate to recognize that the difference between franchise and independent makes a difference in selling the business. Do you think it will be easier to sell it as a franchise or as an independent? Do you think you will be able to get more money for it as a franchise or as an independent? These questions are especially interesting because they can vary according to a range of factors, especially geography.

## The Questions of Advertising Impact and Visibility

Franchise companies, as noted earlier, collect monies from their franchisees for basically three reasons. The first is that they need the money in order to service the franchisees, to be available when a franchisee needs help or advice. The second is that they need money to sell the concept of the franchise to potential franchisees. The third is to advertise the products and services, to bring customers to the franchisees. This advertising generates revenues for the franchisees from whom the franchisor gets royalties and advertising dollars. This is the cycle. The bigger the franchise name and the more recognizable the franchise logo, the more likely that entrepreneurs will want to buy franchises and, presumably, the more likely that franchisees will enjoy a favorable equity position when they sell their franchise.

On the other hand, if the name and logo do not have this commercial impact and if the franchisee no longer feels a need for the services provided by the franchisor, then the question of the franchise name becomes a lower priority. If the franchisee chooses not to renew the contract when it expires, that decision to go independent might not impair his or her ability to sell the business at all. In fact, if the business operates as an independent rather than as a franchise, there are no royalties to pay, so a potential buyer would enjoy greater profits.

Since most businesses are valued, at least in part, on the basis of profit, it is easy to recognize that a business might sell for a higher price as an independent rather than as a franchise. This, of course, is based on the ability of the owner to continue to function equally well as an independent after the franchise relationship ends. This may or not be problematic, depending in great part on the industry, as you will see later on in the chapter.

The owner must also reflect on the fact that the noncompete clause of the franchise contract might prevent him or her from continuing in the same business after the franchise relationship ends.

## The Length of the Contract

Franchises also differ with respect to the length of the contract. Some are for as little as five years and some are for as long as 25 years. Occasionally, you will even run into a franchise contract that suggests it is in perpetuity—in other words, forever. As the old saying goes, time flies when you're having fun. Certainly that's true when you're busy and, as an entrepreneur, you will be busy. The five-year contract or even the 25-year contract comes to an end faster than you might think.

You are constantly told that in business you must always plan ahead. That wisdom applies in this case. You should examine the length of the contract, your long-term plans for yourself and your family, and the limitations on competition specified in the contract.

## The Language of Limitations

The typical franchise contract contains language to the effect that, for a certain period of time and within certain geographical boundaries, the franchisee and any representative or affiliate of the franchisee are precluded from competing with the business. The language of these limitations differs from contract to contract: any franchise candidate should read and understand these differences. Even if you are permitted to continue the business after the franchise contract expires, you might have to give up the telephone number that is listed under the franchise logo in the Yellow Pages. After all, the logo belongs to the franchise company, which is entitled, if not obligated, to protect it from use by any business that is not part of the franchise. In some industries, losing the telephone number in the Yellow Pages could devastate the business.

## The Geography

Since most franchise contracts designate a certain geography for each franchise, the noncompete language usually uses the same geographical boundaries. The language will state that the franchisee is precluded from participating "in any competitive business located or operating within the statistical market area of the terminated franchise."

Some problems are created when the franchisor tries to prevent competition not only within the area that was allocated to the terminated franchise but also within all of its franchise territories anywhere. Such language is contained in a paragraph that precludes the franchisee from operating in a competitive capacity "within a fifteen (15) mile radius of the franchised location or within fifteen (15) miles of any other franchised or company-owned store." Another franchise contract uses the same language, but specifies an area of no less than 25 miles. In the case of a national franchise, such language could preclude the ex-franchisee from working anywhere! Without knowing whether a court in your particular state would enforce this restriction, what would be your immediate reaction to this kind of limitation?

## What Is "Reasonable"?

It is interesting that one franchisor tries to eliminate the question of "reasonable" by asking the franchisee to sign a contract with the following language: "the franchisee acknowledges that the terms and conditions of this covenant are fair and reasonable with respect to both the time and distance restrictions." Some attorneys suggest that this language precludes the need for a court to decide whether the restrictions are fair and reasonable. Other attorneys suggest that the court will not necessarily accept this agreement by the parties and will accept or reject it only after a fair hearing on the facts. The decision will depend on the court and the disposition of the judge, factors over which you as a franchisee would have little or no influence.

## Not Just the Franchisee

In order to prevent former franchisees from the clever strategy of operating under someone else's name, most of the contracts contain language that is quite inclusive. Here's an example: "franchisee and each of its principals agrees not to engage within forty (40) miles of the approved location, either directly or indirectly, as an owner, officer, director, shareholder, partner, employee, consultant, or agent in any activity competitive to the business of the franchisor or which is similar to or conducts its business in a manner similar to, or be involved in any manner."

Here's another example of language that makes the restriction pretty tight: "as a disclosed or beneficial owner, investor, partner, representative or agent or in any other capacity." Some language even attempts to include those who may never have had any relationship to the contract: "through a member of any immediate family of the franchisee or its owners or otherwise."

A franchisor may temper this very restrictive language, as in this example: "the restrictions of this Section shall not be applicable to the ownership of shares of a class of securities listed on a stock exchange or traded on the over-the-counter market that represent 5 percent or less of the number of shares of that class of securities issued and outstanding." It obviously doesn't leave very much room for any sort of participation short of a minor investment in a publicly traded company.

Whether or not any court would enforce much of this restrictive language is conjectural for most attorneys. However, the language stands as valid unless challenged.

## The Adjusted Compromise

Occasionally, you will find language that is somewhat surprising, in favor of the franchisee. You may surmise that it emanates from a company with a different sense of morality or ethics. It might, however, be a compromise that was made between the franchisor and the franchisee to keep peace in the franchise "family—in other words, a compromise that was either designed to avoid litigation or developed during a litigation situation. Here is an example: "For one (1) year following the earlier termination *(but not expiration)* of this agreement, franchisee shall not directly or indirectly, own, operate, or have any interest (as an owner, employee, director, officer, salesperson, representative, or agent or in any other capacity) within the exclusive franchise area or three (3) miles of the location of the store authorized by this agreement." The exclusion of the word "expiration" gives a prerogative to the franchisee that is most unusual.

## Negotiating the Contract Provision

What about requesting a change in the language of the franchise contract before you commit to signing it? Keep in mind that the franchise relationship depends on consistency among the franchisees. If one franchisee finds that another has a much different contract or one in which the language has been seriously changed, the franchise's cohesiveness could be destroyed as a result. It is for this reason that it is not normal for a potential franchisee to make changes in the franchise contract. It is possible, and there are certainly areas where minor adjustments might be made. But, as a general rule, don't think that you can substantially adjust the terms and conditions of a franchise contract. The reasons are obvious. You would not want to find out after the fact that someone else has a more advantageous contract than you do, would you?

## Contract Language Aside

Perhaps the biggest question to be answered in this context is whether there are reasons that will prevent an independent from competing with the franchise after the contract expires because of things that have nothing to do with the noncompete language itself. As one franchisor said, "If there isn't a secret formula or some other exclusive, proprietary item that is susceptible of absolute protection, there better be some special prerogatives that the ex-franchisee, now the independent, cannot enjoy without being a part of the franchise company."

This kind of prerogative can take many forms. In the case of one fast-food company, the franchisor provides the product in frozen form, eliminating the need to measure ingredients, knead dough, or design the product for sale. If the franchisee were to leave the fold when the contract expires, he or she would no longer have access to the product. The owner would have to create an entirely different product that would have neither the quality nor the customer appeal of the franchised product.

In another company, the franchisee is totally dependent on the use of certain vendors whose pricing structure is extremely beneficial to the franchisees because of the quantity of purchases made by the franchisor through its network. If a franchise turned independent, he or she could no longer benefit from this discount structure and the profit margin would decrease to the point that it was unlikely to be sufficient to support the business.

## But I've Got the Customers!

In some cases, building the customer base is the biggest problem in a retail business. If you have loyal customers, it might not make a big difference that you are now selling cookies instead of cake or tea instead of coffee. In some such situations, the product or service may change enough to avoid the non-compete language but still appeal to the customer base. That situation might be unusual, but it does happen.

Of course, this is exactly what many franchisors are trying to protect against. After all, if the franchise product is designed to create a certain ambiance around the sale of the product, is it the product or the ambiance that is the real moneymaker? And if the ambiance can be maintained with a different product, has the franchisee actually used the franchisor's advertising dollars to build a business that can now be used for another product? On the other hand, many franchisors would not care if this happens, since they are more concerned about their product or service than about the customer base.

## The Ultimate Contract Compromise

Many franchisors have recognized the problem of enforcing such restrictive language and have tried to avoid the problem of competition in a different way. They have acknowledged that, whatever the franchisor has invested in the trade name and whatever it has done to help create a successful enterprise for the franchisee, not all franchisees will want to renew their franchise obligations when the contract expires. In fact, long before the contract expires, many don't feel comfortable paying the royalty. Unhappy franchisees are not good for the propagation of the system. The unhappiness, in some cases, has a way of spreading, and it certainly isn't a good idea to suggest that someone interested in buying a franchise talk with a franchisee who may express dissatisfaction.

The answer is to give these unhappy franchisees a way out, one that may be painful to their pocketbook but that will not hurt the franchise. Money is often the answer.

In some cases, the franchisor offers a dollar buyout equivalent to a percentage of the last year's gross income. In other cases, the franchisor tries to create a present value based on the average royalties being paid annually and then multiplied by the number of years left on the contract.

In order to keep this from being considered a "penalty," which the courts are hesitant to enforce, the franchisor describes this buyout as "liquidated damages." This means that the amount is theoretically equivalent to the loss the company would incur when the franchisee leaves and no longer pays the royalty to which the company would otherwise be entitled. Even though the franchisee signs the contract that contains this language, most lawyers feel that whether this dollar amount is reasonable is still subject to the opinion of a court. This is especially true when the percentage or the dollar amount does not appear to be related to the real dollars involved and suggests that it is, in fact, a penalty and thus unenforceable.

For example, "franchisee agrees ... that the damage to franchisor's business arising from a breach of the provisions of this covenant not to compete is difficult to assess and that payment to franchisor of forty-five percent (45%) of the revenues related to franchisee's breach would be reasonable and franchisee agrees to pay and franchisor agrees to accept payment of that amount as liquidated damages for such breach." Would you consider that percentage a reasonable compromise?

Of course, if the amount designated in the contract or a negotiated amount is acceptable to a franchisee who wants out of the contract, then the concept certainly serves its purpose for both parties—they don't end up in court.

The language involved in these noncompete situations is difficult to understand and even more difficult to interpret. It is the kind of question that you must discuss with your attorney. Remember: the long-term consequence of your signature on any contract is something you must consider at the beginning of any relationship.

## Key Points to Remember

- Check the length of the franchise commitment in order to ensure that its expiration coincides with your personal plans for the future.
- Although it may not appear to be a high priority when buying a franchise, it is important to note the conditions under which you can continue in business after your franchise contract expires.
- Do you think your customers will be loyal to you even if you change the name of your business or do you think the absence of the franchise logo will mean losing your customers?

- Have your attorney explain the reasonableness and the potential enforceability of your franchise expiration language in your state.
- Make sure you understand the limitations of staying in business if you choose not to renew your franchise contract.

# PART SIX

# Revisiting the Essentials and Valuing an Internet Business

# CHAPTER 25

# Revisiting the Financial Issues

### Illustration 25-1. The Difference
### Between *Accrual* and *Cash*

When Alice Sparks decided to sell her printing business, it was explained to her that she needed to prepare a profit and loss statement (an income statement) and make it available to the buyer. This would enable the buyer to examine all the expenses against revenues in order to determine the profit of the business. Alice chose to do this on a cash basis. The results were disastrous.

In the printing business, the month of December is notoriously slow. This means that January is a catch-up month during which many obligations are paid for the previous year's activities. In order to catch up on some old debts, Alice prevailed upon her landlord to suspend her rent payments for November and December of 2006. This amounted to $10,000—$5,000 for each of those months. She promised to make these payments in January and February of the following year in addition to the January and February rent payments. As a result of using the cash method of accounting, her P&L reflected rent payments of 10 months for 2006 ($50,000). And, her P&L for 2007 reflected rent payments of 14 months for 2007 ($70,000). This represented the actual cash expenditures for 2006 and 2007, but it was very misleading to the buyer. If the buyer looked at the 2006 figures, the price would be about $50,000 more than it should be. If the buyer looked at the 2007 figures, the price would be about $50,000 less than it should be. The difference between the two years in terms of the expected selling price would be $100,000—not exactly peanuts!

When a potential buyer is looking at the price for a business, he or she is not interested in the manipulations of the seller for personal reasons. A potential buyer wants to know the income and the obligations for each month and whether they are paid or not. This is the accrual method of accounting and, for the most part, ought to be the method used to determine the operational activity of most businesses.

How much do you know about finances? How do you absorb and use financial information? We are all different in our knowledge, experience, and processing. Since understanding financial basics is a predicate for understanding the entire topic of business valuation, this chapter has been added to ensure that, whatever your background, education, or learning disposition, the information is packaged from a slightly different perspective. In this context, this chapter uses definitions as well as charts. If we are to be accused of redundancy, our defense is that we want to make sure that you understand the financial issues.

## The Balance Sheet

The balance sheet is a document to which many entrepreneurs fail to give the proper respect. They think it is a tool that is more important to the accountant at tax time than to the owner in operating the business. Nothing could be further from the truth. This section explains the basic elements and presents some of the reasons why the balance sheet is important, whether you're buying a business, selling a business, expanding a business, or just surviving.

## Structure and Components

The balance sheet consists of three components structured into two sections. The first section is Assets (what you own). The second section is Liabilities (what you owe) and—depending on the legal form of the company—Owner's/Owners' Equity or Stockholders' Equity (what you have invested and earned, the difference between assets and liabilities).

The balance sheet represents the financial position of the company at a moment in time. To understand the financial health of the company, you must see more than one balance sheet over a period of time, so you can understand the direction the company is taking.

The layout of the balance sheet is as follows:

## Assets

*Current Assets*
   Cash
   Marketable Securities
   Accounts Receivable
   Inventory
     Raw materials
     Work in process
     Finished goods
   Prepaid Expenses
*Long-Term Assets*
   Property, Plant, and Equipment
   Furniture and Equipment
   Machines
   Building
   Land
   Accumulated Depreciation
**Total Assets**

**Liabilities**

*Current Liabilities*

Accounts Payable

Accrued Expenses

Income Tax Payable

Short-Term Notes Payable

Total Current Liabilities

*Long-Term Liabilities*

Long-Term Notes Payable

Total Long-Term Liabilities

**Total Liabilities**

**Stockholders' Equity**

Capital Stock/Paid in Capital (cash or other contributions to the business)

Retained Earnings

**Total Liabilities and Stockholders' Equity**

## What Is a Balance Sheet Statement?

A balance sheet statement is a snapshot of the financial support structure you need to be able to make sales. Now, let's look at how we define the structure of the three segments—assets, liabilities, and owner's/owners' or stockholders' equity.

**Assets** are the part of a business that helps support and pay for the work of a business or, to put it another way, the work the business needs to do to complete a sale. Assets divide into two categories: current assets and long-term assets. Current assets include cash, accounts receivable, marketable securities, and inventory. These assets are considered current because they can be easily converted into cash. Long-term assets include equipment, buildings, and land. These assets have a life of over one year and cannot be converted to cash as easily as current assets. Long-term assets make it possible for a company to continue to build widgets or provide a place for a company to do whatever work must be done to complete a sale. Assets include prepaid expenses—expenses paid in advance, such as insurance, leases, and deposits—and accumulated depreciation—a deduction the government allows for certain assets based on the presumed life of the assets.

Cash listed on the balance sheet comes from sales made with cash or from sales made on credit. Cash also comes from investments or from lines of credit that a company maintains with banks. Cash pays for inventory and for the daily operations.

**Liabilities** are commitments (debt) that a company incurs to support business operations. Liabilities are divided, like assets, into two categories: current liabilities and long-term liabilities. Current liabilities include accounts payable, accrued expenses, income tax payables, and short-term notes payable (lines of credit). These debts are totally paid off within one year. Long-term liabilities include long-term notes payable. These are debts that are paid over time, such as an equipment loan or a loan for a building or land.

**Owner's/Owners' or Stockholders' Equity** is the difference between assets and liabilities. Equity is divided into two basic categories: Capital Stock (investments in the company, in cash or other) and Retained Earnings (net income not distributed to the owners or shareholders). The Retained Earnings appear on a balance sheet only after the company has been in business for one year. Retained Earnings maintains the records of earnings and losses directly from the profit and loss statement (income statement).

## The Balance Sheet as a Reference Point

Unlike the profit and loss statement, which shows you a picture of the business in a chronological way, month to month, the balance sheet does not represent a chronology. It's a picture of the business at a moment in time. In order to understand that kind of picture, you will need to compare two balance sheets.

For example, if December 2003 shows a loan outstanding in the amount of $120,000, you will need to look at a month in 2004 to see what the balance is. If the balance of the loan in December 2004 is $60,000, then you know that you paid $60,000 on the principal of the loan between December 2003 and December 2004. It is likely that you paid $5,000 each month during that 12-

month period. You can then plug this figure into your profit and loss statement (which likely contains only the interest payments on the loan) and you have a clearer picture of the monthly obligations of the business.

|  | December 2003 | December 2004 |
|---|---|---|
| **Liabilities** | $120,000 | $60,000 |

What can you learn about the trends in your business?

Your balance sheet will show you, at any given time, your receivables and your inventory. If your receivables were larger this year than last year and your inventory was less this year than last year, you probably made more sales this year than last. *But* what if your receivables are all past due? What if a lot of your receivables are from the previous year's sales? This might mean that many might not be collectable. This is not good news!

|  | December 2003 | December 2004 |
|---|---|---|
| **Assets** | | |
| *Receivables* | $200,000 | $300,000 |
| *Inventory* | $50,000 | $20,000 |

The above scenario could represent an increase in sales from one year to the next, which would be very positive, but if the $300,000 is broken down into $150,000 in current receivables and $150,000 in last year's receivables, still owed, this picture could represent a serious negative situation.

On the other hand, if your receivables were lower this year than last year and your inventory was more this year than last year, you might have made a mistake in the number of units you chose to produce and been unable to sell enough of them. This could be bad. *But* when you look at your sales picture, you might notice that you've sold much more this year than last year. This might mean that you've collected more on your receivables and have an appropriate amount of inventory left at the close of the year. This could be good.

|  | December 2003 | December 2004 |
|---|---|---|
| **Assets** | | |
| *Receivables* | $300,000 | $200,000 |
| *Inventory* | $20,000 | $50,000 |

It is interesting to note that finding the incremental payments on long-term obligations requires reading two or more balance sheets. Although the interest on long-term loans and leases will be found on the P&L, the only way to obtain the principal payments on those loans is to look at two balance sheets. The amount on the current balance sheet will indicate what is still owed. The amount on the previous balance sheet, deducted from the current amount, will show what's been paid during the period of time between the two balance sheets. This amount of principal payments can then be added to the P&L and then divided by months to get a more realistic picture of the incremental payments required to pay off both the interest and the principal. Failure to do this will result in an unrealistic picture of the business and its profit picture.

## The Profit and Loss Statement

The P&L (also known as the income statement) is an ongoing account of the sales and expenses related to those sales during the course of the months and years of a business.

The first section below explains in basic narrative form the line items on a typical P&L. Keep in mind that this is basic. A P&L, initially, is for the benefit of the entrepreneur, so it can have as many line items in each category as the business owner chooses. The owner may want to compare products or services from one time frame to another to see which of them is the most profitable in terms of time, margins, or numbers sold. He or she may want to compare expenses, like advertising expenses, to see which appear to have been more cost-effective from one year to the next. The idea is to make the P&L readable so that it becomes a tool of the business and not an academic exercise.

As has often been said, you don't have to be an accountant or a lawyer in order to properly operate a business. If that were the case, there would be very few small businesses in the American marketplace. The financial paperwork can be as simple or as complex as you like. The better approach is to keep it simple, understand the basics, and only then proceed to make it as complicated as you like. An entrepreneur can deduce many things from a comparative analysis of two or more P&Ls, as will be shown later in this chapter.

## What Is a Profit and Loss Statement?

There are basically five elements involved in a P&L:

- Sales
- Cost of Sales or Cost of Product
- Gross Profit
- Salaries, General, and Administrative Expenses (SG&A)
- Profit

**Sales.** These are the revenues generated by the company. Sales are often broken down into line items so the reader can see which products or services have a larger margin of profit. If the person preparing the financial picture is doing a complete job, he or she will prepare a set of *assumptions* that explain the purpose of each line item under Sales. This will also be important as you examine trends in the business.

**Cost of Sales or Cost of Product.** This represents the cost of raw materials or components necessary to prepare the product for sale. This category should also have a set of assumptions indicating the nature of the materials or components necessary to produce the product or service. Again, the reader will be able to compare the costs and get a better sense of the business on an ongoing basis. The figures will show which items are potentially problematic, in terms of either availability or price.

**Gross Profit.** This is the difference between Sales and Cost of Sales or Product. There are variations due to the approaches that people take to keeping financial records, even in the same business. Some businesses will put sales *commissions* under Cost of Product, since they relate directly to the amount of revenues or sales produced, and put sales *salaries* under SG&A, because they represent expenses of operating the business *regardless* of the volume of sales. This is one of the reasons why it is sometimes very difficult to do a comparative analysis of two like businesses, since each may present its financial picture somewhat differently.

**Salaries, General, and Administrative Expenses (SG&A).** This represents *all* the other costs of operating the business. This is where the problem of most businesses starts, because this section includes rent, telephone, gas and electric, deliveries, cleaning, and every other aspect of keeping the business alive, *regardless* of whether you sell a little or a lot—or any at all! The SG&A section must be carefully examined to ensure that the business can make a profit. The line items under SG&A should be sufficiently designated to allow for a comparative analysis. If, for example, a line item says "Advertising," how will you know how much of that figure is for Yellow Pages (an expense that created sales) and how much is for mailers (an expense that didn't create sales)? If you don't find the answer to this in the assumptions, be sure to ask. Also, be sure that you understand the discussion above, What Is a Balance Sheet? to ensure that you include both the principal and the interest payments in the SG&A section of your P&L. Failure to do so will give you a deceptive profit picture.

**Profit.** This is the bottom line. It can be a positive number or a negative number, indicated by parentheses ($) or angle brackets <$>. A positive number means that the company made money after all the expenses of properly operating the business. The accountants then differentiate among different kinds of profit. For example, they will use terms like EBITDA—earnings before interest, taxes, depreciation, and amortization.

In examining the profit of a company, there are some key factors to look for. One of these is to ask if the owner's salary is included in the SG&A or if the owner takes his or her compensation out of the profit of the business. You should recognize the tremendous difference in the answer to this all-important question.

## The Difference between Accrual and Cash

The P&L is usually built on the accrual method of accounting. This ensures that the sales (even if not yet collected) and the equivalent expenses against sales (even if not yet paid) will show how the business is doing. The difference between building a P&L on an accrual basis and building it on a cash basis is significant. You need to understand both, as they indicate, in different ways, the financial status of the business. (See Figures 25-1 and 25-2.)

Figure 25-1 shows a cash flow projection using the accrual method. Figure 25-2 shows the cash flow projection using the cash method.

|  | Jan | Feb | Mar | Apr | May | Jun | Jul | Aug | Sep | Oct | Nov | Dec | Total |
|---|---|---|---|---|---|---|---|---|---|---|---|---|---|
| Sales Made | $5,000 | $5,000 | $5,000 | $5,500 | $6,000 | $6,500 | $7,000 | $7,000 | $8,000 | $8,000 | $9,000 | $12,000 | $84,000 |
| Cash Collection | $– | $– | $2,500 | $2,500 | $5,000 | $5,000 | $6,000 | $6,000 | $7,000 | $7,500 | $8,000 | $4,000 | $53,500 |
| Cost of Sales | $2,500 | $2,500 | $2,500 | $2,750 | $3,000 | $3,250 | $3,500 | $3,500 | $4,000 | $4,000 | $4,500 | $6,000 | $42,000 |
| Gross Profit (accrual) | $2,500 | $2,500 | $2,500 | $2,750 | $3,000 | $3,250 | $3,500 | $3,500 | $4,000 | $4,000 | $4,500 | $6,000 | $42,000 |
| SG&A |  |  |  |  |  |  |  |  |  |  |  |  |  |
| Rent | $2,000 | $2,000 | $2,000 | $2,000 | $2,000 | $2,000 | $2,000 | $2,000 | $2,000 | $2,000 | $2,000 | $2,000 | $24,000 |
| All Other Expenses | $1,000 | $1,000 | $1,000 | $1,000 | $1,000 | $1,000 | $1,000 | $1,000 | $1,000 | $1,000 | $1,000 | $1,000 | $12,000 |
| Profit (Loss) | ($500) | ($500) | ($500) | ($250) | $– | $250 | $500 | $500 | $1,000 | $1,000 | $1,500 | $3,000 | $6,000 |
| Cumulative | ($500) | ($1,000) | ($1,500) | ($1,750) | ($1,750) | ($1,500) | ($1,000) | ($500) | $500 | $1,500 | $3,000 | $6,000 | $6,000 |

Note that on an accrual basis it doesn't make any difference whether money was received or not.

The accrual method shows the progress of the business, not the progress of collections.

Costs are deducted from sales made rather than from cash collections.

When using an accrual basis, at the end of the year the company shows a cumulative profit of $6,000. Do you think you ought to know the difference between cash and accrual?

When trying to find a true value for your business, you might want to understand both.

**Figure 25-1.** Basic cash flow projection—accrual basis

| | Jan | Feb | Mar | Apr | May | Jun | Jul | Aug | Sep | Oct | Nov | Dec | Total |
|---|---|---|---|---|---|---|---|---|---|---|---|---|---|
| Sales Made | $5,000 | $5,000 | $5,000 | $5,500 | $6,000 | $6,500 | $7,000 | $7,000 | $8,000 | $8,000 | $9,000 | $12,000 | $84,000 |
| Cash Collection | $– | $– | $2,500 | $2,500 | $5,000 | $5,000 | $6,000 | $6,000 | $7,000 | $7,500 | $8,000 | $4,000 | $53,500 |
| Cost of Sales* | $2,500 | $2,500 | $2,500 | $2,750 | $3,000 | $3,250 | $3,500 | $3,500 | $4,000 | $4,000 | $4,500 | $6,000 | $42,000 |
| Gross Profit (cash) | ($2,500) | ($2,500) | $– | ($250) | $2,000 | $1,750 | $2,500 | $2,500 | $3,000 | $3,500 | $3,500 | ($2,000) | $11,500 |
| SG&A | | | | | | | | | | | | | |
| Rent | $2,000 | $2,000 | $2,000 | $2,000 | $2,000 | $2,000 | $2,000 | $2,000 | $2,000 | $2,000 | $2,000 | $2,000 | $24,000 |
| All Other Expenses | $1,000 | $1,000 | $1,000 | $1,000 | $1,000 | $1,000 | $1,000 | $1,000 | $1,000 | $1,000 | $1,000 | $1,000 | $12,000 |
| Profit (Loss) | ($5,500) | ($5,500) | ($3,000) | ($3,250) | ($1,000) | ($1,250) | ($500) | ($500) | $– | $500 | $500 | ($5,000) | ($24,500) |
| Cumulative | ($5,500) | ($11,000) | ($14,000) | ($17,250) | (18,250) | ($19,500) | ($20,000) | ($20,500) | ($20,500) | ($20,000) | ($19,500) | ($24,500) | ($24,500) |

Note that the people to whom the company sold goods in January and February don't even start paying for the goods until March. This is a business profile of those that don't sell for cash. Note also that, although payments are good for most of the year, December is good for sales but not for collections. As a result, you might be short of cash in December and you might make arrangements to pay your December rent in January, in addition to January's rent, when you have better collections.

Even though you have accrued $84,000, the company received only $53,500 in cash. Note that, when you pay the December rent in January of the following year, your cash costs for the current year will be $2,000 less and your cash costs for the following year will be $2,000 more. This will change the profit picture on a cash basis in both years. It will not change the picture on an accrual basis.

*Note that this is money paid for the goods when purchased, whether or not the company sold any or collected for any.

**Remember that the profit (or lack of it) is being recorded on a cash basis, deducted from collections, not from sales. On a cash basis, you will be in the hole $24,250 at year-end. Do you think the business will be worthwhile?

**Figure 25-2.** Basic cash flow projection—cash basis

## What Is Cash Flow?

In analyzing a business in terms of making a loan or an investment, a lender or a potential equity participant will want to see a cash flow analysis. This person with the money will want to know which periods will require a cash reservoir to achieve the anticipated goals or, in the case of a new business, how long it will take the business to reach a breakeven point (when the income will be equivalent to the costs necessary to produce that income) and begin to register a real, bottom-line profit.

Forecasting cash flow is especially important, aside from what your P&L may look like at the end of the year. After all, the P&L is usually developed on the basis of sales made but not necessarily collected and purchases made but not necessarily paid for—accrual accounting. On the other hand, cash flow is the difference between actual dollars spent and actual dollars collected—cash accounting.

Although cash flow is particularly important in a business involved in seasonal activity, where monthly sales rise and decline, most businesses need to address the subject for other reasons. Whether buying products for resale, hiring a salesperson, or creating an advertising campaign, it is essential that you anticipate the dollars needed for the expenditure long before you expect to earn the dollars.

Working on the basis of day-to-day requirements can be terribly problematic without having the necessary cash available. If you need to buy inventory or parts or start making payments on equipment or additional personnel, you will be paying out in advance, sometimes significantly in advance, of bringing in the money to meet these payment obligations. If you don't have a sufficient working capital reservoir (enough money in the bank), you must have a lending source that will take you over this financial hurdle. This will invariably mean you will need a relationship with a lending institution that allows you to borrow money in some way, such as a simple loan or a line of credit.

Every lender will want to understand the reasons for this temporary financial problem and they will insist on seeing a cash flow forecast. The best forecast will obviously be based on the previous year's activities—providing, of course, that you had a previous year. If you have no such history, you need to back up your forecast with assumptions that are credible based on the marketplace, with the support of purchase orders, current inventory, and the like.

The lender will want to look at your balance sheet, particularly at your cash availability, your current inventory, your purchase orders, your accounts receivable, your accounts payable, and your current and long-term obligations. Essentially, they will make judgments based on the ratios of your assets to your liabilities. They will often give you an advance based on your receivables, but only a percentage of this figure, depending on the age of these accounts and the reputation of the people who owe you the money. They will consider advancing dollars based on the amount of your inventory, on the assumption that this inventory will convert into sales. They will note the purchase orders for new goods or services and, depending on the credibility of those accounts, may advance money against those purchases. In other words, lenders want to assess the validity of your business practices, the financial position of the company, and the time and dollars you've already invested in your business.

## What Is a Borrowing Base?

When a company applies for a loan, it may grant the lender a security interest in its receivables and/or inventory as collateral. This security interest is the borrowing base, determined by multiplying the value of the assigned collateral by a discount factor. A bank uses the borrowing base to monitor the financial health of the company to determine that it can lend money or to evaluate the financial performance of a company to which it has made a loan.

The type of loan that will require a borrowing base is a revolving line of credit. Banking institutions of all kinds will use a borrowing base when making a loan to a company, to determine how well a company is performing and achieving its goals relative to its projections. The bank and the company will agree on a borrowing base when a loan is executed. If a company is overperforming or underperforming its goals, the bank will use the borrowing base to evaluate the situation and determine how to help the company. The terms of a note may require that the company submit a borrowing base to the bank monthly, quarterly, or annually.

Key ratios that help determine the company's ability to repay its debt include the current ratio (current assets divided by current liabilities) and the total debt/equity ratio (total debt divided by total equity). For manufacturing companies, key ratios will also include accounts receivable days (average gross receivables divided by the quotient of annual net sales divided by 365), accounts payable days (average payables divided by the quotient of annual purchases divided by 365), and inventory days (average inventory divided by the quotient of cost of goods sold divided by 365).

A borrowing base certificate will look like the sample in Figure 25-3.

The compliance ratios used in this certificate measure management's ability to manage the assets and liabilities on the balance sheet. For instance, the top ratio of debt to tangible net worth is simply debt divided by net worth. The bank is requiring that the debt/worth ratio be equal to or less than 5.0:1. This means that, in the most extreme case, for every $5 of debt, the company has $1 invested in net worth. If the company goes over that ratio, the bank can no longer lend it any money. The actual figure shows that the company has $1.91 of debt to $1 of net worth. This is evidence to the banker that the company knows how to manage its finances appropriately and that the bank can keep lending money to the company.

## And What about a New Business?

When you have a new business and want to show your potential lender, partner, or investor how you intend to handle the money that you're seeking, you have a problem: no history. So you need to create the future of the business in financial terms. Sophisticated businesspeople, including lenders, are aware that a new business will not likely generate a profit immediately. The question is "When will that happen?" By creating a future year, based on serious and credible investigation, you should be able to show how long it will take for the business to reach its breakeven point.

In the early stages of the business, you will be spending more than you're earning and go deeper into the hole each month, using the investment dollars. This will represent a cumulative loss. Lenders expect this to be the case. What lenders want is a credible picture of the time when you will not only have

**Borrowing Base/Compliance Certificate For XYZ Trading Co.**
**As of March 31, 2004**

**Borrowing Base**

| | | |
|---|---|---|
| 1. | Total US A/R book value as of 3/31/2004 | $507,442 |
| 2. | Less: A/R 91 days or more past due | $222,195 |
| 3. | Eligible accounts (line 1 – line 2) | $285,247 |
| 4. | Loan value of accounts (80% of line 3) | $228,198 |
| 5. | Total A/R book value as of 3/31/2004 | $106,112 |
| 6. | Less A/R 90 days or more past due | $36,369 |
| 7. | Eligible accounts (line 5 – line 6) | $69,743 |
| 8. | Loan value of accounts (80% of line 7, $800,000 max) | $55,794 |
| 9. | Inventory as of 3/31/2004 | $493,537 |
| 10. | Loan value of inventory (50% of line 9) | $246,769 |
| 11. | Sales purchase orders as of 3/31/2004 | $7,263,321 |
| 12. | Loan value of sales purchase orders (60% of line 11) | $4,357,993 |
| 13. | Maximum line amount $5,000,000* | $4,888,753 |
| 14. | Banker's acceptance owing lender | $94,869 |
| 15. | Present line of credit balance owing lender | $860,000 |
| 16. | Total due to lender | $954,869 |
| 17. | Line amount due or available unused line amount | $3,933,884 |

*Combined loan value of Lines 4, 8, 10, and 12.

| Compliance Ratios | Notes | Required | Actual |
|---|---|---|---|
| Debt to | | | |
| Tangible net worth | = or < | 5.0:1 | 1.91:1 |
| Tangible net worth | = or > | $1,000,000 | $710,376 |
| Consecutive days out of debt | = or > | 30 | 30 |
| Personal liquidity – A/R XYZ | = or > | $500,000 | $500,000 |

The undersigned represents and warrants that the foregoing is true, complete and correct, and that the information reflected herein complies with the representations and warranties set forth in the loan agreement between the undersigned and the bank dated _____.

XYZ Trading Company, Inc.

By _____

Title _____

**Figure 25-3.** Borrowing base/compliance certificate

reached the breakeven point but also have earned back the dollars spent—that is, when you will start generating a profit. This will give the lender (and yourself) a timeline for your success.

Although this may present a fairly simplistic view of the lender relationship, it should give you an idea of the parameters that your company should contemplate when borrowing. It is clearly essential for you to take advantage of professional advice to ensure that your presentation is prepared most appropriately.

## A Real Example with Assumptions

Figure 25-4 is the cash flow statement for a new school, with income projections for the first three years.

# The Comparative Analysis

It is obvious that looking at longer periods for a comparative analysis will give you a better definition of "differences" than looking at shorter periods. The month-to-month activity change could easily be an aberration caused by any number of factors. A comparative analysis of year-to-year activity change is much more likely to give you a better sense of the differentials in real terms. In this context, see Figure 25-5 (page 368).

Compare services and products in the years referenced. Such an analysis should give the reader good reason to consider a change in the direction of the company.

Sales (revenue) shows the same decline for both Company A and Company B. However, with Company A revenue from services carries a cost of product of 10%, while revenue from products, which remains the same for all four years, carries a cost of product of 50%. What if these were reversed, as with Company B? Would you think that this trend required your serious attention? It certainly would if you were concerned about the difference in profit! In addition, it would also tell you what direction your company is taking.

SG&A stays the same whether you are generating greater or fewer sales. If you no longer need space for product, could you save money on your SG&A? What about rent and utilities?

| Assumptions | | | | 2 classes | 3 classes | 4 classes | 4 classes | 5 classes | 5 classes | 6 classes | 6 classes | 6 classes | | 6 cl/mo | 8 cl/mo |
|---|---|---|---|---|---|---|---|---|---|---|---|---|---|---|---|
| | Jan | Feb | Mar | Apr | May | Jun | Jul | Aug | Sep | Oct | Nov | Dec | Yr 1 Total | Yr 2 Total | Yr 3 Total |
| Sales* | 0 | 0 | 0 | $2,304 | $3,456 | $4,608 | $4,608 | $5,760 | $5,760 | $6,912 | $6,912 | $6,912 | $47,232 | $82,944 | $110,592 |
| COS | | | | | | | | | | | | | | | |
| Teacher Salaries | $- | $- | $- | $480 | $720 | $960 | $960 | $1,200 | $1,200 | $1,440 | $1,440 | $1,440 | $9,840 | $17,280 | $23,040 |
| Class Supplies | $- | $- | $- | $30 | $45 | $60 | $60 | $75 | $75 | $90 | $90 | $90 | $615 | $1,080 | $1,440 |
| Total COS | $- | $- | $- | $510 | $765 | $1,020 | $1,020 | $1,275 | $1,275 | $1,530 | $1,530 | $1,530 | $10,455 | $18,360 | $24,480 |
| Gross Profit | $- | $- | $- | $1,794 | $2,691 | $3,588 | $3,588 | $4,485 | $4,485 | $5,382 | $5,382 | $5,382 | $36,777 | $64,584 | $86,112 |
| Expenses | | | | | | | | | | | | | | | |
| Phone | $75 | $50 | $50 | $50 | $50 | $50 | $50 | $50 | $50 | $50 | $50 | $50 | $600 | $600 | $600 |
| Legal/Accounting | $- | $- | $- | $700 | $700 | $700 | $700 | $- | $75 | $- | $75 | $75 | $225 | $225 | $225 |
| Advertising | $500 | $500 | $700 | $700 | $700 | $700 | $700 | $700 | $600 | $600 | $700 | $700 | $7,600 | $7,600 | $7,600 |
| Postage | $200 | $- | $1,000 | $- | $1,000 | $- | $- | $- | $1,000 | $300 | $- | $- | $3,200 | $1,000 | $1,000 |
| Mailing List Referral | $- | $300 | $- | $- | $- | $300 | $- | $- | $- | $- | $- | $- | $900 | $900 | $- |
| Printing | $- | $1,050 | $- | $- | $- | $- | $- | $- | $- | $- | $- | $- | $- | $- | $- |
| Cleaning | $- | $- | $- | $- | $- | $- | $- | $- | $- | $- | $- | $- | $- | $600 | $600 |
| Office Staff Salaries | $- | $- | $- | $- | $- | $- | $- | $- | $- | $- | $- | $- | $- | $20,000 | $30,000 |
| Maintenance | $- | $- | $- | $- | $- | $75 | $75 | $75 | $75 | $75 | $75 | $75 | $675 | $- | $- |
| Utilities | $- | $- | $- | $75 | $- | $- | $- | $676 | $- | $- | $- | $- | $- | $675 | $675 |
| Insurance | $- | $- | $- | $- | $- | $- | $- | $- | $- | $75 | $- | $- | $675 | $- | $- |
| Rent | $4,500 | $- | $- | $1,000 | $1,000 | $1,000 | $1,000 | $1,000 | $1,000 | $1,000 | $1,000 | $1,000 | $9,000 | $12,000 | $12,000 |
| Start-up Costs | $100 | $- | $- | $- | $- | $- | $- | $- | $- | $- | $- | $- | $4,500 | $- | $- |
| Banking Costs | $- | $- | $- | $25 | $25 | $25 | $25 | $25 | $25 | $25 | $25 | $25 | $325 | $300 | $300 |
| SG&A Expenses | $5,375 | $1,900 | $1,750 | $1,850 | $2,850 | $2,150 | $2,550 | $1,850 | $2,750 | $2,050 | $2,050 | $2,125 | $29,250 | $43,900 | $53,900 |
| Net Income | ($5,375) | ($1,900) | ($1,750) | ($56) | ($159) | $1,438 | $1,038 | $2,635 | $1,735 | $3,332 | $3,332 | $3,257 | $7,527 | $20,684 | $33,112 |
| Cumulative Income (Loss) | ($5,375) | ($7,275) | ($9,025) | ($9,081) | ($9,240) | ($7,802) | ($4,129) | ($2,394) | ($3,921) | $938 | $4,270 | $7,527 | | | |

Assumptions: 8 students per class @ $144.00 each
Teachers = $240.00 per class

*Note: Many businesses account for sales when the invoices are mailed, even though not paid until 30, 60, or 90 days later. This is accrual accounting. Cash accounting is when business collects cash at the time of a sale and accounts for all sales in this manner.

**Figure 25-4.** Pro forma cash flow statement

| Company A | | | | |
|---|---|---|---|---|
| | 2004 | 2003 | 2002 | 2001 |
| Sales (Revenue) | | | | |
| Services | $30,000 | $40,000 | $50,000 | $60,000 |
| Products | $30,000 | $30,000 | $30,000 | $30,000 |
| Total | $60,000 | $70,000 | $80,000 | $90,000 |
| Cost of Product | | | | |
| Services | $3,000 | $4,000 | $5,000 | $6,000 10% |
| Products | $15,000 | $15,000 | $15,000 | $15,000 50% |
| Total | $18,000 | $19,000 | $20,000 | $21,000 |
| Gross Profit | $42,000 | $51,000 | $60,000 | $69,000 |
| SG&A (Salaries, General, and Administrative Expenses) | | | | |
| Advertising | $1,000 | $1,000 | $1,000 | $1,000 |
| Legal/Accounting | $200 | $200 | $200 | $200 |
| Rent | $3,000 | $3,000 | $3,000 | $3,000 |
| Utilities | $800 | $800 | $800 | $800 |
| Total | $5,000 | $5,000 | $5,000 | $5,000 |
| Net Income or Loss | $37,000 | $46,000 | $55,000 | $64,000 |
| Company B | | | | |
| | 2004 | 2003 | 2002 | 2001 |
| Sales (Revenue) | | | | |
| Services | $60,000 | $60,000 | $60,000 | $60,000 |
| Products | $0 | $10,000 | $20,000 | $30,000 |
| Total | $60,000 | $70,000 | $80,000 | $90,000 |
| Cost of Product | | | | |
| Services | $6,000 | $6,000 | $6,000 | $6,000 10% |
| Products | $0 | $5,000 | $10,000 | $15,000 50% |
| Total | $6,000 | $11,000 | $16,000 | $21,000 |
| Gross Profit | $54,000 | $59,000 | $64,000 | $69,000 |

**Figure 25-5.** Profit and loss statement (income statement) for a comparative analysis (continued on next page)

| SG&A (Salaries, General, and Administrative Expenses) | | | |
|---|---|---|---|
| Advertising | $1,000 | $1,000 | $1,000 | $1,000 |
| Legal/Accounting | $200 | $200 | $200 | $200 |
| Rent | $3,000 | $3,000 | $3,000 | $3,000 |
| Utilities | $800 | $800 | $800 | $800 |
| Total | $5,000 | $5,000 | $5,000 | $5,000 |
| **Net Income or Loss** | **$49,000** | **$54,000** | **$59,000** | **$64,000** |

**Figure 25-5.** Profit and loss statement (income statement) for a comparative analysis (concluded)

# Key Points to Remember

- A balance sheet represents a moment in time. You will always need to compare two or more balance sheets to note the movement of the business's financial position.
- A profit and loss statement (also known as an income statement) is usually prepared on an accrual basis. This shows what the business looks like, assuming that all receivables are collected and all payables are paid, even though they might not be.
- Showing a business's activity on a cash basis will be significantly different in most cases from showing the same financial picture on an accrual basis.
- A borrowing base includes the totality of the financial picture of a business, which allows a lender to properly assess and minimize risk.
- In the cash flow forecast of a new business, assumptions explaining the details of line items are especially important for a potential lender or equity participant.

# Revisiting the Core Elements of This Book

**Illustration 26-1. Deciding What to Do**

Allison and Bob operated a very successful printing business. The growth curve was pretty spectacular every year. They had finally reached a point where selling the business was an interesting option. They had been told that the best time to sell a business is when it's doing very well. And, as good as business was, the partners thought it might be a good idea to buy some equipment that would enable them to increase the sales volume. This would allow them to ask a higher price for the business. But there was a problem.

When they approached their business consultant, they were surprised at her advice. She explained that buying additional equipment should be based on the time at which they expected to sell the business. She further explained that the reason for this is that additional expenses against revenues would decrease the bottom-line profit on which the valuation of the business would depend. In other words, they would need the new equipment to generate not only the cost of the equipment but also an additional profit. If they didn't do this, the monthly cost of the equipment would actually cause the price of the business to decrease. In other words, if they expected the new equipment to pay for itself in three or four years and to increase the profit of the company in four or five years, then selling the company at the end of that period could make sense. On the other hand, if they wanted to sell the business right away, then acquiring the new equipment would probably be a bad idea. It was an interesting conundrum and a lesson to be learned.

Allison and Bob reconsidered this situation and decided to buy the new equipment and to delay the sale of the business until the equipment had built a new customer base, developed a new profit center, and given them enough bottom-line profit to increase the potential sale price of the business. They were glad to have examined this problem with their consultant before making the decision.

As you speak with professionals about the valuation process, you will find that they consider a variety of approaches. They will invariably discuss a comparative analysis of other businesses in the same field. For public companies, they will reference the stock prices and ratios. In fact, they will boggle your mind with figures that can be manipulated in various ways.

It is interesting that buyers' and sellers' goals, although sometimes taken into consideration, are pretty low on the totem pole. And yet, the entire buying-selling process depends on these people at the center of this process. You cannot lose sight of this fact.

To ensure that the basics of the people involved are never excluded from the process, this penultimate chapter begins with a discussion of why people buy businesses and why people sell businesses.

## For a Seller: Why Does Someone Buy a Business?

It is certainly easier to recognize the reasons why a buyer wants to acquire a business than it is to understand a seller's motives. But be careful—all is not necessarily what it appears to be.

A buyer's reasons are important because most small businesses (businesses with gross revenues of $10,000,000 per year or less) are not normally sold for cash. The buyer makes a down payment and then pays the balance over time, usually in the form of a promissory note, often carried by the seller for five to ten years. If this seems like an inordinate period of time, it would be appropriate to remember that most franchise relationships last between 10 and 20 years. It is important, then, to know the buyer's qualifications, including education, experience, family involvement, and financial history, including current assets and liabilities. A seller can't make a careful judgment without knowing these elements.

Here are a half-dozen potential problem areas in the sale of a business that should cause a seller to take precautions.

The buyer who can pay cash is clearly the least problematic sale from the seller's perspective. So long as the seller's presentation doesn't contain misrepresentations that could be the basis for a lawsuit, the seller will be out of the picture and have no financial interest in the success or failure of the business after the sale. The only disadvantage is that the buyer who is willing to pay all cash will likely want a substantial reduction in price, to which he or she would be entitled.

The buyer who says that the compensation available to him or her after the sale will be adequate to support the family can be problematic. If the seller is going to carry back a promissory note for the balance of the purchase price after a down payment, he or she better be sure that buyer is telling the truth and that exigencies won't change that truth. If the buyer needs to take more money from the business, it might be at the expense of making complete and timely payments on the seller's promissory note. There are ways to protect against this contingency; be prepared to discuss it with your professional.

A buyer with substantial dollars may be acquiring the business as an investment with the idea that he or she will be an absentee owner. Even if the operation is handled by a family member, the seller needs to be careful about this situation. It is well known in the business community that absentee ownership, more often than not, can spell disaster. If this appears to be the case, the seller will need additional protections.

If the seller will be carrying a note for the balance of the purchase price, whatever the situation, it is always appropriate to ask for financial protection in addition to the business itself as security. This can be in the form of additional equities such as stocks, bonds, and second or third trust deeds (mortgages) on real property. Even if there is little equity left in the real estate after existing mortgages, using it as security represents a very substantial and intimidating risk to the buyer and his or her family.

In most businesses, a key factor to maintaining the business is to have adequate working capital for growth, for continuity, and for the unexpected. If a buyer is taking over the business with little or no additional capital available, any glitch in the normal business activity may cause the business to falter. In such a case, the buyer usually needs to ask the seller for a hiatus on note payments. As a seller, be sure that you don't get caught in this situation. You will essentially be financing a business that you no longer own just to protect the payments on your note. In addition, most of those problems get worse before they get better. Be cautious.

If a buyer wants to change the format of a business, the seller needs to be sure that it doesn't change the original concept to the extent of hurting the buyer's ability to operate successfully. Converting a successful women's clothing shop to a children's clothing shop might seem like a good idea. If this is the buyer's plan, he or she should have purchased a children's clothing shop. (The exception to this caveat is noted earlier in the book relative to the franchise alternative.) If the buyer converts to an entirely different competitive marketplace, the change may very well prove disastrous and he or she may never pay the seller's note. On the other hand, a creative buyer may want to augment the products or services offered and this may be a great idea. As a seller holding a promissory note, it is your obligation to ensure that the decisions are appropriate to the survival of the business. It is an ongoing obligation until the promissory note has been completely paid.

Although it is impossible to examine all the potential problem areas in the sale of a business, the above examples should cause any seller to seek the appropriate professional advice before making the commitment.

## For a Buyer: Why Does Someone Sell a Business?

It is impossible to cover all the myriad possible reasons why the owner of a business might put it up for sale. If you're buying, you should be aware of at least the following half-dozen reasons, because they may affect you.

Age has its prerogatives as well as its failings. The physical and intellectual demands of a business can be wearing. As time passes and an owner gets closer to the golden years, it may become more difficult for him or her to operate the business. Those who can anticipate the difficulties early enough will decide to sell while the business is still healthy and needs only a strong leader to continue its success. Others maintain their health and abilities, but decide that the time has come to stop working and start enjoying life more fully.

Illness of the owner or illness in the family that forces a move to a different climate or a simpler way of life is often a compelling reason to sell. If this is the premise for the sale, keep a sharp eye for the possibility that it might not be the whole story. Remember: even a covenant not to compete, an essential document for the buyer in just about every business sale, might not provide sufficient protection, if it applies only to the owner but not to his or her family or key employees. You should not be consistently cynical, but certainly you should exercise the appropriate cautions. In legal terms, this is called *due diligence*. In lay terms, it's basic protective thinking.

Some business owners hadn't thought about selling until they were approached by a competitor or a "downsized" executive looking for a new opportunity. These sellers are not any easier to deal with; in some cases, they may be even more difficult than most. Although they do not come to the decision to sell as much as the decision comes to them, they will now be as anxious to maximize their equity as anyone who has prepared the business for market many months before presentation.

There are younger owners for whom the romance or excitement of the business has worn off. They may or may not have been really successful, but have handled the business at least adequately. They are now ready for their next adventure and want to convert the equity of the business into dollars for their next business. There is nothing particularly problematic about these buyers, so long as you have some comfort in knowing that they are not going to create a business like the one they're selling across the street. Very often, these sellers will not have maximized the potential of their business because they've always had the second dream on their minds. This might be an interesting opportunity.

The caution in dealing with more sophisticated sellers, is that they may be selling the business because they can read the writing on the wall; they may recognize the next level of sophistication in their trade or industry and innovations that might obsolete their current product or service and the cost of upgrading might be prohibitive. It is something to consider when you are investigating the industry of which this business is a part.

This is a good reason to consult someone who knows more about the business than you. It is the old franchise axiom: "investigate before investing."

And then, of course, there is the owner who knows something that you don't know. Maybe it's something about his or her source for raw materials, components, equipment, and the like. Maybe some of his or her key employees are about to leave, possibly taking some key clients along. Maybe a giant competitor is opening shop close enough to the business to cause a problem. Maybe the city is going to restructure the street on which the business is located. It might be almost anything! If you're going to buy a business, it is your obligation to become knowledgeable about every aspect relative to its survival and potential success. Anyone who suggests that you rush to judgment before taking adequate time for this necessary examination is giving you bad advice.

Although it is certainly true that you could hold an auction for the sale of your business, it is also true that you could merely close the door and sell off your assets. Neither of these approaches would likely result in a satisfactory conversion of your equity into cash. The idea is to find the parameters within which to arrive at a price that is logical for both buyer and seller. If you do this far enough in advance, you will have an opportunity to maximize the sales and minimize the costs of operation, leading to the highest price potential for the business.

## Why Value a Business?

Valuing a business is very much like writing a business plan. It is usually intended to serve a specific purpose—the business valuation in anticipation of selling, the business plan in anticipation of borrowing. But these should not be the primary goals. The real goal is to give the owner an idea of where he or she stands and what must be done to maximize the conversion of equity to retirement or to satisfy the requirements of a lender.

Building a valuation should not be done the day before preparing a selling presentation. It should not be done because a buyer is waiting for the answers. It should be done because you need to know the answers in advance in order to work on those things that need attention long before a presentation is anticipated. Remember Allison and Bob who wanted to buy new equipment just prior to selling.

As you look at your preliminary valuation, you should examine the last few years on the basis of a comparative analysis. And always start with the basics.

Are profits up because you've improved your margins by buying raw materials or component parts at lower prices? Or are profits up because you've increased your sales to customers? If you've improved your margins but sales are down, you will want to know why.

Are you taking less compensation from your business? Is your lesser compensation predicated on increased costs of doing business? You will want to know what these increased costs are. Are your competitors dealing with the same problem? How have they handled the problem to maintain profits?

Are you spending more time at the business but not seeing any improvement in either sales or profits? You certainly want to know why this equation is not more positive. If any of these questions and answers suggests a trend in your business, you will need to know this and factor it into the risk aspect of your selling presentation. Is your business vulnerable because your customer base is small, because the loss of any customer could cause chaos? This is certainly another of the risk factors that the buyer will be looking at.

Are you aware of your competitors and what they are doing to market and advertise? You must be sure that your marketing approach and use of advertising dollars is most cost-effective. It's very difficult to explain to potential buyers that they can improve their sales by adjusting their marketing and advertising after the sale. They will invariably want to know why you didn't do it before selling.

Is your inventory up and are your receivables down? This is a simple barometer that should take you to your sales department. Why did you order as many products or as much production in anticipation of sales that didn't materialize? Did you make a mistake or did the economy cause a few surprises? And you will need to see how many of your receivables are recent and how many have not paid for a long time. Are you still doing business with the people who have not paid? They may be using you as their banker—which is not likely the business that you intended.

Have you analyzed each employee's job category and whether employees are performing up to expectations? Where are your key people and what is their performance rating? In the event of a sale, which of them are likely to stay under new management? Are any in a position to become competitors to your buyer?

Have you ever thought of such a situation? If you're going to carry a promissory note for the balance of the purchase price, this issue could become particularly problematic.

The problem of valuing a business is that most entrepreneurs don't attend to this very important matter until the 11th hour—just before they need to make a selling presentation. The key to selling is to understand the valuation concept long in advance of any such sale.

The above references represent only some of the elements of the business that you need to consider. Waiting too long will invariably mean that you will be leaving money on the table during selling negotiations. Remember: in any negotiations, you need to be in control. In order to do that, you must be able to anticipate the questions and have credible answers. Losing this credibility means losing the negotiating battle. Don't let this happen. Get a valuation done early.

## Key Points to Remember

- Most businesses are not sold for cash. The buyer usually makes a down payment and then pays the balance of the purchase price over time.
- Both buyer and seller should be sure that the buyer has adequate working capital to ensure against any glitch in the economy or other problem with the business.
- The buyer should make sure that the seller (together with family, friends, and associates) will not become a competitor after the sale.
- The purpose of a business valuation is to help the seller increase his or her equity in the business long before a sale become necessary or appropriate.
- A business valuation should ensure that, after the sale, there is sufficient profit for the buyer to draw an income and make payments to seller on the balance of the purchase price.

# CHAPTER 27

# Valuing an Internet Business

### Illustration 27-1. What's It Worth?

Nathan Ross was a business consultant who had achieved a reputation as a business valuation expert. He had written a book on the subject as well as articles in various magazines. Since his book, which he published in 1993, was in its fourth edition and, as a result, he had achieved a certain credibility in the business community, Nathan was confident that his methods were correct.

When the dotcom craze was at its zenith, Nathan was asked almost daily to create business valuations for businesses that were not yet businesses. They were merely ideas on which businesses might eventually be predicated. Nathan considered creating a valuation of a business that was not yet a business to be a matter of total conjecture rather than a calculation of any kind. As a matter of fact, Nathan felt that to give credence to a business idea that had not yet been formed into a business venture would completely destroy his credibility in the business community. He refused to do this.

As time went on and as companies acquired many of these "not yet businesses," it became a real challenge to people like Nathan to avoid total speculation in an area where buyers and sellers needed at least a rough valuation. After a number of years of avoiding the process of valuing dotcoms, Nathan began working with entrepreneurs involved in internet businesses. This chapter is an exposition of the conceptual aspects that allowed Nathan to maintain his credibility and his reputation in this new world of business.

### Illustration 27-2. Collateral Value to the Purchase Price

Bernie McDougal had developed a method of dissipating the heat from lamps, which allowed for a much hotter, more pervasive light from the strongest bulbs without risk of fire. As a result of this new type of canister, he developed a lamp that could be used for purposes previously impossible in the commercial marketplace. His business grew quite quickly, as his lamp was popular among commercial businesses. He also developed a smaller lamp, using the same technology, which could be used in art museums, supermarkets, and smaller retail locations. He produced the prototype for this product but had not yet entered the marketplace when he decided to sell his business. The business was valued at a substantial sum based entirely on the products in the marketplace and the profit already achieved. The question is, does a new product, not yet in the marketplace, have a value that can be calculated and that could raise the selling price of the business?

The reason for this example being relevant to this chapter is that, even if a prototype exists, the future of the product is conjectural at best. As a result, it is difficult to assess the dollar value of the product's future. In the case of a website attracting many visitors, some making purchases and others merely checking it out, the value of the customer potential is equally conjectural. On the other hand, the mere fact that the customer base is growing has a value, albeit difficult to quantify, to a company acquiring the website.

In Bernie's case, he is precluded from putting the lamp into the marketplace after selling his business because of the usual noncompete provisions in the sale agreement. And, if the buyer decides to enter the marketplace, he or she may have to spend many dollars for marketing, advertising, production, and delivery before enjoying any profit. Bernie made the prototype a part of the sale with the understanding that, if the buyer decided to produce and sell the lamp, Bernie would be entitled to a license fee of 2 percent of the gross sales for a period of five years, but only after the buyer recouped all the dollars spent to place the product in the hands of customers. This kind of situation is not unusual and will likely find its place in the sale of websites that have created similar types of potential activity.

## The Bottom Line in Terms of Valuation

Although the internet and its websites may generate a broader spectrum of product/service activity, the basic concept of buyer/seller remains the same. If an average buyer, a person of average financial capability, acquires a website business and can't produce enough bottom-line profit to pay the family bills and amortize the price of the business over an appropriate period of time, then the sale is going to be problematic. On the other hand, a bigger business may have different motives and, certainly, different expectations.

The difference lies in the fact that a bigger business can afford to pay the purchase price based on other factors. The acquiring company may consider that it would save a certain amount of time (which has its equivalent in dollars) to reach the plateau already achieved by the company it is acquiring, even if that company has not yet reached a profit position. The bigger company may need to acquire the expertise or the creative abilities of the management team that created the smaller company or the domain name that it owns. There are many reasons why such an acquisition could help the bigger company grow and it would not need to amortize the acquisition cost over a reasonable period of time, as a smaller company might do in making the purchase.

## How to Value an Internet Business

There are a few basic concepts in the valuation of any business. These include the following:

1. Buyers tend to use the bulk of their dollars to buy a business—their philosophy: the bigger the investment, the bigger the business, the bigger the anticipated income. Although this is not necessarily the case, it is nonetheless the predicate for most acquisitions. This being so, the buyer will need to generate the family income from the business being purchased, since any other cash flow is likely to have been exhausted. This seems so simplistic, but often the cause of a failed acquisition is that buyers don't take this into account.

2. The money for a business acquisition is, more often than not, borrowed from some source. This could be a lending institution, but in the case of the small business community, this is not likely. The money could be from the seller, who understands the difficulty of borrowing from a lender to buy a small business and who agrees to carry the balance of the purchase price after a down payment by accepting a promissory note payable over some years. This difficulty with borrowing from a lender and the sale of small businesses with a down payment and a promissory note are both examined in previous chapters. It's also possible that the buyer has, in a sense, "borrowed" from himself or herself by liquidating stocks, bonds, or other equities. He or she must pay back this money to reestablish the family reservoir. In any case, the payback of the balance of the purchase price must be amortized over a reasonable period of time based on the risk involved in the business and in the industry.

3. The profit of the business to be acquired must be sufficient to provide a sufficient income and make the scheduled payments on the promissory note. In other words, the business must be able to buy itself or the buyer may forever be in a position of subsidizing the purchase with additional funds. This is not a good acquisition in most cases.

4. The seller should be able to convert into dollars whatever equity the seller has earned. Although the seller would like a piece of future profits, these

profits belong to the buyer who will ultimately earn them. After all, the seller would never be willing to share the losses should the business fail after the buyer takes over. Why, then, should the seller expect to share in the profit?! Note, however, the difference in the Bernie McDougal scenario where the future has a sharing aspect.

The question is, should these basic concepts prevail in the sale of an internet business? The facts that fly in the face of these concepts are the phenomenal stories about Google™ and the like where the acquisition is based "on the come," so to speak, and has little to do with the concept of converting earned equity into dollars for a seller. Which of these is valid for the internet business? Do you think it has to do with the difference between big business and small business? It certainly deserves an examination.

## The Internet

What is the internet? It is actually a vast, global network of computers to which anyone can connect. And, although it is considered "boundaryless," it has political boundaries, as shown by the fact that China has instituted a number of restrictions. The question of whether an internet business is different from any other business is probably best resolved by the statement: "We consider ourselves business people first, as opposed to internet people."

A website is certainly an expanded environment within which to do business. It can be formatted to work like a newspaper or a magazine, a catalog of products and services, an audio/video presentation, a text messaging service, a store, and more. The reality is that a business can market and sell throughout the world.

## The Dynamic Difference

A big company can afford to make an investment and wait for the possibilities to develop. The small businessperson needs to enjoy the profits of a business … now! The difference between investing and gambling is the difference between enjoying the profit and anticipating it.

# The Phenomenal Growth Potential

Because of the phenomenal growth potential of an internet business, the acquisition process must be separated into at least two concepts: primary selling and collateral income. Keep in mind that the internet is theoretically "boundaryless" even though the basic business tenet is that it is still a "storefront." As such, a storefront website still functions to supply products, services, or information to customers and, in that context, still represents a business for profit. The biggest difference, of course, is that being virtual eliminates the problems of traffic, parking, proximity, zoning restrictions, etc. Other advantages include not needing to maintain significant inventory and not paying overhead for retail premises. A disadvantage is that the customer doesn't get to touch the goods until after the purchase and delivery is not instantaneous. To what extent a business valuation needs to consider any or all of these differences deserves a closer look.

## The Usual Method

The usual method for valuing a going business is to look to the bottom-line profit. When a business hasn't yet earned a bottom-line profit, valuing involves other approaches, such as determining a liquidation-of-assets value, or developing a time-line equivalent to the dollars necessary to reach the level of activity achieved by the fledgling business. Using top-line gross revenues is not normally a good idea, since two businesses with the same top-line revenue stream could be producing very different bottom-line profits. However, the unique nature of the internet necessitates a further examination.

## The Peculiarity Involved

The internet business is peculiar to the extent that it has a value not only in terms of the sales it achieves but also in terms of the number of people who know how to find it. In other words, people who visit a website can be considered potential customers and thus of significant value to the future of the business. How to quantify this value is somewhat conjectural, but the internet gurus know, in each category, what this potential is worth: the evidence is the enormous sums paid for some businesses that have tremendous traffic (visits) or that have generated dynamic excitement over their content, even if they have not produced any actual profit. Keep in mind that these metrics in the internet world can be quantified and there are services that can make these statistical evaluations available to those who want to calculate the value in their own ways and for their own purposes. Also, keep in mind that you can do these evaluations on your own.

## Recommendations and Referrals

Take a look at another difference: recommendations and referrals. If you visit a store in your neighborhood and can't find exactly what you're looking for, you can always ask the clerk to recommend another local store in which you might find that item. He or she should do so as a basic business courtesy. When visiting a website, you will likely find advertisements with links to other websites carrying similar or collateral products or services. Many websites earn a good deal of their revenue from advertising of this nature, either through selling ad space or through earning commissions on click-throughs (when a visitor follows an ad link to another website) or on sales resulting from click-throughs. Thus a website owner can make money from referring visitors, which is not the case for the local vendor within a confined geography, except under extraordinary circumstances.

## Acquisition for Growth

Another way in which an online business is similar to a conventional business is in value in terms of acquisition for growth. It isn't surprising for a business to acquire a competitor just to take control of the customer base, or one or more members of its management team, or its relationship with vendors. Taking over a competitor is one way of accelerating the expansion of a business, as opposed to the more conventional incremental growth. This is a *horizontal* growth pattern, expanding to other geographic areas but selling the same products or services. The margins are increased by the ability of the business to enjoy quantity discounts. A *vertical* growth pattern would be to find more ways to profit from the same product or service by acquiring another level of activity, such as when a retailer acquires a manufacturer, a manufacturer acquires a distributor, a manufacturer acquires a retailer, and so on. These approaches to growth are possible as well on the internet.

## The Domain Name

For any small business, helping customers find the location is always a challenge that the owner needs to address. The advertising for the location must stand out and the name of the store must be specific enough that customers recognize it immediately. Is it any different on the internet?

The storefront website is similar. The domain name is the address of the location and is often referred to as "real estate."

One difference is that a domain name is exclusive to the business. And, because the internet is so pervasive, the exclusivity has a value. With businesses that have a physical location, you may have a wine store in every neighborhood. On the internet, there is only one *winestore.com*. Since wine is not unique to any particular neighborhood, as might be an auto body shop, the virtual location—the website at *winestore.com*—can serve customers all over the country and all around the world!

For this reason, whatever value a business online may have based on profit, the domain name is an added value that has no specific value. The quantitative or qualitative value depends on the person or the company making the valuation. In a sense, it's an update of the old adage, "Beauty is in the eyes of the beholder." That's why the the dollar value of a domain name defies even the most brilliant expert, unless he or she knows the specific purpose for which a company may be considering acquiring it.

The domain name also has a branding aspect and is entitled to the same protection. In the business marketplace before the internet, names were entitled to the protection of the law: a company could be prevented from using a name that was "confusingly similar" to another name already in use by the same type of business or a business selling a similar product or service. Do you think that using "cocoa cola" for a beverage would likely be precluded by the courts, even though it is not exactly the same as the more recognizable name?

## Hits and Misses

The reason why many retail businesses have newsletters is to tell customers about new items or special deals. This is building a customer list that has a value by virtue of the belief that it is easier to sell a product or service to a current or former customer than to find a new customer. If the belief has any validity, and conventional wisdom suggests that it does, then the visitors to a website have a value to the business, conjectural though it may be.

This is where the metrics come into play. Visiting a website is one thing. How long the visitor (potential customer) stays on the site may be revealing whether that customer makes a purchase or not. And then, there are variables to consider. For example, a customer may leave the site by backtracking through each page he or she has visited; this activity may count as so many "visits," yet be meaningless. Again, it serves the business well to understand the various metrics and to use a service that differentiates among the metrics. As you get more sophisticated about monitoring the quality as well as the quantity of "customer visits," there are services, as mentioned, some free, that will give you a much more definitive analysis of these visits, depending on what you want to know.

## What's the Real Answer?

The answer to the question of valuing an internet business is twofold.

For the average person acquiring an online business, the standard protocols must prevail. The buyer must be able to enjoy sufficient income to feed his or her family and must also be able to amortize (pay back) the purchase price over a reasonable period of time based on the risk.

For the company that is focused entirely on the future and has sufficient resources (dollars) to wait for the future to unfold, the acquisition of an internet company is an entirely different investment. Woe be unto you if you can't afford the waiting game!

## Key Points to Remember

- When acquiring another business, a big business will often have different motives and different expectations than a small business.
- Selling a business, for the most part, is the conversion of earned equity to cash.
- The buyer of a business usually needs to have the profit service the family's needs and amortize the balance of the purchase price over a reasonable period of time based on risk.
- An internet business, although ultimately predicated on actual profit, has some unique properties that can represent extraordinary profit potential.
- The competitive aspects of an internet business are substantially different from the competitive elements of a conventional small business.

# Glossary

**Accelerated Growth:** The growing of a business within an extraordinarily short time frame.

**Accounts Payable:** Money owed by a business for the purchase of goods or services.

**Accounts Receivable:** Money owed to a business for the purchase of goods or services.

**Accounts Receivable Turnover Period:** The length of time between the sale of goods and the receipt of payment. Receivables turnover is a measure of how quickly a business firm collects on its accounts receivables. It is calculated by dividing the accounts receivable balance by the average daily credit sales (annual credit sales divided by 365).

**Accrual Accounting:** The method by which revenues and expenses are computed as incurred even though payment has not been received.

**Acquisition:** Takeover of one company by another.

**Advisor:** A person who acts in an advisory capacity to a business.

**Agent:** A person or business that has the authority to act on someone else's behalf.

**Amortization:** The method by which a "soft" asset (e.g., a franchise) can be expensed over a period of time based on a fictional "asset life."

**Angel Investor:** A person who invests in a company with expectations of a return of a multiple of his or her investment.

**Balance Sheet:** A picture of the assets, liabilities, ratios, and equity of a business at any given moment in time. Comparing one balance sheet with another will show activity and change in a business. Also known as a statement of financial condition or statement of financial position.

**Balloon Mortgage:** A fixed-rate mortgage with monthly payments that are not large enough to pay off the loan during the term. Balloon mortgages terminate after a specified time, usually five to seven years, at which time the remaining balance must be paid in one balloon payment.

**Balloon Payment Scheme:** A variation on a purchase money payment note, using the logic of the *balloon mortgage*. It's basically taking a ten-year fully amortized note and converting it to a five-year note, amortizing the full amount over ten years but making the balance of the principal due at the end of the five years.

**Bankruptcy:** A legal declaration of inability or impairment of ability of an organization or an individual to pay creditors. The three more common types are Chapters 7, 11, and 13. Chapter 7 allows an individual or a business owner to transfer his or her nonexempt assets to a bankruptcy trustee, who liquidates the assets and distributes the proceeds to the unsecured creditors and the debtor is generally entitled to a discharge of debt. Chapter 11 allows an individual to retain ownership and possession of all of his or her assets, but requires that he or she pay a specified portion of future income to the creditors, generally for three to five years. Chapter 13 allows any business or any individual with debts in excess of $307,675 (unsecured) or $922,975 (secured) to reorganize.

**Borrowing Base:** Amount that a lender is willing to advance against the value of pledged collateral, such as accounts receivables, inventory, and equipment. The borrowing base is determined by multiplying the value of the assigned collateral by a discount factor.

**Breakeven:** The point at which operating income is neither a profit nor a loss.

**Bulk Sale Transfer:** Legal conveyance of a business and its assets from seller to buyer.

**Business Model:** A particular method of operating a business for profit.

**Business Plan:** A written analysis of a business, its state of affairs, and its road map to the future.

**Business Valuation:** The value of the earned equity in a business at any moment in time.

**Cadre:** The internal group of people making up the operational capability of a business.

**Carryback (loan):** A loan that is financed by the seller of a property through a (purchase money) promissory note. Also known as a *seller carryback*.

**Cash Accounting:** The method by which revenues and expenses are computed only when payment is received or paid for goods and services.

**Cash Flow:** The movement of money into and out of a business for goods or services purchased or sold. This is a measure of the financial solvency of a business, calculated as cash receipts minus cash payments over a specified period of time or net profit plus any amounts charged off for depreciation, amortization, and depletion.

**Chart of Accounts:** A list of all the account names and values used by an organization.

**Click-Through/Clickthrough:** The act of clicking on a link in an advertisement on a website to follow it to the website of the advertiser, a measure of the effectiveness of the advertisement.

**Clone:** A potential buyer of a business similar in most respects to the seller.

**Collateral:** Assets used as security.

**Competition:** Other businesses of like kind with which a business shares its potential customers.

**Competitive Analysis:** An exposition of the relative values of a product or service in relation to the same or similar products or services offered by competitors.

**Confidentiality Agreement:** A written agreement that precludes all signatories from disclosing proprietary information. Also known as a *nondisclosure agreement*.

**Confidential Information:** Information that should not be shared with anyone other than the responsible people in a business.

**Consultant:** A person whose experience in business allows him or her to act as a business advisor.

**Consumer Price Index (CPI):** A number used as a measurement of the average price of consumer goods and services purchased by households, prepared monthly by the Department of Labor, Bureau of Labor Statistics.

**Contract:** A relationship between or among two or more parties, each of whom has obligations to perform and prerogatives to enjoy.

**Copyright:** A method of protecting proprietary information by designating date of first use.

**Corporation:** A legal entity that protects investors from any liability or loss beyond the original investment.

**Cost of Labor:** The wages and salaries of employees and any employer costs that are based on payroll—taxes, insurance, and benefits paid by the employer.

**Cost of Sales / Cost of Product:** The cost of goods or components or raw material necessary to produce or have products or services available for sale.

**Deep Pocket:** Wealth or a person or an entity with wealth, generally the member of a business entity or other organization who is the target of lawsuits against the entity or organization.

**Depreciation:** A method by which capital investments are deducted from revenues over an arbitrary period of years for tax purposes.

**Dilution:** The issuance of additional shares of stock in a corporation to a new investor that changes the current investors' percentages of participation.

**Directors and Officers Liability Insurance (D&O Policy):** Insurance policy to insulate members of a board of directors from lawsuits directed against them as individuals.

**Disclosure Document:** A written record of facts about a business, containing information about the basic business concept, the people involved, the number and location of units, any pending litigation, and many other disclosures about the history, financial stability, management structure, and operation of the franchise (parent) company. The disclosure document required when selling a franchise is called a *Uniform Franchise Offering Circular (UFOC)* in some states and a *Federal Trade Commission disclosure document* in others.

**Disclosures:** Facts about a business, including ownership and financial information, especially as required by state and/or federal law. The Uniform Franchise Offering Circular (UFOC) is a federal requirement for selling a franchise in any of the states.

**D&O Policy (Directors and Officers Liability Insurance):** Insurance policy to insulate members of a board of directors from lawsuits directed against them as individuals.

**Due Diligence:** The process of investigating a business for the purpose of acquiring all material statements, documents, and other information that may influence the outcome of the transaction.

**EBITDA:** Earnings before interest, taxes, depreciation, and amortization. One of several kinds of profit, among which are earnings before interest and taxes (EBIT), earnings before taxes (EBT), and earnings after taxes (EAT).

**Encumbrance:** A legal issue attached to a property that devalues it. That issue can be a claim, a lien, a charge, a zoning ordinance, or any other legal action.

**Equity:** Amount of ownership in a company. Also, that realm of the law in which a judge is empowered to issue a remedy that will either prevent or cure a wrong that is about to happen; an *equitable action* or an *equity matter* is an action that may be brought for the purpose of restraining the threatened infliction of wrongs or injuries and the prevention of threatened illegal action, in instances in which payment of money damages would not be adequate compensation.

**Escrow:** A trust account held by a third party who is charged with the responsibility of holding all monies and papers until all conditions of the escrow are observed.

**Executive Summary:** The first page or so of a business plan, which acts as a concise summary of the plan.

**Executory Contracts:** A contract of which some or all of the obligations of either party are yet to be completed and which can be affirmed or rejected in a bankruptcy.

**Exit Strategy:** The method by which a partner or an investor is expected to be compensated or by which a partner or an investor expects to exit a business venture.

**Expenses Against Revenues:** The concept of costs against sales leading to profit.

**Feasibility Study:** A document that examines whether a business has the potential for success in the marketplace.

**Federal Trade Commission:** Agency that regulates franchises through the Bureau of Consumer Protection, Division of Marketing Practices.

**Federal Trade Commission Disclosure Document:** A disclosure document that some states require that a franchisor provide to any person who expresses an interest in buying a franchise. This document contains information about the basic business concept, the people involved, the number and location of units, any pending litigation, and many other disclosures about the history, financial stability, management structure, and operation of the franchise (parent) company.

**Fiduciary:** A person or other entity that has the responsibility to protect the goods or monies of someone who has created this relationship.

**Financial Assumptions:** Narrative explanations that clarify the numbers in a financial document.

**Finder of Fact:** In a legal proceeding, the one who decides if facts have been proven. This may be a judge, a jury, or someone appointed by the judge to investigate and report on the facts. Also known as *fact finder*.

**Fixed Expenses:** Business costs that do not increase or decrease with the volume of business, such as rent, insurance payments, and most utilities.

**Franchise:** A method of replicating a business that involves the investment and participation of an individual owner and a fee or royalty to the originator for use of the business name and marketing concept.

**Franchise Disclosure Document:** See *Disclosure Document*.

**Franchisee:** Owner of a franchise.

**Franchisor:** Franchise company.

**General Ledger:** Formal record containing all the accounts that make up a business entity's financial statements, with separate accounts for individual assets, liabilities, stockholders' equity, revenue, and expenses.

**Golden Parachute:** The reservoir of dollars and retirement benefits offered to an executive on termination or retirement.

**Growth by Acquisition:** The growing of a business by acquiring other businesses in the same or a related trade or industry.

**Guru:** A person whose credentials suggest that he or she knows all about a particular issue.

**Homestead Act:** Legislation in most states that allows a homeowner to protect a certain amount of his or her equity in the residential property in which he or she is living.

**Horizontal Growth:** Growing a business by replicating its activity in a different venue.

**Income Statement:** See *Profit and Loss Statement.*

**Incremental Growth:** The growing of a business by small but constant moves from one plateau of success to another.

**Inevitable Disclosure:** The concept of an individual using what he or she has learned by virtue of experience in a particular trade or industry.

**Inhouse Capability:** The ability of a business to handle operating elements by using equipment and personnel inside the parameters of the company.

**Indictment:** The legal term indicating that the State is putting a person on trial for an illegal act.

**IPO (Initial Public Offering):** The creation of a stock participation in the equity of a company by outsiders.

**IRS P&L:** The income statement prepared for tax purposes. Compare with the *reconstituted P&L.*

**Joint and Several Liability:** A legal principle by which each of two or more parties who have acted together (e.g., are partners in a business, have signed a contract, have caused an injury) is legally liable for the total amount of debts, payments, penalties, damages, or other obligation.

**Joint Venture:** Agreement by two or more parties to work on a project together, in a temporary relationship, to take advantage of their synergy.

**Junior Position:** Status of a security with lower priority claim on assets and income than a senior security.

**Key Person Insurance:** Insurance policy to pay for the loss of a partner in a business.

**Lien:** Claim of a party, typically a creditor, to hold or control the property of another to ensure satisfaction of a debt, a duty, or a liability.

**Matrix:** A vertical and horizontal chart that creates a comparative analysis of the products, values, and prices of competition in the marketplace.

**Memorandum:** Any written record that proves that a relationship exists between two parties.

**Memorandum of Intent:** A nonbinding document that sets forth the terms under which a seller and a buyer agree to transfer the business in the future. Also known as a *letter of intent.*

**Memorandum of Sale:** A letter of agreement committing a party to purchasing a property, representing a purchase contract in preparation for a formal purchase and sale agreement.

**Merger:** Combination of two or more companies into one with a single identity, typically that of the larger or largest of the companies, although a new identity could be created.

**Negligence:** The failure of a person to act properly and in accordance with reasonable caution.

**Negotiation:** The process by which two parties come to a position that satisfies both in part and neither completely.

**Net Profit:** Amount of money earned after deducting from the gross revenues of a business all expenses, including overhead, employee salaries and benefits, manufacturing costs, inventory costs, distribution costs, and marketing and advertising costs.

**Niche Position:** A place in the competitive community that makes a business unique.

**Nondisclosure Agreement:** A written agreement that precludes all signatories from disclosing proprietary information. Also known as a *confidentiality agreement.*

**Operating Profit (or Loss):** Amount of money that remains of the gross revenues of a business after paying all the related costs and expenses, excluding income from sources other than its regular activities and before income deductions. Also known as operating income (or loss), net operating profit (or loss), and net operating income (or loss).

**Option:** A contractual right to take advantage of a purchase opportunity on specific terms and within a specific time frame.

**Outsourcing:** The use of other businesses to handle certain aspects of a business.

**P&L:** See *Profit and Loss Statement*.

**Partnership:** A legal entity formed by two or more individuals or businesses or, more generally, any relationship involving two or more people or entities for business purposes.

**Patent:** The method by which a method or product can be protected against unfair use by others.

**Phantom Partnership:** A relationship created to give comfort to clients for a transition period as part of the sale of a business.

**Pro Forma:** A presentation of information, typically on financial statements, that represents an "as if" situation. For example, a pro forma balance sheet and a pro forma income statement are similar to a standard balance sheet and a standard income statement, but they represent projections of how a business will be managing its assets and income in the future.

**Profit and Loss Statement (P&L):** A financial statement, usually done on an accrual basis, designed to show a picture of the business's "expenses against sales."

**Promissory Note:** A contract signed by a party borrowing money to repay the party lending the money according to specified terms and conditions.

**Protocol:** The method by which operations are best handled in a business.

**Purchase Money Promissory Note (PMPN):** A *promissory note* for the balance of a purchase price after a down payment is made.

**Receivable Turnover Period (Accounts Receivable Turnover Period):** The length of time between the sale of goods and the receipt of payment. Receivables turnover is a measure of how quickly a business firm collects on its accounts receivables. It is calculated by dividing the accounts receivable balance by the average daily credit sales (annual credit sales divided by 365).

**Reconstituting the P&L:** A method by which a profit and loss statement is adjusted to include only those expenses against revenues that are necessary for the proper picture of a business for sale.

**Return of Investment:** The money returned to an investor or the "bonus" returned to an investor for the use of his or her money.

**Right of First Refusal:** The right of an owner to acquire another owner's stock position instead of allowing an outside third party to do so.

**Senior Position:** Status of a security with higher priority claim on assets and income than a junior security.

**Status Quo:** The state of affairs that a court decides not to change until all the facts are examined in a legal dispute.

**Strategic Alliance:** A working relationship in which two or more companies benefit from *synergy*, each using its best strengths to combine for an effort that neither or none of the allies could generate as well on its own.

**Subordination of Security Interest:** Establishment of the right of a creditor to receive the proceeds of a sale of property before the subordinated creditor. See *Junior Position* and *Senior Position*.

**Synergy:** The interaction of two or more entities such that their combined effect is greater than the total of their separate effects.

**Trade Secrets:** Proprietary information about a business or product or service of a business.

**Tort:** Intentional interference with someone's right to privacy, property, and the like.

**Tortious Conduct:** The activity by a person that creates a tort against another person or his or her property.

**Trespass:** The act of intruding on a person or a person's space.

**Uniform Commercial Code:** The longest and most elaborate of a number of state laws drafted by the National Conference of Commissioners on Uniform State Laws in order to harmonize the law of commercial transactions in all 50 states.

**Uniform Franchise Offering Circular (UFOC):** A disclosure document that some states require that a franchisor provide to any person who expresses an interest in buying a franchise. This document contains information about the basic business concept, the people involved, the number and location of units, any pending litigation, and many other disclosures about the history, financial stability, management structure, and operation of the franchise (parent) company.

**Usury Statutes:** State laws that specify the maximum interest rate at which loans can be made legally.

**Variable Expenses:** Business costs that increase or decrease with the volume of business, such as advertising costs and manufacturing costs.

**Vertical Growth:** Growing a company by generating an inhouse capability for the component parts or raw materials necessary to create a product.

**Working Capital Reservoir:** The money available to a business for operating expenses and contingencies.

# Index

**A**

Absence of competition, 101

Absentee ownership
   concerns about, 374
   costs of, 174–176
   manager's salary with, 27–28

Acceleration-upon-default clauses, 187

Acceptance from lenders, 322–323

Accountants. *See also* Financials
   brokers working with, 305, 308
   major services for buyers, 274–281
   major services for sellers, 271–274
   reasons to involve, 52

Accounts payable days, 364

Accounts receivable. *See* Receivables

Accounts receivable days, 364

Accrual method of accounting, 102, 352, 359, 360

Accumulated depreciation, 354–355

Acquisitions for growth, 387–388

Advertising
  to attract buyers, 182–184
  brokers' assistance with, 304
  evaluating, 220, 269–270
  franchisor requirements for, 339
  franchisor support, 123–126, 341
  of professional practice for sale, 257–258

Advice, assessing, 53, 58, 146–147

Advisors. *See* Professional advisors

Age as reason for sale, 375

All-cash deals, 35, 262, 272

Allocation of purchase price monies, 47–48

Amortization periods, 38–39

Amortization tables, 40, 41

Answering machines, 81

Asking price
  accountants' help with, 272
  attorneys' help with, 286–287
  calculating maximum, 41–45
  down payment negotiations and, 36–37, 38
  factoring referrals into, 259–266
  impact of equipment purchases on, 371–372
  impact of financing method on, 34–36
  relation to operating profits, 5–6, 7–8, 44, 167–168
  structuring for professional practices, 252–255
  variables affecting, 300–301

Asset purchases, 89–90

Assets
  on balance sheets, 353, 354–355
  bulk transfer, 294
  of buyer, to secure purchase, 46–47, 374
  evaluating prior to purchase, 90–101, 294
  pledging to investors, 109
  protecting personal holdings, 221
  vulnerability after sale of family business, 12–13

Attitude for success, 82–83

Attorneys
  brokers working with, 305, 308
  for help with creditor negotiations, 222
  including in meetings with buyers, 244–245
  reasons to involve, 52–53, 285–286

**B**

Backup systems, 80–81

Balance sheets
  accountant's analysis, 277
  buyers' need for, 102
  comparing, 355–357
  elements of, 352–355
  showing to lenders, 363

Balance sheet statements, 354–355

Balloon payments, 48–49, 223

Bankers. *See also* Lenders
  knowing, 314
  presentations to, 316–321
  reluctance to fund business purchases, 23
  responding to rejections or acceptance from, 322–323
  venture capitalists versus, 315

Bankruptcy
    alternatives to, 231–232
    Chapter 7, 226–227
    Chapter 11, 228–229, 323
    Chapter 13, 230
    major considerations, 215–217,
        224–226, 230–231
    selling a business in, 245
Bankruptcy loans, 323
Baseball center illustration, 145–146
Benefit plans, 334
Body language, 70–71
Bonus programs, 177, 189
Bookkeeping systems, 301
Borrowing, 280–281, 307–308. *See also*
    Lenders; Purchase money promissory
    notes
Borrowing base, 363–364, 365
Brand names, 388
Breakeven point, 182, 364–366
Brokers. *See* Business brokers
Buildings, 94. *See also* Leases
Bulk sales transfer notices, 217–218, 294
Business brokers
    benefits of using, 54–58, 298
    for buyers, 305–310
    multiple, 297–298
    reviewing agreements with, 290
    for sellers, 299–305
Business contacts, finding buyers
    through, 182
Business forms, 114–115, 185–186,
    291–292
Business plans
    brokers' assistance with, 302
    form and purpose, 312–313
    importance, 82, 315–316
    myths about, 311

Business styles, 210–211
Business valuation. *See* Valuation of
    businesses
Buyers
    accounting services for, 274–281
    attorney services for, 289–295
    basic financial considerations for,
        21–24
    business brokers for, 305–310
    employees as, 192–193
    financial statements from, 273–274,
        275
    finding, 182–185
    importance of income to, 4–6, 7–8
    information needs of, 63–68
    learning the business, 212–213
    motivations of, 205–210, 373–375
    noncompete agreements with,
        328–329
    pressures on, 144–145
    protections for, 185–186, 289–290
    research strategies for, 84–86
    wrong candidates, 180–181
Buyers' assets, backing purchases with,
    46–47, 374
Buying versus building a business,
    202–203
Buyout clauses, 46, 346–347

C
Capital gains taxes, 35
Capital stock, 355
Cash basis of accounting, 102, 351–352,
    359, 361
Cash businesses, 28
Cash flow forecasts, 360–363
Cash flow statements, 367
Cash on balance sheets, 355

Cash returns, importance to buyers, 21–22

C corporations, 280

Chapter 7 bankruptcy, 226–227

Chapter 11 bankruptcy, 228–229, 323

Chapter 13 bankruptcy, 230

Chart of accounts, 277–278

Click-throughs, 387

Client-attorney relationships, 285–286

Client-practitioner relationships, 250

Closing costs, 278

Collateral
    in addition to business, 46–47, 53, 374
    borrowing base, 363–364
    inventory as, 92
    for investors, 108–109
    showing to prospective lenders, 319

Collections, 102, 293

Commercial lenders. *See* Lenders

Commissions (broker)
    costs to sellers of, 54–55
    incentives in, 56
    post-contract, 57, 298
    varying conditions for earning, 299

Commissions for salespeople, 335

Compatibility with business opportunities, 83

Competitors
    buyers' need to understand, 63–64
    discussing with buyers, 159–160
    evaluating prior to business purchase, 101
    franchisor experience against, 122, 128
    including in prepurchase research, 85, 86
    learning from, 149

Computers
    evaluating prior to purchase, 99–100

for homebased businesses, 80–81
    impact on homebased business growth, 77

Confidential Business Application, 206–209, 274

Confidentiality protection by brokers, 303

Consent from franchisors, 130–132

Consideration for noncompete agreements, 331

Consistent payments, 222

Consultants. *See also* Franchises; Professional advisors
    costs of, 139–140
    debtors in bankruptcy as, 245
    evaluating advice from, 146–147
    franchisors versus, 136–138, 139
    obtaining services of, 111, 138–139, 140–141
    sellers as, 133–134

Consulting businesses, 202–203

Consumer Price Index (CPI), 161

Contracts. *See also* Noncompete agreements
    for equipment purchase, 174
    evaluating prior to business purchase, 96
    examination by buyer's attorney, 291, 293–294
    executory, 228–229
    to keep key employees, 188–190
    purchase agreements, 185

Control by investors, 107–110

Copying business concepts, 149

Copyrights, 158

Corporations, 114–115, 280

Cosigners, 47

Cosmetic improvements, 56

Cost of labor, 5, 176–177
Cost of product, 5, 358
Cost of sales
   adjusting prices for increases in, 219
   defined, 5
   on profit and loss statements, 25, 358
Counterpersons, 176
Creative financing options, 45–49
Credibility, preserving, 222–223
Credit, impact of bankruptcy on, 231
Credit applications, 280–281
Credit cards, 28
Credit checks, 274
Creditors. *See also* Bankruptcy
   discussing bankruptcy with, 226
   negotiating with, 221–222
   nonjudicial settlements with, 231–232
   notifying of business sales, 217–218,
     221
Curiosity seekers, 65
Current assets, 354
Current liabilities, 355
Current ratio, 364
Customer base
   buyers' need to understand, 64–65
   discussing with buyers, 158–159
   evaluating prior to business purchase,
     95–96
   increasing sales to, 220
   introducing to new practitioners,
     249–250
   retaining after leaving franchise,
     345–346
Customer contracts, 96
Customer lists
   as assets in bankruptcy, 224
   building, 389
   protecting, 334

   requests from buyers for, 61, 62
Customer volume, 245–246

**D**
Debt collection, 221
Debtor in possession, 228
Debt problems, selling a business with,
   221–224. *See also* Bankruptcy;
   Creditors; Troubled businesses
Debt/worth ratio, 364
Delegation, 211
Deposits, 185
Depreciation
   allocation of purchase monies for, 48
   as asset, 354–355
   as tax deduction, 20
   valuing for sales, 25–26
Diluting ownership interest, 111–112
Discipline, for homebased businesses,
   78–79
Disclosures
   buyers' needs, 63–68
   early in negotiations, 61–63, 101–103
   for investors, 107–108
   prohibiting, 330–335
   required for franchises, 121, 131, 184,
     291
   sellers' needs, 68–70
   when selling troubled businesses,
     240–242
Discretionary expenses, 20
Disgruntled employees, 191–192
Dissolution of partnerships, 113
Do-it-yourselfers, 210–211
Domain names, 388
Double taxation, 280
Down payments, 36–37, 38, 70
Downsizing, 77–78

Due diligence, 375
Dues, 30

**E**
Elderly parents, 77
Emotional involvement, 82–83
Employee benefits, 334
Employee compensation, 279–280
Employees
   assessing in business valuation, 378
   as buyers, 192–193
   evaluating prior to business purchase,
     94–95, 279–280, 293–294
   informing of sale, 188–192
   noncompete agreements with,
     329–331
Encumbrances on equipment, 91
Endgames, 216–217
Entrepreneur bug, 210
Entrepreneurship, 78–79, 210–211
Equipment
   evaluating franchise advantages for,
     126–127
   evaluating prior to purchase, 91, 99,
     100
   for homebased businesses, 80–82
   impact of contracts on business sales,
     174
   timing purchases of, 371–372
   valuing for sales, 25–26
Equity categories, 355
Escrows
   with all-cash deals, 262
   creating to pay creditors, 218, 222
   to discourage moving to competitors,
     335
Excess profits, 281

Excitement, conveying to prospective
   lenders, 318–319
Exclusive authorization to sell, 299
Exclusive geographical areas, 126
Executory contracts, 228–229
Existing franchises, 127–128, 130–131.
   *See also* Franchises
Exit interviews, 333
Exit strategies, 314, 320–321
Expectations, adjusting, 15–16
Expenses, removing from P&L state-
   ments, 20, 29–30
Experts. *See also* Consultants;
   Professional advisors
   costs of, 139–140
   obtaining services of, 111, 138–139,
     140–141

**F**
Facilities, 220. *See also* Leases
Failing businesses, selling, 222–224. *See
also* Troubled businesses
Families, impact of business purchase
   on, 150–151
Family businesses, 9–15
Fast-food restaurants, 309
Fastframe USA, 75–76
Fax machines, 81
Federal Trade Commission disclosure
   documents, 67
Final documents, 287–288
Financial reports
   balance sheet basics, 352–357
   borrowing base and key ratios,
     363–364
   breakeven forecasts, 364–366
   cash flow forecasts, 360–363

comparative analysis, 366
profit and loss statements, 357–359
Financials. *See also* Accountants
   absentee ownership costs, 174–176
   assessing condition of, 273
   in business plans, 313, 315
   buyer disclosures, 65, 69–70
   buyers' basic considerations, 21–24
   early requests for, 61–62
   major financing options, 34–36, 45–49
   mentioning requirements in ads,
      183–184
   pie chart approach, 168–174, 178
   prepurchase research into, 86–87,
      149–150
   sellers' basic considerations, 24–29, 307
Financial statements of buyers
   accountant's analysis, 273–274, 275
   evaluating with broker, 302–303, 307
Financing methods. *See also* Purchase
   money promissory notes
   importance to buyers, 23–24
   major options, 34–36, 45–49
Fixed expenses, 177
Focus of product mix, 160
Follow-up with lenders, 321–322
Food courts, 309
Format changes, 374–375
Formulas
   for managers' salaries, 27–28
   maximum asking price, 42
   valuation, 7–9
Franchise agreements, 290–291
Franchisees
   including in prepurchase research, 85,
      86
   learning the business, 212–213
   long-term goals of, 339–340

   selling to, 183
Franchise magazines, 182
Franchises
   advantages and disadvantages,
      117–119, 121–122, 135–138, 340
   contractual differences among,
      338–339, 341–342
   historic development, 119–121
   importance of reputation to, 98
   long-term goals for, 339–340
   mandatory disclosures with, 67–68,
      121
   marketing and advertising support,
      123–126
   noncompete agreements with, 186,
      342–347
   parents' long-term obligations to,
      12–13
   required disclosures, 121, 131, 184,
      291
   selling a business with or without,
      157–158, 340–341
   training with, 212
   variables in purchase decisions,
      121–123, 126–132
Fraud, 242
Future profits, 8–9, 181

**G**
General ledgers, 277–278
General managers, 10, 27–28
General partnerships, 114, 284
Geographical boundaries for noncom-
   pete agreements, 342–343
Gifts, family businesses as, 14
Google, 385
Gross profit, 358
Gross revenues, 25

Gross sales, ratio of manager's salary to, 27
Growth potential
  discussing with buyers, 162, 192
  of internet businesses, 386, 387–388

**H**
Homebased businesses, 76–82
Home equity, protecting, 224
Homestead acts, 224
Horizontal growth, 387
Husbands and wives, 150–151, 163

**I**
Ice cream shops, 124–125
Ideal ratios, 170
Illness forcing sale, 375
Incentive programs, 177
Income, importance to buyers, 4–6, 7–8
Income statements. *See* Profit and loss (P&L) statements
Information packets, 66
Information sharing
  body language in, 70–71
  buyers' needs, 63–68
  early in negotiations, 61–63, 101–103
  sellers' needs, 68–70
Initial memorandum, 287
Innovations, evaluating prior to purchase, 91
Inspecting businesses, 66–67
Insurance, 80, 187
Interest rates, negotiating, 39–41
Internet businesses, 381–389
Inventories, 92, 356, 378
Inventory days, 364
Investment advice, 281
Investor motivations, 106–110

**J**
Jargon of professionals, 57–58
Job loss, as incentive to buy business, 144–145
Joint and several liability, 114, 292

**K**
Key employees, 94–95, 188–190
Key person insurance, 113
Key ratios, 364

**L**
Labor costs, 5, 176–177
Labor law specialists, 295
Language of professionals, 57–58
Law practices, selling, 252–259
Lawsuits
  avoiding from creditors, 218, 222
  Chapter 11 protections, 228
  legal specialists in, 295
  new owners' liability, 89–90
Lawyers. *See* Attorneys
Layoffs, 144–145
Leadership, 211
Learning the business, 212–213
Leases
  discussing with buyers, 160–162
  evaluating prior to purchase, 92–93, 103
  examination by attorney, 290, 291
  as executory contracts, 228–229
Legal issues for franchises, 121, 130–132
Lenders
  knowing, 314
  presentations to, 316–321
  reluctance to fund business purchases, 23
  responding to rejections or acceptance from, 322–323

showing business plans to, 315–316
showing financial reports to, 362–366
understanding goals of, 313–314
Length of franchise contract, 341–342
Letters of intent, 184–185, 287
Liabilities, 354, 355
Liability
  acquiring with stock purchases, 89–90
  advising accounting clients about, 280
  with different business forms,
      114–115, 185–186
  in general partnerships, 284
  joint and several, 292
Liens on equipment, 91
Life insurance, 187
Limited liability, 284–285
Limited liability companies, 115
Limited partnerships, 14, 114
Liquidated damages, 346–347
Loans, 307–308, 323. *See also* Lenders
Location. *See also* Leases
  discussing with buyers, 160–162
  evaluating prior to purchase, 97, 101,
      103
  for franchises, 122–123, 128
Logos, 97–98, 137, 342
Long-term assets, 354
Long-term goals, 339–340
Long-term liabilities, 355
Long-term obligations
  on balance sheets, 355
  examination by buyer's attorney, 291,
      293
  with sales of family businesses, 12–13

**M**
Magazine advertising, 257–258
Magazine subscriptions, 81–82

Maintenance costs, 30
Management
  discussing with lenders, 317
  investors' influence, 107–108, 109
Managers
  calculating salaries of, 27–28
  offering to sell businesses to, 191–192
  styles of, 210–212
Mandatory disclosures for franchises,
      67–68, 121
Manufacturing businesses, 269–270
Marketing
  brokers' assistance with, 303–304
  in business plans, 313
  franchisor support, 123–126
  of professional practices, 256–259
Market research by franchisors, 124–125
Material facts, 240, 241
Maximum asking price, 41–45
McDonald's, 97
Metrics on web traffic, 389
Microsoft, 97
Misrepresentation, 242
Monthly payments, 40, 41
Mortgages, 47, 48–49
Motivation
  of buyers, 205–210, 373–375
  of sellers, 204–205, 375–377
Multiple brokers, 297–298

**N**
Name recognition, 97–98
Negotiation
  of down payments, 36–37, 38
  early information sharing, 61–63,
      101–103
  of franchise contracts, 344–345
  preparing seller's position, 302

of promissory note length and interest rate, 38–41
of purchase price, 41–45
sales of troubled businesses, 242–246
Net profits, 37, 38
New franchises, existing versus, 127–128
New ownership, potential of, 237–240
Newspaper advertising, 182, 183
Noncompete agreements
with departing employees, 329–331
forced on employees, 327–328
with franchises, 186, 342–347
required of sellers by buyers, 328–329
Nondisclosure agreements, 330–335
Nonjudicial settlements with creditors, 231–232
Nonverbal communication, 70–71

**O**
Old debts, 235–236
Operating profits
absentee ownership costs to, 174–176
fixed expenses and, 177
future, 8–9, 181
improving, 219–221
labor costs and, 176–177
pie chart approach to, 168–174, 178
relation to asking price, 5–6, 7–8, 44, 167–168
as return on investment, 21–22
valuing internet businesses without, 386–387
Options to buy, 162
Orthodontist's practice, 259–262
Owner's compensation, 26–27
Owner's equity, 354, 355

**P**
Packaging loans, 307–308

Parents remaining in family businesses, 11–12
Parking, 162
Partnership agreements, 113, 293
Partnership period, 250–251
Partnerships
attorneys' advice on, 293
evaluating, 146
liability in, 284
motivations for, 110–113
temporary, 46, 140
to transfer family business ownership, 14
to transfer professional practices, 248–249, 251
Patient-physician referral valuation model, 263–265
Patients
introducing new owners to, 249–250
referrals of, 259–266
Pension plans, 334
Personal assets, securing purchase with, 46–47, 374
Personal guarantees
attorneys' advice on, 292
for bank loans, 323
in bankruptcies, 225
on promissory notes, 186
Personal liability. *See* Liability
Personal relationships, 250
Personal visits to businesses, 66–67
Pie charts, 168–174, 178
Portfolios for selling, 163
Post-term, noncompete covenants, 186
Posturing, 242–243, 245
Prepaid expenses, 354
Prepurchase research, 84–86, 308–310
Presentations to lenders, 316–321

Present value of money, 35

Price (of business). *See* Asking price; Selling price

Pricing guides, 158

Prime rate, 39

Print advertising, 182–183

Print shops. *See* Quick printing businesses

Product mix, 160

Professional advisors
accountants for buyers, 274–281
accountants for sellers, 271–274
accounting services overview, 52–53
attorney services overview, 52–53, 285–286
attorneys for buyers, 289–295
attorneys for sellers, 286–288
business brokers' services, 54–58, 298
buyers' brokers, 305–310
including in meetings with buyers, 242–243, 244–245
including in prepurchase research, 85
sellers' brokers, 299–305
when to involve, 52

Professional practices
creating partnerships to transfer ownership, 248–249
degradation during ownership change, 251–252
introducing new owners to clients, 249–250
marketing techniques, 256–259
predicting referrals, 259–266
selling price determination, 252–255, 259–262
unique nature of, 247–248

Profit and loss (P&L) statements
accountant's analysis, 276–277
comparative analysis, 368–369
elements of, 357–359
reconstituting for sales, 24–25, 29–30, 168–174
for tax versus selling purposes, 19–20, 169
when to request, 101–102

Profits, 359. *See also* Net profits; Operating profits

Profit-sharing plans, 334

Protecting the sale, 185–188, 288

Protective clauses, 161–162

Purchase agreements, 185

Purchase money promissory notes
interest rates on, 35
negotiating duration and interest rates, 38–41
potential terms of, 23–24
profits versus payment on, 6, 8
as reason for sellers to remain involved, 68–69, 288
seller protections in, 186–187, 374
successful payment as sellers' goal, 16, 23

Purchase price. *See* Selling price

**Q**

Questions, preparing, 84–85

Quick printing businesses
absentee ownership costs, 175
labor costs, 176–177
operating profit pie charts, 168–174

**R**

Ratios, 364

Real estate, 92–94

"Real estate" (virtual), 388

Reasonable terms for noncompete agreements, 328–329, 343

Receivables
    accounts receivable days, 364
    assessing in business valuation, 378
    on balance sheets, 356
    buyers' purchase of, 23
    turnover periods for, 28
Reconstituting P&L statements, 24–25,
    29–30, 168–174
Referrals
    all-cash deals and, 262
    difficulties presented by, 259–262,
        265–266
    valuation models, 263–265
    on web sites, 387
Rejection from lenders, 322
Rent, 160–162
Repair costs, 30
Repayment periods, negotiating, 38–39
Reputation, 98
Research, 84–86, 308–310
Restaurant businesses, 84, 159–160, 309
Retained earnings, 281, 355
Return on investment
    describing to prospective lenders,
        320–321
    importance to buyers, 21–22
    investors' expectations, 108–109
Right of first refusal, 132, 162
Right to cancel leases, 161
Risk, 22, 318
Royalties. See also Franchises
    consultant fees versus, 136–137
    differences among franchises, 338–339
    restrictions accompanying, 117–118,
        155–156

S
Salaries, general, and administrative
    expenses, 358–359

Sale of business
    disclosing to employees, 188–192
    documentation for, 184–185
    finding buyers, 182–185
    overview of process, 180–181
    preparing business for, 56, 156–157,
        167, 217, 301–302
    protecting, 185–188, 288
    with or without a franchise, 157–158,
        340–341
Salespeople, 333–334, 335
Sales (product), 84, 358
Sales taxes, 47–48
Sample Confidential Business
    Application, 206–209
S corporations, 280
Scott, John, 75–76, 210
Second mortgages, 47
Secret formulas, 98–99
Securities law specialists, 295
Security interests. See also Collateral
    additional, 374
    borrowing base, 363–364
    of investors, 108–109
Seller-carry financing, 35–36. See also
    Purchase money promissory notes
Sellers
    accounting services for, 271–274
    attorney services for, 286–288
    basic financial considerations for,
        24–29
    business brokers for, 299–305
    as consultants, 133–134
    information needs of, 68–70, 307
    interest in buyers' success, 6
    motivations of, 204–205, 375–377
    noncompete agreements with,
        328–329

protections for, 186–188, 287–288, 374

risks of selling to wrong buyers, 180–181

training by, 212–213

Selling portfolios, 163

Selling price. *See also* Asking price
accountants' help in obtaining, 272
attorneys' help with, 286–287, 289
brokers' input on, 306
explaining to buyers, 275–276
impact of financing method on, 34–36

Service contracts, 127

SG&A expenses, 358–359

Skills, 83–84, 148–149

Social contacts, finding buyers through, 182

Soft entrepreneurs, 210

Software, 80, 99–100

Sole proprietorships, 114

Solvency problems, 221–222

Specialty lawyers, 295

Specialty practitioners, 259–262

Spouses
impact of business purchase on, 150–151
including in meetings with buyers, 242
selling to, 163

Standing debt, 221

Stock, 108

Stockholders' equity, 354, 355

Stock purchases, 89–90

Subordination agreements, 109

Subscriptions, 30, 81–82

Success, 82–84, 123

Supervisors, 210–211

Supplies, 80–82, 175

**T**

Tax deductions, 78

Taxes
accountant's advice on, 272–273, 278
allocation of purchase monies for, 47–48
capital gains from all-cash deals, 35
continuing obligations in bankruptcy, 227
on corporations, 280
with sales of family businesses, 14–15

Tax returns, 19–20, 25–26

Teachers, business owners as, 211

Technology
evaluating, 91, 99–100, 220
impact on homebased business growth, 77

Telephone lines, 81

Temporary partnerships, 46, 140

Temporary restraining orders, 332

Terminology of professionals, 57–58

Thank-you notes, 321–322

Third-party lenders. *See* Lenders

Time pressures, 147–148, 165–167

Timing in negotiations, 243–244

Total debt/equity ratio, 364

Trade magazines, 85

Trade names, 97–98, 137

Trade organizations, 137, 158

Trade secrets, 330

Training, 212, 220

Transfer fees, 144

Troubled businesses. *See also* Bankruptcy
disclosures when selling, 240–242
negotiating sale, 242–246
new ownership potential for, 237–240
seeking help with, 222–224

Trust, establishing with buyers, 241
Trust deeds, 47

**U**
Unemployment, 144–145
Uniform franchise offering circulars, 67
Usury statutes, 40

**V**
Valuation of businesses
    differing viewpoints in, 204–205
    internet businesses, 381–389
    major considerations, 6–9, 377–379
Vendors, 85
Venture capitalists, 315
Vertical growth, 387–388
Vested-dollar incentives, 334–335
Visibility of homebased businesses,
    79–80

Visiting businesses, 66–67
Voting privileges for investors, 108

**W**
*The Wall Street Journal*, 183
Waste, 175
Web-based businesses, 381–389
Working capital
    evaluating need for, 102
    for franchisees, 122, 128
    inadequate, 374
    mentioning in ads, 183–184
    reservoirs, 28–29, 45

**Y**
Yellow Pages advertising, 342

**Z**
Zoning restrictions, 79–80